UNDERSTANDING MOTOR BEHAVIOUR IN DEVELOPMENTAL COORDINATION DISORDER

Although Developmental Coordination Disorder (DCD, sometimes referred to as 'Dyspraxia') has received less attention than other developmental disorders, its impact can be severe and long-lasting. This volume takes a unique approach, pairing companion chapters from international experts in motor behaviour with experts in DCD. Current understanding of the motor aspects of DCD are thus considered in the context of general motor behaviour research.

Understanding Motor Behaviour in Developmental Coordination Disorder offers an overview of theoretical and methodological issues relating to motor development, motor control and skill acquisition, genetics, physical education and occupational therapy. Critically, Barnett and Hill ground DCD research within what is known about motor behaviour and typical development, allowing readers to evaluate the nature and extent of work on DCD and to identify areas for future research.

This unique approach makes the book invaluable for students in developmental psychology, clinical psychology, movement science, physiotherapy, physical education, and special education, as well as researchers and professionals working in those fields.

Anna L. Barnett is Professor of Psychology at Oxford Brookes University. Her general area of interest is perceptual-motor development, which focuses on various aspects of DCD – including diagnosis and assessment in children and adults with this condition.

Elisabeth L. Hill is Professor of Neurodevelopmental Disorders at Goldsmiths, University of London. Her research focuses primarily on DCD and the relationship between social and motor development in typical and atypical populations.

Current Issues in Developmental Psychology

Series Editor: Margaret Harris
Professor of Psychology, Oxford Brookes University, UK

Current Issues in Developmental Psychology is a series of edited books that reflect the state-of-the-art areas of current and emerging interest in the psychological study of human development. Each volume is tightly focused on a particular topic and consists of seven to ten chapters contributed by international experts. The editors of individual volumes are leading figures in their areas and provide an introductory overview.

Example topics include: developmental disorders, implicit knowledge, gender development, word learning and categorisation.

Published titles in the series

Gender and Development
Edited by Patrick Leman and Harriet Tenenbaum

Trust and Skepticism
Children's Selective Learning from Testimony
Edited by Elizabeth J. Robinson and Shiri Einav

Current Issues in Developmental Disorders
Edited by Chloë R. Marshall

New Perspectives on Moral Development
Edited by Charles C. Helwig

Early Word Learning
Edited by Gert Westermann and Nivedita Mani

Understanding Motor Behaviour in Developmental Coordination Disorder
Edited by Anna L. Barnett and Elisabeth L. Hill

UNDERSTANDING MOTOR BEHAVIOUR IN DEVELOPMENTAL COORDINATION DISORDER

Edited by Anna L. Barnett and Elisabeth L. Hill

Routledge
Taylor & Francis Group

LONDON AND NEW YORK

First published 2019
by Routledge
2 Park Square, Milton Park, Abingdon, Oxon OX14 4RN

and by Routledge
52 Vanderbilt Avenue, New York, NY 10017

Routledge is an imprint of the Taylor & Francis Group, an informa business

© 2019 selection and editorial matter, Anna L. Barnett and Elisabeth L. Hill; individual chapters, the contributors

British Library Cataloguing-in-Publication Data
A catalogue record for this book is available from the British Library

Library of Congress Cataloging-in-Publication Data
Names: Barnett, Anna Louise, editor. | Hill, E. L. (Elisabeth L.), editor.
Title: Understanding motor behaviour in developmental coordination
   disorder / Anna Barnett and Elisabeth Hill.
Description: First edition. | New York : Routledge, 2019. | Series: Current
   issues in developmental psychology
Identifiers: LCCN 2018055133 (print) | LCCN 2019005162 (ebook) |
   ISBN 9781315268231 (Ebook) | ISBN 9781138287501 (hardback) |
   ISBN 9781138287570 (pbk.) | ISBN 9781315268231 (ebk)
Subjects: LCSH: Movement disorders in children. | Motor ability in children.
Classification: LCC RJ496.M68 (ebook) | LCC RJ496.M68 U43 2019
   (print) | DDC 616.8/3—dc23
LC record available at https://lccn.loc.gov/2018055133

ISBN: 978-1-138-28750-1 (hbk)
ISBN: 978-1-138-28757-0 (pbk)
ISBN: 978-1-315-26823-1 (ebk)

Typeset in Bembo
by Apex CoVantage, LLC

For images in colour, please visit the eResource at www.routledge.com/
9781138287570

Printed and bound by CPI Group (UK) Ltd, Croydon, CR0 4YY

This book is dedicated to Sylvia Rodger
30th Aug 1961–28th April 2017
Brisbane, Australia.

Professor Sylvia Rodger's contribution to what is known about developmental coordination disorder was both broad and deep. She was instrumental in raising the profile of this condition and its impact on the lives of children and their families. Sylvia was part of a research team which gave children and their families a voice (Mandich, Polatajko, & Rodger, 2003; Rodger & Mandich, 2005), demonstrating the impact of this condition on daily life and emphasising the need for early intervention. She championed multidisciplinary assessment of children with DCD in a bid to reduce the burden on families (Rodger et al., 2007; Rodger et al., 2003) and successfully demonstrated that the Cognitive Orientation to Occupational Performance approach could be used with younger children than previously thought (Bernie & Rodger, 2004; Rodger & Liu, 2008). Always generous with her time and committed to capacity building, one of the key ways Sylvia contributed to the field was through supporting others to conduct research; through her passion for the field and her focus on collaboration and team-building, her influence will continue to be felt. Her leadership (and laughter) will be greatly missed.
Ann Kennedy-Behr, BAppSc(OT), MOccThy, PhD,
School of Health and Sports Sciences,
University of the Sunshine Coast
Queensland, Australia

References

Bernie, C., & Rodger, S. (2004). Cognitive strategy use in school-aged children with developmental coordination disorder. *Physical and Occupational Therapy in Pediatrics, 24*(4), 23–45.

Mandich, A. D., Polatajko, H., & Rodger, S. (2003). Rites of passage: Understanding participation of children with developmental coordination disorder. *Human Movement Science, 22*, 583–595.

Rodger, S., & Liu, S. (2008). Cognitive orientation to (daily) occupational performance: Changes in strategy and session time use over the course of intervention. *Otjr-Occupation Participation and Health, 28*(4), 168–179.

Rodger, S., & Mandich, A. (2005). Getting the run around: Accessing services for children with developmental co-ordination disorder. *Child: Care, Health and Development, 31*, 449–457.

Rodger, S., Watter, P., Marinac, J., Woodyatt, G., Ziviani, J., & Ozanne, A. (2007). Assessment of children with Developmental Coordination Disorder (DCD): Motor functional, self-efficacy and communication abilities. *New Zealand Journal of Physiotherapy, 35*, 99–109.

Rodger, S., Ziviani, J., Watter, P., Ozanne, A., Woodyatt, G., & Springfield, E. (2003). Motor and functional skills of children with developmental coordination disorder: A pilot investigation of measurement issues. *Human Movement Science, 22*, 461–478.

CONTENTS

CONTRIBUTORS

Anna L. Barnett, Perception and Motion Analyses (PuMA) Lab, Faculty of Health and Life Sciences, Oxford Brookes University, UK.

Martin E. Block, Kinesiology Department, University of Virginia, USA.

Nancy Getchell, Kinesiology and Applied Physiology, College of Health Sciences, University of Delaware, USA.

Beth Hands, Institute for Health Research, The University of Notre Dame Australia.

Kathleen M. Haywood, College of Education, University of Missouri-St. Louis, USA.

Elisabeth L. Hill, Department of Psychology, Goldsmiths, University of London, UK.

Ann Kennedy-Behr, School of Health and Sports Sciences, USC University of the Sunshine Coast, Australia.

Cara Law, Department of Psychology, Health and Professional Development, Oxford Brookes University, UK.

Melissa K. Licari, Telethon Kids Institute, University of Western Australia, Australia.

Dianne F. Newbury, Department of Biological and Medical Sciences, Oxford Brookes University, UK.

Karl M. Newell, Department of Kinesiology, University of Georgia, USA.

Matheus M. Pacheco, Department of Kinesiology, University of Georgia, USA.

Helen E. Parker, Institute for Health Research, The University of Notre Dame Australia, Western Australia.

Jan P. Piek, School of Psychology, Faculty of Health Sciences, Curtin University, Australia.

Daniela Rigoli, School of Psychology, Faculty of Health Sciences, Curtin University, Australia.

Sylvia Rodger, The University of Queensland, Australia and Cooperative Research Centre for Living with Autism (Autism, CRC), Australia.

Nichola Stuart, Department of Psychology, Health and Professional Development, Oxford Brookes University, UK.

Kate Wilmut, Perception and Motion Analyses (PuMA) Lab, Faculty of Health and Life Sciences, Oxford Brookes University, UK.

FOREWORD

Understanding motor behaviour in Developmental Coordination Disorder

Problems of motor skill learning in children (or Developmental Coordination Disorder – DCD) is one of the most commonly occurring issues of childhood, one that often has far-reaching implications for the child's academic achievement, participation, adjustment and well-being. Parents and teachers often observe these motor difficulties from an early age, and frequently have a sense of associated issues. The intrigue of DCD is that the condition is not explained by known medical disorders like cerebral palsy, muscular dystrophy, brain injury and so on. And yet the impact of motor coordination can be quite profound in the world of the child who is so dependent on and defined by their motor actions, their ability to explore the world through movement, and their playful (motoric) interactions with the environment and others. The idea that these abilities are somehow "impaired" is compelling and demands an enquiring and dedicated research eye. Perhaps one of the more landmark developments in our understanding of DCD was its recognition in the latest DSM-5 as a *neurodevelopmental disorder*, a conceptual epiphany that has opened up further debate and enquiry about its causal origins. In this text, we see some of the leading academic experts on DCD, from all corners of the globe, addressing various aspects of the condition, and from various perspectives. Uniting these is an awareness that knowledge of typical development is critical to understanding atypical development. In the first section we see typical motor development presented as the backdrop against which our knowledge of DCD is understood. As well, the acquisition of control, coordination and skill in DCD is then explored. Importantly, in these modern perspectives on motor development we see a shift away from traditional models of development, whether they be purely cognitive or dynamical in their orientation. Researchers are today more willing to adopt what some (including myself) see as a hybrid approach, blending principles from cognitive neuroscience, ecological psychology, and dynamical systems theory. This is not to deny the fact that some tensions in the literature still exist – a field without strong debate would be very rare indeed. However, we are seeing more and more that researchers are willing to adopt and sometimes adapt principles from different fields – this in an effort to understand the many constraints (individual, task-related, and environmental) that act synergistically to determine behaviour and its developmental unfolding. In the section on biological aspects of development we see some of the more powerful (individual-level) constraints that act not only within the child but also in interaction with the environment – "nature via nurture" in the language of some authors. We also see how technological advances in neuroimaging are casting a new light on development and DCD. This still promises to be one of the most exciting periods in DCD research as different groups join force to use "big data" in order to better model developmental pathways in DCD. In the final section on education and therapy, we see how basic research and theory are translating into the coalface strategies that will help children with DCD achieve optimal development into the future. Adapted physical activity and approaches derived from the science of occupational therapy are outlined by leading figures in these fields. What is very evident from this work is that innovation in therapy is built on the back of well-principled basic research and applied research – nothing less! This text is a remarkable and timely contribution to the field, and one that will contribute knowledge to and benefit the practice of people from diverse backgrounds, from students in the allied health disciplines to teachers, fellow researchers, as well as any professional with an interest in the development of children. The authors are to be congratulated for their expertise, and for their sensitivity to the cause of children with DCD.

Peter Wilson
Professor of Developmental Psychology
Co-Director, Centre for Disability & Development Research (CeDDR)
School of Psychology, Faculty of Health Sciences
Australian Catholic University
Australia

INTRODUCTION

Understanding motor behaviour in Developmental Coordination Disorder (DCD)

Elisabeth L. Hill and Anna L. Barnett

Movement has been the unsung hero through history. Motor skills are essential for activities of daily life and without this we are unable to act in, or with, others and the world. Furthermore, our ability to move around and to manipulate objects and engage with people impacts our understanding of the world (Pezzulo, 2011; Piaget, 1953). Arguably, its pervasiveness leads us to take this skill for granted. However, significant consequences arise when motor skill is atypical and this is the motivator for the development of this book on Developmental Coordination Disorder (DCD).

The focus of this book is solely on issues related to motor skill. The majority of the work included relates to children since most of the research and practice relating to DCD has focused on children. However, with an increasing recognition of the presence, and impact of DCD in adulthood it is clear that there are serious and long-term consequences of living with a developmental motor disorder. Perhaps the most significant of these consequences relate to social-emotional difficulties in child- and adulthood, as well as school achievement and employment outcomes. These have not been the focus of the book since they have been addressed elsewhere (e.g., Cairney, 2015; Harrowell, Hollén, Lingam, & Emond, 2017; Kirby, Williams, Thomas, & Hill, 2013; Tal-Saban, Zarka, Grotto, Ornoy, & Parush, 2012).

Research has also identified that for many people with DCD there are co-occurring non-motor difficulties including in mental and physical health, organisation, attention, language processing and other cognitive skills. Understanding is needed of the impacts of these on one another and on participation over the life-span, addressed, for example, through Cairney's environment stress model (Cairney, Veldhuizen, & Szatmari, 2010; Mancini, Rigoli, Cairney, Roberts, & Piek, 2016).

Some developmental disorders have been recognised for many decades, with substantial amounts of scientific research being focused on them during this time. For example, Dyslexia, Autism Spectrum Disorder (ASD) and Attention Deficit Hyperactivity Disorder (ADHD) are familiar terms to lay people, and psychologists have developed and tested theories to help understand the mechanisms that underlie the behavioural characteristics commonly associated with these disorders. This work has led to a range of psychological and educational interventions being developed that, to varying degrees of success, have provided support to those affected with these disorders. While there is still a lot to learn about these disorders, significant progress has been made. Much less attention has been paid to DCD.

Developmental coordination disorder

Developmental Coordination Disorder (DCD) has been less well known than other developmental disorders, although it affects around 2–5% of the population (American Psychiatric Association [APA], 2013; Lingam, Hunt, Golding, Jongmans, & Emond, 2009), equating to 1 child per class or around 1 person in 20. DCD is a neurodevelopmental disorder characterised by significant difficulties with the acquisition and execution of motor skill (DSM-5, APA, 2013, for full details see Table 0.1). People with DCD demonstrate a level of motor skill out of keeping with their age and intellectual ability. Difficulties acquiring adequate motor skill significantly interfere with activities of daily living (e.g., dressing, eating) and educational attainment and, importantly, cannot be accounted for by a sensory or neurological impairment, or general medical condition. As noted previously, while most research has focused on children, more recent work shows that motor difficulties often persist into adulthood (Kirby et al., 2013; Tal-Saban et al., 2012). Adults with DCD tend to report poorer mental and physical health, as well as employment experiences than their typical peers (see earlier). In addition, DCD is commonly seen in those affected with a range of other developmental disorders not least dyslexia, ASD and ADHD.

TABLE 0.1 DSM-5 diagnostic criteria for developmental coordination disorder 315.4 (F82), taken from p. 74

Criterion A	The acquisition and execution of coordinated motor skills is substantially below that expected given the individual's chronological age and opportunity for skill learning and use. Difficulties are manifested as clumsiness (e.g., dropping or bumping into objects) as well as slowness and inaccuracy of performance of motor skills (e.g., catching an object, using scissors or cutlery, handwriting, riding a bike, or participating in sports).
Criterion B	The motor skills deficit in Criterion A significantly and persistently interferes with activities of daily living appropriate to chronological age (e.g., self-care and self-maintenance) and impacts academic/school productivity, prevocational and vocational activities, leisure and play.
Criterion C	Onset of symptoms is in the early developmental period.
Criterion D	The motor skills deficits are not better explained by intellectual disability (intellectual developmental disorder) or visual impairment and are not attributable to a neurological condition affecting movement (e.g., cerebral palsy, muscular dystrophy, degenerative disorder).

In the last decade, awareness of this condition has increased enormously in the general public and among health and educational professionals. From a slow start over several decades, there has been a relative explosion of research into the biological, cognitive and motor characteristics in more recent years. There has also been research into the impact of the condition on the physical and psychological well-being and participation of children and adults. This growing interest has been evident in the increased number of research papers published on the topic, growth of the national and international conferences on DCD and publication of a set of European recommendations for those working with individuals with DCD (Blank et al., 2019). Despite these developments, relative to other conditions, there is still a small body of expertise, and this is disproportionate to the scale of those affected with the condition. Moreover, given that motor difficulties are at the core of this disorder, there has been very little specific focus on the actual motor core of the condition.

Thus, despite this growing interest in, and understanding of DCD, the research in this area often fails to draw fully on our broader knowledge of motor behaviour and biological systems, areas of research which themselves have a much longer history. It seems to us that the disorder will be better understood against a backdrop of this work from different disciplines and professions, including those with expertise in development, motor control, genetics, physical education and occupational therapy among others. Focusing on motor behaviour from those with differing perspectives and expertise should be invaluable in moving forward both in terms of theoretical understanding and practical applications. Finally, we see these as co-dependent: successful strategies and interventions will emerge from understanding motor development, learning and control from a theoretical point of view. Similarly the success of particular strategies and interventions will inform the theories which formed the basis of their development. Thus, without collaboration among many disciplines, significant advances will be slow to occur and will have limited impacts.

In this book we take a unique approach to understanding DCD through the presentation of pairs of companion chapters. In the first of each pair international experts give an overview of current theoretical and methodological issues relating to various aspects of motor behaviour and biological systems. These include a focus on motor development, motor control and skill acquisition, genetics, physical education and occupational therapy. In the second of each pair, experts in DCD extend the discussion of these topics, outlining and evaluating the literature to reflect on our current understanding of DCD.

Outline of the book

DCD is a developmental disorder and poor development of motor skill is fundamental to a diagnosis. Children with DCD experience difficulties with the development of motor skill from the early years and throughout childhood. The first section of this book therefore focuses on motor development and skill acquisition. In the first pairing of chapters, Haywood and Getchell outline the typical development of fundamental motor skills (chapter 1). They show that this is a continuous and age-related change process driven by interacting genetic and environmental factors that influence movement, allowing more proficient movements to be produced over time. They outline the development of fundamental skills of locomotion, object projection and object manipulation. These developmental trajectories show consistency over decades and across cultures while individual differences in timing and sequencing arise from the unique experiences of individuals. Barnett, Law and Stuart introduce DCD in their companion chapter (chapter 2) and review what is known about the development of motor skill in this condition. First, they outline the range of motor assessments used in studies to track the developmental progression of motor skill in DCD. They then draw on a variety of cross-sectional and longitudinal research on infants, children and adults, which shows the persistence of general motor difficulties across these age groups. A more detailed examination of performance within the three areas outlined by Haywood and Getchell illustrates the nature and range of motor difficulties experienced in DCD from early childhood to early adulthood.

Newell and Pacheco explain how both development (or maturation) and learning of motor skill can be considered in the same way, both emerging from an interaction of sub-systems within a dynamical system and ecological framework. They advocate a constraints-based approach to consider how factors relating to the individual, the task and the environment impact on motor behaviour. Using Bernstein's (1967) model for the acquisition of movement coordination and control, they provide examples to show the mastery of redundant degrees of freedom (chapter 3). Such work has been the focus of many decades of research and yet has rarely been applied to inform understanding of DCD. Against this backdrop, Wilmut and Barnett (chapter 4) outline and interpret studies of motor skill learning in children with DCD. They note a number of limitations of such studies, not least the lack of consideration of individual differences in performance, short timescales of adaptation over trials and lack of ecological validity of some tasks employed to date. They also outline research highlighting the capacity to learn motor skills in children with DCD, evidenced by pre- to post-intervention improvements in performance of (some) motor tasks when practice is highly structured and supported.

Over the past few years, huge strides have been made in studying biological mechanisms and these have been applied to understanding neurodevelopmental disorders. While less focus has been paid to biological mechanisms and *development*, and this work in relation to DCD is in its infancy, this is nonetheless an important area for the future. Thus the second section of this book focuses on biological aspects of development, and particularly on understanding the genetic contributions to neurodevelopmental disorders, as well as biological factors at play in DCD. In her chapter, Newbury provides a primer on genetic contributions to neurodevelopmental disorders (chapter 5). In this she outlines how the development of genetic technologies has enabled the identification of an increasing number of contributory genetic risk factors that change the way in which we conceptualise genetic disorders. This has helped understand complex genetic effects such that where neurodevelopmental disorders run in families, but without following a simple inheritance pattern, some understanding of the matrix of risk factors at play is now possible. These factors might include genetic elements, epigenetic effects and environmental influences. In outlining how future studies may address outstanding issues such as epigenetic elements and interactive influences in neurodevelopmental disorders, Newbury provides the basis for work in this area in relation to DCD. Licari, Rigoli and Piek pick up this theme in relation to DCD (chapter 6), highlighting a variety of biological and genetic approaches that have been applied to the study of DCD including structural and functional MRI, brain connectivity analyses and EEG studies. From genetic paradigms, it is evident that familial factors are implicated, while environmental influences also play an important role. Although each of these approaches has only been applied in a handful of studies, their potential for developing understanding of DCD, particularly through collaborative working, is now established. However, the heterogeneity evident in DCD seems to indicate a complex interplay between environmental and genetic factors. These need to be better understood in order for appropriate strategies and interventions to be designed for individuals.

While it is important to focus on theory and techniques, the findings of these investigations must inform, and be informed by, practical applications to support those with DCD as well as those who interact with them. This includes their families, friends, educators, employers and health care professionals. A wide range of educational and health interventions are 'on offer' although many of these have yet to be subject to appropriate degrees of scrutiny. Such scrutiny will be important for the future, although it is not in the scope of the current book. In section three, the focus is, however, on physical education and occupational therapy as two key areas of consideration. Teachers play an important role in the physical development of all children, particularly in the early and primary school years (4–11 years in the UK). Research has shown that children with neurodevelopmental disorders can often feel excluded from school-based physical activities both within formal lessons and playtime activities. They are also at increased risk of poor self-esteem and mental health symptoms. Given the importance of equality of opportunity and inclusion for all, teachers need to identify approaches to catering for the physical abilities of all children in their classroom when planning and delivering their lessons, while also supporting their well-being. Block's chapter on adapted physical activity in physical education (chapter 7) includes both general principles for inclusion of children with a range of disabilities as well as practical examples of adaptations that can be made. Block describes a *differentiated instruction* approach as a model for making inclusive physical education settings more appropriate and inviting for children with disabilities. These principles are invaluable when planning to teach and Hands and Parker develop this area specifically in relation to children and adolescents with DCD (chapter 8), highlighting how teachers and other physical educators can provide developmentally appropriate activities to ensure children and adolescents with DCD engage with, rather than avoid, physical activity opportunities. Primarily this is most successful by identifying and building on an individual's strengths. Hands and Parker also consider motor learning theory and how this relates to practice, highlighting how the integration of both areas allows progress to be made. These two companion chapters represent a very small body of literature and it is our hope that placing them together in this way will support teachers to work with the children and adolescents in their classes, as well as researchers to evaluate different approaches and extend the techniques outlined for the benefit of individuals with DCD.

Allied health professionals often work alongside educators to support those with DCD. In the final chapter pairing, occupational therapy is the focus. Here the late Sylvia Rodger, along with her colleague Ann Kennedy-Behr provide a general overview of the role of occupational therapy with children and their families, focussing on how a child's independence and participation is enabled (chapter 9), and embedding this within the World Health Organisation's International Classification for Functioning Disability and Health (ICF) (WHO, 2001). Their companion chapter on occupational therapy for children with DCD (chapter 10) illustrates how occupational therapists work with children with DCD to facilitate their occupational performance. This chapter includes an overview of a range of occupational therapy interventions including Cognitive Orientation for daily Occupational Performance; Occupational Performance Coaching for parents and teachers; supporting play and social skills; and Partnering for Change. The importance of addressing secondary consequences of DCD is also flagged, and a case study illustrates an example of this process. Occupational Therapy is just one example of intervention in DCD. There are of course a range of other approaches (including physiotherapy/physical therapy) which we have not addressed here. Illustration of other areas of work and professional practice in different countries was beyond the scope of this volume. Consideration of a wider range of approaches will be important in future work to more fully understand the contribution of different professions in countries across the world.

Future directions

Understanding Motor Behaviour in Developmental Coordination Disorder takes a unique approach to understanding both typical motor skill and motor skill in DCD by pairing the work of those who research motor activity in typical populations, or across a range of disabilities, with those who work specifically in relation to DCD. Through presenting a series of topics in this way, we hope to encourage those interested in motor behaviour more generally to learn about DCD; help those working with people with DCD to consider DCD in the context of current knowledge of motor behaviour; and to encourage new directions for research in the field of DCD. We are confident that these approaches will facilitate significant new developments within understanding of both typical and atypical motor development, and their consequences, thus making scientific advances as well as developments in practical interventions and support across the lifespan.

Acknowledgements

We are grateful to Professor Margaret Harris for first suggesting a contribution on Developmental Coordination Disorder for this series. Our heartfelt thanks go to our authors for responding so quickly and positively to our vision for this book, and for their desire to be part of it. For the most part we paired chapters together with authors who live on alternate sides of the globe and have never previously worked together. Not only did they rise to our challenge to write their own chapters, but they engaged with one another in doing so. We hope that the juxtaposition of their work will encourage researchers to cross boundaries of all sorts in order to move forward our understanding of motor development and learning in DCD. We are also grateful to Lucy Kennedy for her commitment to this concept and for her advice and support throughout the process of creating this book.

References

American Psychiatric Association (2013). *Diagnostic and statistical manual of mental disorders* (5th ed.). Arlington: Author.

Bernstein, N. A. (1967). *The coordination and regulation of movements*. London: Pergamon Press.

Blank, R., Barnett, A.L., Cairney, J., Green, D., Kirby, A., Polatajko, H., Rosenblum, S., Smits-Engelsman, B., Sugden, D., Wilson, P., & Vinçon, S. (2019). International clinical practice recommendations on the definition, diagnosis, assessment, intervention, and psychosocial aspects of DCD. *Developmental Medicine & Child Neurology*. https://doi.org/10.1111/dmcn.14132

Cairney, J. (Ed.). (2015). *Developmental coordination disorder and its consequences*. Toronto: University of Toronto Press.

Cairney, J., Veldhuizen, S., & Szatmari, P. (2010). Motor coordination and emotional-behavioral problems in children. *Current Opinion in Psychiatry, 23*, 324–329.

Harrowell, I., Hollen, L., Lingam, R., & Emond, A. (2017). Mental health outcomes of developmental coordination disorder in late adolescence. *Developmental Medicine & Child Neurology, 59*, 973–979.

Kirby, A., Williams, N., Thomas, M., & Hill, E. L. (2013). Self-reported mood, general health, wellbeing and employment status in adults with suspected DCD. *Research in Developmental Disabilities, 34*, 1357–1364.

Lingam, R., Hunt, L., Golding, J., Jongmans, M., & Emond, A. (2009). Prevalence of Developmental Coordination Disorder using the DSM-IV at 7 years of age: A UK population-based study. *Pediatrics, 123*, e693–e700.

Mancini, V., Rigoli, D., Cairney, J., Roberts, L., & Piek, J. (2016). The elaborated environmental stress hypothesis as a framework for understanding the association between motor skills and internalizing problems: A mini-review. *Frontiers in Psychology, 7*, 239.

Pezzulo, G., & Dindo, H. (2011). What should I do next? Using shared representations to solve interaction problems. *Experimental Brain Research, 211*, 613–630.

Piaget, J. (1953). *Logic and psychology*. Manchester: Manchester University Press.

Tal-Saban, M., Zarka, S., Grotto, I., Ornoy, A., & Parush, S. (2012). The functional profile of young adults with suspected Developmental Coordination Disorder (DCD). *Research in Developmental Disabilities, 33*, 2193–2202.

World Health Organisation (2001). *International classification of functioning, disability, and health: ICF*. Geneva: World Health Organization.

SECTION I

Development and skill acquisition

1

THE SYNERGETIC, PROBABILISTIC PATHWAYS OF TYPICAL MOTOR DEVELOPMENT

Kathleen M. Haywood and Nancy Getchell

Introduction

The development of motor skills is a continuous and age–related change process shaped by interacting influences, both internal and external to an individual (Clark & Whitall, 1989a; Haywood, Roberton, & Getchell, 2012). There is not a single pattern or trajectory of this change process that is considered 'typical' development. Rather, variations in the interacting influences create a multitude of developmental trajectories, all of which are considered representative of human motor development. Typically developing individuals acquire motor milestones and fundamental motor skills within an age range that broadens over time. Most will become competent in many motor skills and a few will become highly proficient at specific skills such as the ability to play the piano or participate in tennis. To understand what is typical motor development, or for that matter what is atypical motor development, it is important to understand how internal and external influences shape motor development and why some variations in the change process fall within a typical range while others fall outside of it.

Universality versus variability

The basic principles that allow for a 'family' of typical developmental trajectories are known as universality and variability. Universality refers to the great similarity observed as members of a species proceed through development. In fact, when developmentalists refer to "stages of development" they are tracking the emergence of universal behaviors, the changes that are almost stereotypical for a species. An example in infants is the sequence of "motor milestone" skills that emerge in the first year: holding the head erect, rolling over, sitting, pulling to stand, walking, and so on. These will be discussed in more detail later, but typically developing infants move through a sequence of emerging, universal, fundamental motor skills.

At the same time, there are differences across the individuals of a species, even in the emergence of universal behaviors. These differences are termed variability. The variability can be in both process and developmental outcome (Thelen & Ulrich, 1991). Infants acquire even motor milestone skills at slightly different ages. They might also arrive at a similar developmental outcome having traveled different trajectories to get there. For example, Langendorfer and Roberton (2002) observed different developmental trajectories in children acquiring the overarm throw. Consider, too, identical twins who share many commonalities but who have different experiences resulting in individual differences.

The co-existence of universality and variability might seem to be a paradox, but they are like layers woven into development, influencing development at the same time. Often universality is easier to observe early in development. Genetic make-up, an internal influence, drives much of the universality in development. Genetics dictate the formation of the human form and organs in a predictable way, in the absence of a genetic defect, of course. The human form, in turn, tends to drive the development of the skills that can be performed by the human body. At the same time, genetic make-up contributes to variability in development. Some individuals mature faster than average, others mature at the average rate, while still others mature slower than average. This can create great variability in size as well as coordination and skill, even among those of the same chronological age.

Over time, external influences, also termed environmental factors, have more and more impact on an individual, especially after emergence from the relatively protected womb. These external influences tend to vary greatly among individuals of a species and as they accumulate over time, the variability among individuals tends to increase. The same environmental influence can tend to have a similar impact on the emerging movement of all individuals. For example, all individuals can throw a small ball one-handed, but with all individuals increasing the size of the ball eventually causes a change to throwing two-handed. Ball size can have a universal effect on all individuals. At the same time, the exact ball size that causes the switch can be different across individuals. Generally, the smaller the individual's hand, the sooner a change must be made. We can see that both internal and external influences drive motor development that is universal and motor development that is variable.

Developmentalists must be continuously aware that even with universality in development, environmental factors are always present to shape the motor behavior observed. With the same individual, a slight change in environmental factors can change the movement that emerges from these conditions. The same environmental factors can elicit different movements across different individuals. Studying typical motor development, then, requires constant attention to the existing internal and external influences that help shape a movement at any point on the developmental trajectory, particularly considering that early differences result in greater variability over the course of development.

Sensitive periods

The timing of influences on motor development is well illustrated by sensitive periods in development. A sensitive period is an age span during which the developing individual is particularly sensitive to influence, whether the influence is one that contributes to healthy, normal development or one that contributes to slowed, arrested, or atypical development. Sensitive periods also have been described as critical periods, emphasizing the potential importance of an influence to eventual developmental outcomes.

There are many examples of critical or sensitive periods in physical growth and maturation. For example, if an embryo is exposed to the rubella virus during the first four weeks of life, the impact on growth can be wide-ranging: impaired growth, deafness, cataracts, and cardiac defects, among others. Exposure to the virus at eight months, though, has none of these devastating results. It is more difficult to associate a failure to engage in certain behaviors, or for that matter enhanced engagement in other behaviors, with a change in development. Yet, Held and Hein conducted a well-known study of kittens in 1963 that suggested a failure to experience self-directed movement through the environment at a young age resulted in impaired depth perception and paw placing at an older age.

While there is a dearth of knowledge about specific associations of movement experience and later motor skill competency, developmentalists generally advocate for rich experiences in movement during development. Any condition that would limit the exposure of an individual to appropriate motor activities has the potential to impact later movement outcomes, even though humans can display a degree of plasticity, or ability to adapt. Relevant to our discussion here, though, is the relationship between internal and external influences, be they supportive or detrimental to development, and variability in typical development. Both the presence of influences and their timing, especially considering the possibility of sensitive periods during development, results in numerous developmental trajectories that can be considered typical developmental trajectories.

Foundation of skill development: infancy

Infant motor development received formal attention as early as the 1920s and 1930s, if for no other reason than a sense that early motor skill acquisition formed the foundation for later motor development. Early investigators (e.g. Bayley, 1969; Shirley, 1963) observed the sequence and timing of early skill emergence. The sequence of skill emergence was found to be very consistent across children. While an average age of skill onset was identified, so was an age range of typical skill onset (see Table 1.1). This age range widened for later-developing skills.

Early developmentalists attributed the consistent sequence and somewhat tight age ranges of skill emergence to strong genetic influence, but more recent work (see Adolph & Berger, 2006; Thelen, 1995) has explored the intersection of genetics and environment in early development.

TABLE 1.1 Selected motor milestones and associated age ranges

Age range (months)	Milestone
0.1–1.0	Lifts head in prone; Lateral head movements
0.3–2.0	Arm thrusts in play; Leg thrusts in play
0.3–3.0	Retains (i.e. grasps) red ring
0.7–4.0	Lifts head and chest in prone; Turns from side to back
1.0–5.0	Sits with slight support
2.0–7.0	Turns from back to side
4.0–8.0	Unilateral reaches; Grasps object; Rotates wrist; Sits alone momentarily
4.0–10.0	Rolls from back to front
5.0–9.0	Sits alone steadily, Complete thumb opposition
5.0–11.0	Pre-walking progression; Partial finger prehension
5.0–12.0	Pulls to stand with help
7.0–12.0	Walks with help; Creeps
9.0–16.0	Stands alone
9.0–17.0	Walks alone

Source: Adapted from Bayley (1969) and Shirley (1963) scales.

While genetic factors are certainly a strong influence on the development of these motor milestone skills in a fairly regular sequence across individuals, many types of environmental factors also play an important role in this process. Certainly, the timing of skill development is subject to varying environmental and task-related factors.

An example of the role of genetic factors is related to the cephalocaudal direction of physical growth that results in newborns who are rather short-legged and top heavy. These proportions are a challenge to standing on two legs early in life. Hence, the onset of standing can reflect genetically driven development in the neurological system, the skeletal system, and the muscular system. At the same time, cultural practices can introduce particular environmental influences that lead to greater variability in timing, sequencing and later performance of motor skills (Adolph, Karasik, & Tamis-LeMonda, 2010; Karasik, Adolph, Tamis-LeMonda & Bornstein, 2010). For example, a cultural practice of exercising and placing infants in a walking position on a daily basis leads to an earlier onset in walking in several cultures (see Karasik et al., 2010).

It is clear that multiple internal and external factors can influence an individual's developmental trajectory during infancy. Early influences can play a large role in the ultimate developmental trajectory by shifting that trajectory even slightly at a young age. The range of behaviors that we would describe as typical fall into a rather narrow span early in life, but with time, this range widens to include an increasingly larger span of behaviors.

Atypical behaviors are often labeled as such because they fall outside the range of behaviors encompassing a large number of developing individuals. For example, an infant who initiates sitting at the 'old' end of the typical age range for the onset of sitting is considered typically developing, while an infant who initiates sitting at a much older age than the typical age range is considered atypical. A pattern of consistently acquiring fundamental skills at an age much beyond average suggests atypical development.

The emergence of skill proficiency after infancy

While fundamental motor skills such as walking and reaching appear to be ubiquitous early in development, environmental influences impact skill development almost immediately. Culture, opportunity, equipment and ability to practice, among a myriad of other factors, contribute to the development of motor skill (Adolph et al., 2010; Haywood & Getchell, 2014). Therefore, the development of proficient motor skill execution appears to depend on skill-specific experiences such as practice, instruction, or imitation. Such experiences guide further changes in proficiency with high levels of proficiency requiring significant amounts of practice within the context in which the skill will be used (Brian, Goodway, Logan, & Sutherland, 2016). Therefore, variability in motor performance exists even at high levels of proficiency since individuals vary in specific experiences and possess different physiques.

As a result of this variability in motor development, individuals reach different levels of proficiency in fundamental motor skills at different ages. In the typical motor development of young children, timing differences might be a matter of weeks or months. However, individuals who are significantly delayed in motor development across many skills exhibit atypical development. Unfortunately, this situation easily leads to a curtailment of the experiences facilitating development, causing an even larger gap between typically and atypically developing individuals.

In the next sections, we will describe developmental changes in locomotor, ballistic, and manipulative skills. As we noted, researchers have found sequential, cumulative, stage-like changes in movement patterns within these skills.

Development of locomotion

By definition, the act of locomotion is moving the body from one place to another. While the human body allows for many different types of locomotion using different limb configurations and types of coordination, the most commonly used forms of locomotion after infancy involve using the legs and feet to project an upright torso. The first upright bipedal form of locomotion to emerge is walking, which involves symmetrically alternating legs. For new walkers, controlling postural stability in order to maintain balance is the most difficult challenge to overcome in order to move independently on two feet. Walking requires the ability to balance on one foot while moving the entire body forward to plant the other foot. If movers cannot maintain an upright posture while shifting the center of gravity over their base of support (either one or both feet) while responding to reactive forces generated by their own movements, they will fall. Early walkers accomplish postural stability by using a 'stability' strategy, assuming limb configurations that maximize their overall steadiness, which in turn minimizes their odds of falling.

Within just a few months, new walkers acquire the ability to run. Both walking and running are ubiquitous skills that emerge in typically developing children independent of culture, race or ethnicity. Variations of these skills such as hopping, galloping, and leaping, on the other hand, do not automatically appear, but rather emerge as a result of individual experiences and environmental interactions. However, the different forms of locomotion tend to change similarly as individuals gain proficiency. Further, they change from movement strategies that favor stability to ones that elicit greater mobility. The ability to maintain balance (e.g. postural support) is a major precursor to proficient performance across all locomotor skills. As with walking and running, individuals adopt movement strategies that ensure maximum stability early on. For those who have a plethora of early movement experiences, adoption of movement strategies that trade stability for additional mobility lead to a progression to increased skill proficiency. For example, movers produce more force by alternatively pumping arms and swinging legs through a wide range of motion in proficient running, hopping, jumping, and leaping. By forgoing stability as a means to maintain postural stability and balance, individuals can manipulate force production to adapt their movements to task context (e.g. moving faster, jumping farther). Within limbs, segment movements optimize transfer of energy using an open kinetic chain. As a result, mobility increases. In the following sections, we describe specific changes in walking and running to serve as general examples for changes seen in other forms of locomotion as a function of increasing proficiency.

Walking. Most typically developing infants begin walking anywhere from ten to eighteen months of age, when they can maintain an upright posture while alternating actions of their legs and feet (Haywood & Getchell, 2014). Unlike running and other more advanced forms of locomotion, walking does not contain a moment of flight where both feet leave the ground making it a highly stable form of locomotion. One foot will support the body as the alternate leg swings forward, then the body is supported by both feet and then the original support leg swings forward while the opposite foot supports; this pattern of single-double-single support (termed a step cycle) is repeated. Because no flight exists, walking requires a relatively small amount of leg strength to move the body's center of gravity forward. Since it lacks a moment of flight, walking is also the most stable of the foot locomotor patterns. By having two feet on the ground between leg swings, it is easier for the walker to maintain balance.

Because new walkers have just mastered balance and postural control in order to walk, it is not surprising that their movements optimize stability. Ivanenko, Dominici, and Lacquaniti (2007) described the early levels of leg action as a combination of stepping in place with forward progress. They speculated that toddlers sacrifice energy efficiency in order to maintain upright posture. Biomechanically, stability can be accomplished through widening the base of support: Toddlers spread their feet wide apart and point toes outward. In addition, young movers limit the range of motion used at any given joint (i.e. 'freezing degrees of freedom'). For example, new walkers lock their arms into 'high guard' and ankles such that feet remain flat or flexed and then take independent steps moving primarily at the knee and hip of the swinging leg (see Figure 1.1.a).

While a stability-centered movement pattern ensures that movers will not fall over, it also ensures that they will not move fast or far. In order to increase walking velocity, they must 'trade' the body configuration that provides optimal stability for one that allows a greater degree of mobility. New walkers transition to these more proficient movement patterns over a period of several years and most children will have the essential ingredients of an advanced walk by about 4 years old (Sutherland, 1997). Single foot support time increases, especially between 1.0 years and 2.5 years of age (Sutherland, Olshen, Cooper, & Woo, 1980). The length of each stride increases, both because of growth and from greater application of force and greater range of motion at the hips, knees, and ankles. Pelvic rotation increases, allowing full range of leg motion and oppositional movement of the upper and lower body segments. Walkers also reduce out-toeing and narrow the base of support laterally to reduce out-of-plane movements (Figure 1.1.b). Intersegmental leg coordination changes to that of a 'double knee lock', such that the knee extends at heel strike (first knee lock), flexes slightly as the body weight moves forward over

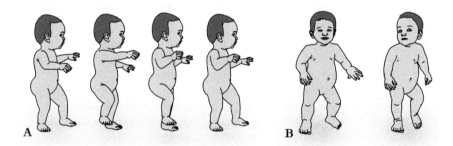

FIGURE 1.1   A new walker exhibiting a gait pattern used to improve stability through reducing the number of active joints. A. From the side, where the legs reduced range of motion and the arms in high guard are apparent. B. From the front, which shows the out-toeing and wide placement of the feet.

Source: A. Reprinted by permission from film tracing drawings taken in the former Motor Development and Child Study Laboratory, University of Wisconsin-Madison. B. Adapted, by permission, from R.L. Wickstrom, 1983, Fundamental motor patterns, 3rd ed. (Philadelphia: Lea & Febiger), 29 © Mary Ann Roberton.

the supporting leg, then extends once more at foot push-off (second knee lock). As a result of these changes, walking velocity increases, especially between 1.0 and 3.5 years of age (Sutherland et al., 1980). The rhythm and coordination of a child's walk improve observably until age 5 or so, but beyond this age, pattern improvements are subtle.

Developmentally, running follows walking. While modifications to walking patterns result in greater mobility, the velocity gains are limited by the double support period. Therefore, toddlers soon transition to a form of locomotion that allows for even greater speed. Children typically start to run about 6 to 7 months after they begin to walk (Clark & Whitall, 1989b; Whitall & Getchell, 1995). Walking and running are similar in that action of the legs is symmetrical and anti-phase. However, one critical difference exists: Running includes a period of flight wherein both feet are off the ground, which results in greater stride length. In order to propel their bodies into flight, toddlers must generate substantially more force in the stance leg. The production of more force with the resultant increase in landing velocity coupled with the loss of double support leads to a challenging postural control scenario. Characteristically, early running patterns exhibit a return to some of the earlier body configurations used in early walking that preserve stability (Burnett & Johnson, 1971). For example, when first learning to run, the child may adopt a wide base of support, a flat-footed landing, leg extension at midsupport, and the high-guard arm position without a concomitant return to these patterns in walking patterns.

As children grow, these qualitative changes in running pattern, together with increased body size and strength and improved coordination, typically result in improved quantitative measures of running speed and time in flight. Such changes have been well documented in several University of Wisconsin studies of children between ages 1.5 and 10 years (Beck, 1966; Clouse, 1959; Dittmer, 1962) and in other studies (Branta, Haubenstricker, & Seefeldt, 1984; Roberton, 1984). The gait pattern changes that occur are similar to those seen as individuals become more proficient in walking, such as a decrease in out-toeing and elimination of out of plane movements. In addition, movement changes reflect an increased generation of force, such as full extension of the knee as the support leg pushes off the ground and faster acceleration of the thigh during swing phase, or a conservation of energy, such as the 'tucked' position of the leg during forward swing (Figure 1.2).

Other forms of locomotion. While an almost limitless variety of locomotor patterns have the potential to exist after walking and running, only approximately six are seen with relative frequency. All six include a flight period where both feet are off the ground. Hopping is defined as a take-off into the air from one foot and a landing on the same foot. Jumping is defined only by its landing: it is a take-off into the air from one or two feet with a landing simultaneously on two feet. Leaping is a run that exaggerates the moment of flight by making it longer in time and frequently higher than would be seen in the run. The remaining three forms consist of combinations of other locomotor patterns, including the gallop, skip, and slide. The gallop is composed of a step-leap; the skip of a step-hop. The slide, a sideways

FIGURE 1.2   An advanced runner exhibiting a running pattern that biomechanically maximizes mobility e.g. arms and legs move in opposition through a wide range of motion.

Source: Adapted, by permission, from R.L. Wickstrom, 1983, Fundamental motor patterns, 3rd ed. (Philadelphia: Lea & Febiger), 29. © Mary Ann Roberton.

gallop, is the only foot pattern for which the direction of movement is specified. All the others may be performed forwards, backwards, sideways, or diagonally.

Development of ballistic skills

In locomotion, individuals generate force through their movements to project their bodies as a means to move from place to place. Compare this to ballistic skills, where individuals generate and apply force to an external object in order to project it. The most frequently researched ballistic patterns involve sports skills such as throwing, kicking or striking. Interestingly enough, the developmental changes leading to more proficient movement forms are similar, primarily because the same biomechanical principles leading to optimal performance apply. In other words, early movements maximize stability whereas later movements maximize force production. As they become more proficient at projecting objects, movers begin to take advantage of body configurations that optimize force production and energy transfer among limbs. These complex movements all tend to begin proximally with action of the trunk muscles; energy is then passed from limb segment to limb segment of the open, kinetic link system until it reaches the distal effecter, usually the hand or foot.

In the case of striking, kicking, and throwing this energy exchange occurs superimposed on a running or stepping base of support. Another interesting commonality across these complex, projectile skills is that they employ backswings to place the body segments in position to move forward. In the advanced form of striking, throwing, and kicking the backswing and forward swing partially overlap: proximal segments begin to move forward while more distal segments are still moving backward. The advanced form of these movements also shows strong acceleration of the distal segment just milliseconds before contact/release, thus yielding high, distal angular velocity. This acceleration seems to result partially from the inertia of each distal segment against the motion of its adjacent, proximal segment. The "lagging" segment stretches the agonist muscles of the distal segment, which may in turn excite reflexes that augment the latter's muscular contractions (Roberts & Metcalfe, 1968). As we will see, "lag" is one aspect of object projection which develops only gradually over time.

Throwing. Throwing can take many forms depending on interactions among the individual within the movement environment and any task-related goals, rules or equipment. Young children may use a one or two-hand underhand throw due to ball size or weight. As children become involved in organized sport, throwing form often changes as a function of specific, sport related task goals (e.g. speed vs. accuracy) or rules. For example, within both cricket and baseball, players use over-arm or sidearm throws to project balls forcefully and with accuracy; however, the movement pattern differs based on requirements of the individual sport.

Early throwing. Young children's throwing patterns, especially those of children under 3 years, tend to be restricted to arm action alone, without leg movement or trunk rotation (Marques–Bruna & Grimshaw, 1997). No backswing is used; instead, new throwers lift their arm into position. Once in front of the body, children merely position the upper arm, often with the elbow up or forward, and execute the throw by elbow extension alone or including minimal extension/flexion of the trunk. By configuring the body this way, stability is maximized (limiting challenges to balance) but mechanical efficiency is low and little force is generated to project the ball (see Figure 1.3.a).

Proficient throwing. As individuals become more proficient at throwing, they move in characteristic ways. A backswing, used as a windup is added, during which weight shifts to the back foot, the trunk rotates back and the arm makes a circular, downward motion. In addition, throwers will take a step (see Figure 1.3.b). Initially, children frequently step with the foot ipsilateral to their throwing arm; this is later replaced with a contralateral step. This contralateral step facilitates trunk rotation, with the trunk bending laterally, away from the side of the throwing arm. The action of the arm changes as well. The upper arm forms a right angle with the trunk and comes forward just as (or slightly after) the shoulders rotate to the point at which the individual releases the object (called front facing). The thrower holds the elbow at a right angle during the forward swing, extending the arm when the shoulders reach the front-facing position. Extending the arm just before release lengthens the radius of the throwing arc. Finally, the forearm lags behind the trunk and upper arm during the forward swing. All of these movements occur sequentially, progressively adding the contributions of each part to the force of the throw (see Figure 1.3.b).

In sum, individuals gain proficiency when they move in ways that allow them to generate more force in order to move the projectile farther or faster, just as with locomotor skills. This represents a change from a movement strategy based on stability to one of greater mobility. The body configurations, while sometimes difficult to describe at the segmental level, take advantage of a relatively small set of

FIGURE 1.3   The developmental progression of overarm throwing. A. A novice thrower reduces joint degrees of freedom by isolating movements to primarily flexion/extension of her throwing arm. This improves her overall stability in order to accomplish the task. B. A more proficient thrower takes a contralateral step and uses a backswing prior to throwing, and uses a greater range of movements within the throwing arm.

Source: Reprinted from permission from drawings from film tracings taken in the former Motor Development and Child Study Laboratory, University of Wisconsin-Madison. © Mary Ann Roberton.

biomechanical principles such as increasing distance over which a force is applied through truck rotation, increased range of motion or taking a step (Gagen & Getchell, 2008).

Development of manipulative skills

The third broad category of motor skills are 'manipulative' and reflect instances where individuals receive, maneuver, or direct objects rather than project them. Most developmental research has focused on the development of reaching and grasping in infancy and later the development of interception skills such as catching.

It is not intuitive that these types of skills are categorized together. Yet, they share an element of anticipation and timing that are essential for successful performance. In other words, individuals must plan their actions so that their hands move to the appropriate place within a narrow time range. Indeed, the anticipation involved in these skills makes the study of their development both complex and intriguing since perception of the object plays a large role.

Over the course of development, individuals acquire a smooth, seamless reach for and grasp of an object. The reach and grasp are adapted for the location of the object, as well as for the object's characteristics such as size, shape, and even anticipated weight. These adaptations underscore the importance of sensory (e.g. vision, proprioception) and perceptual information to movement success. Therefore, much of the research on the emergence of manipulative skills deals with the relative roles of the various sensory-perceptual systems as well as neuromuscular control of the upper limbs. Despite execution of the skilled reach and grasp as a seamless movement, researchers often have focused on reaching and grasping separately to better understand each component of the movement. Let us start our discussion with grasping.

Grasping. Adults shape their hands to grasp differently shaped and sized objects without conscience thought. The hand and fingers adeptly grasp a coin, a table knife, or a tennis racket as needed. Researchers began to study the development of this ability in the 1930s. Early research focused on how infants shaped their hands to grasp a 1-inch cube. A transition was identified around 9 months of age. In the early months infants tended to use power grips that position the object in the palm with counter pressure from the thumb but later infants could use precision grips that pinched the object between the fingers and thumb (Halverson, 1931; Napier, 1956). Adults are able to use both grips, and select the one appropriate to the task.

Later research on infant grasping focused on infants' use of a wide range of grips depending on the size and shape of the object (Hohlstein, 1982; Butterworth, Verwerj, & Hopkins, 1997). Newell, Scully, Tenebaum, and Hardiman (1989) proposed that selection of a grip was dictated by the relative size of the hand and the size and shape of the object. This notion is termed body scaling. One grip might be used with a small object, but enlargement of that object, even if its shape is maintained, might trigger the use of another grip because the ratio of hand size to object size had changed. So, too, a change in object size might trigger a switch to grasping with two hands. Researchers have suggested a hand-to-object size ratio of .6 to .7 is the relationship that triggers a switch from one-handed grasping to two-handed grasping in both toddlers (Newell et al., 1989) and children (Van der Kamp, Savelsburgh, & Davis, 1998).

Barrett, Traupman, and Needham (2008) additionally demonstrated that even infants as young as 5 months of age adapted the shape of their hands in preparation for a grasp according to visual inspection of the object to be grasped. The researchers presented balls to the infants that appeared either hard and rigid or soft and compressible. Infants readied a grip that was appropriate for nature of the ball. At very young ages, then, infants are developing the ability to shape their hands according to the nature of an object to be grasped, although there is some indication that younger children still use a wider hand opening to grasp an object than adults do, perhaps providing a safety margin.

Task and environmental conditions continue to influence choice of grip as children learn to use objects as tools. Braswell, Rosengren, and Pierroutsakos (2007) observed 3- and 4-year-olds copying shapes with a pencil. The children used various grips, including the adult-like tripod grip, but those with relatively stable grips copied shapes more accurately. Presumably, with typical development children settle on the tripod grip as the most efficient for writing.

Reaching. An arm reach obviously brings the hand or hands to an object to be grasped. Newborns progress from arm thrashing to reaching toward objects to reaching successfully to objects at approximately 4 months of age. These early reaches tend to be jerky and inaccurate. The work of Thelen et al. (1993) suggested that infants learn to reach accurately in a flexible way, arriving at accurate reaches through exploration of a variety of patterns (see also Gonçalves et al., 2013). In addition to exploring movement paths, infants explore movement speed (Corbetta & Thelen, 1996). With some weeks of reaching experience, infants generally develop acceptable control of the speed and path of their reaches around 8 months of age (von Hofsten, 1991). It should be noted that development of stable sitting posture around this age could well be related to the stability of reaches. Corbetta and Thelen also observed bimanual reaching in infancy, finding that infants tended to alternate between periods of unimanual reaching and bimanual reaching. More intentional use of unimanual and bimanual reaching comes gradually after 8 months of age when infants can better inhibit responses across the limbs.

The role of vision in the development of reaching has long been of interest to researchers but questions about the role of vision remain. By studying reaches in both light and dark conditions researchers (Berthier & Carrico, 2010; Carrico & Berthier, 2008) observed that visual guidance of a reach to a graspable object becomes more important to infants over the age span of 6 to 15 months. This is particularly true as the precision demands of the reach-and-grasp increase. Likely, the later phase of the reach is slowed as vision guides the hand to the object requiring a precision grasp (Jeannerod, 1981).

While researchers have often studied the development of grasping and reaching independently, the authentic task is a reach and grasp as an action. Zoia et al. (2006) compared the reach-to-grasp of 5-year-olds to that of adults, using cylinders of three sizes at two distances away. The researchers used shutter glasses that could be switched from clear to opaque to provide two viewing conditions. In the vision condition participants could see the target cylinder throughout the reach and grasp while in the no-vision condition the glasses were opened for 400 msec then closed before the reach.

Movement duration and deceleration was longer and the grip opening was made earlier and wider in the no vision condition compared to the vision condition. The 5-year-olds had longer movement durations, wider grips (relative to hand size), and decelerated over a long time to the longer distance than adults. Vision plays an important role throughout the life span when the task requirements become more precise.

The development of reaching and grasping appears to be similar for stationery objects and moving objects (von Hofsten & Lindhagen, 1979; von Hofsten, 1980). At 8 months of age infants display a bias to reach for moving objects with the right hand. By 10 months of age infants show more diverse strategies and more ipsilateral reaches that correspond to the direction of object approach (Domellöf, Barbu-Roth, Rönqvist, Jacquet, & Fagard, 2015; Fagard, Spelke, & von Hofsten, 2009). Thus, reaching to grasp moving objects becomes more efficient with age.

Catching. Infants can intercept moving objects when seated. The challenge of childhood is learning to anticipate an object's arrival when it moves in variable trajectories, at variable speeds, and in variable directions. Additionally, the catcher must learn to move to another location to catch the object. For children, then, attaining proficiency in catching typically comes at a later age than many other fundamental skills. Generally children must learn to position their hands with fingers up or down and the palms adjusted to the arrival point of the object relative to the body and to object size. They must transition from stiff, outstretched arms to a relaxed position that allows the arms to 'give' and possession of the object in the hands to be maintained (Strohmeyer, Williams, & Shaub-George, 1991).

Moving distances to catch balls likely involves a subconscious learning of the relationships in the environment and keeping one or more of those relationships invariant as one moves to the ball. Children might learn these relationships through experience. Initially, when they are stationary only balls with a certain relationship of the trajectory to themselves actually come to them. As they learn to move to catch, they only reach the balls when they keep that relationship (McLeod & Dienes, 1993, 1996). Experience with many situations, then, is important in learning complex catching skills.

Conclusions: foundations of atypical development

We have focused on typical motor development in childhood throughout this chapter – those changes we might expect in individuals without genetic disorders or dispositions who develop in 'typical' environments. Basically, this is motor development "on average", encompassing a broad range of ages and motor activities and allowing for universality as well as variability among humans. Infants acquire motor milestones that lead up to the ability to sit and stand unassisted, reach and grasp objects and move from place to place. Early goal directed movements frequently optimize individuals biomechanical and postural stability. Through experiences, growth and maturation, children gain proficiency in fundamental motor skills, relinquishing stability strategies for ones that provide more mobility or generate more force. Each individual's developmental trajectory will depend on the interaction between experiences and genetic make-up over time.

At the same time, trajectories exist that can deviate from the average developmental course in a variety of ways. Of concern to both practitioners and parents are situations where children experience significant delays or differences in acquisition of motor milestones and subsequent fundamental motor patterns which interfere with their activities of daily living and academic performance. If the motor delays or differences vary significantly from the age ranges seen in typical development, this can indicate some underlying issue such as Developmental Coordination Disorder.

References

Adolph, K. E., & Berger, S. A. (2006). Motor development. In W. Damon & R. Lerner (Series Eds.) & D. Kuhn & R. S. Siegler (Vol. Eds.), *Handbook of child psychology: Vol. 2. Cognition, perception, and language* (6th ed., pp. 161–213). New York: Wiley.

Adolph, K. E., Karasik, L. B, Tamis-LeMonda, C. S. (2010). Motor skills. In M. H. Bornstein (Ed.), *Handbook of cultural developmental science* (pp. 61–88). New York: Taylor & Francis.

Barrett, T. M., Traupman, E., & Needham, A. (2008). Infants' visual anticipation of object structure in grasp planning. *Infant Behavior & Development, 31*, 1–9.

Bayley, N. (1969). *Manual for the Bayley scales of infant development.* New York: The Psychological.

Beck, M. (1966). *The path of the center of gravity during running in boys grades one to six.* Unpublished doctoral dissertation, University of Wisconsin, Madison.

Berthier, N. E., & Carrico, R. L. (2010). Visual information and object size in infant reaching. *Infant Behavior & Development, 33*, 555–566.

Branta, C., Haubenstricker, J., & Seefeldt, V. (1984). Age changes in motor skill during childhood and adolescence. In R. L. Terjung (Ed.), *Exercise and sport science reviews* (Vol. 12, pp. 467–520). Lexington, MA: Collamore.

Braswell, G. S., Rosengren, K. S., & Pierroutsakos, S. L. (2007). Task constraints on preschool children's grip configurations during drawing. *Developmental Psychobiology, 49*, 216–225.

Brian, A., Goodway, J., Logan, J. A., & Sutherland, S. (2016). SKIPing with teachers: An early years motor skill intervention. *Physical Education and Sport Pedagogy*, 1–13. http://dx.doi.org/10.1080/17408989.2016.1176133

Burnett, C. N., & Johnson, E. W. (1971). Development of gait in childhood, part II. *Developmental Medicine and Child Neurology, 13*, 207–215.

Butterworth, G., Verweij, E., & Hopkins, B. (1997). The development of prehension in infants: Halverson revisited. *British Journal of Developmental Psychology, 15*(2), 223–236.

Carrico, R. L., & Berthier, N. E. (2008). Vision and precision reaching in 15-month-old infants. *Infant Behavior & Development, 31*, 62–70.

Clark, J. E., & Whitall, J. (1989a). What is motor development? *Quest, 41*, 183–202.

Clark, J. E., & Whitall, J. (1989b). Changing patterns of locomotion: From walking to skipping. In M. H. Woollacott & A. Shumway-Cook (Eds.), *Development of posture and gait across the life span* (pp. 128–151). Columbia, SC: University of South Carolina Press.

Clouse, F. (1959). *A kinematic analysis of the development of the running pattern of preschool boys.* Unpublished doctoral dissertation, University of Wisconsin, Madison.

Corbetta, D., & Thelen, E. (1996). The developmental origins of bimanual coordination: A dynamic perspective. *Journal of Experimental Psychology: Human Perception and Performance, 22*, 502–522.

Dittmer, J. (1962). *A kinematic analysis of the development of the running pattern of grade school girls and certain factors which distinguish good from poor performance at the observed ages.* Unpublished master's thesis, University of Wisconsin, Madison.

Domellöf, E., Barbu-Roth, M., Rönnqvist, L., Jacquet, A. Y., & Fagard, J. (2015). Infant manual performance during reaching and grasping for objects moving in depth. *Frontiers in Psychology, 6*, 1142.

Fagard, J., Spelke, E., & von Hofsten, C. (2009). Reaching and grasping a moving object in 6-, 8-, and 10-month-old infants: Laterality and performance. *Infant Behavior & Development, 32*, 137–146.

Gagen, L., & Getchell, N. (2008). Applying Newton's apple to elementary physical education: An interdisciplinary approach. *Journal of Physical Education, Recreation, and Dance, 79*, 43–51.

Gonçalves, R. V., Figueiredo, E. M., Mourão, C. B., Colosimo, E. A., Fonseca, S. T., & Mancini, M. C. (2013). Development of infant reaching behaviors: Kinematic changes in touching and hitting. *Infant Behavior & Development, 36*, 825–832.

Halverson, H. M. (1931). An experimental study of prehension in infants by means of systematic cinema records. *Genetic Psychology Monographs, 10*, 107–286.

Haywood, K. M., & Getchell, N. (2014). *Life span motor development* (6th ed.). Champaign, IL: Human Kinetics.

Haywood, K. M., Roberton, M. A., & Getchell, N. (2012). *Advanced analysis of motor development*. Champaign, IL: Human Kinetics.

Held, R., & Hein, A. (1963). Movement-produced stimulation in the development of visually guided behavior. *Journal of Comparative and Physiological Psychology, 56*, 872–876.

Hohlstein, R. E. (1982). The development of prehension in normal infants. *American Journal of Occupational Therapy, 36*, 170–176.

Ivanenko, Y. P., Dominici, N., & Lacquaniti, F. (2007). Development of independent walking in toddlers. *Exercise and Sport Science Review, 35*, 67–73.

Jeannerod, M. (1981). Intersegmental coordination during reaching at natural visual objects. In J. Long & A. Baddeley (Eds.), *Attention and performance* (pp. 153–168). Hillsdale, NJ: Lawrence Erlbaum Associates.

Karasik, L. B., Adolph, K. E., Tamis-LeMonda, C. S., & Bornstein, M. H. (2010). Weird walking: Cross-cultural research on motor development. *The Behavioral and Brain Sciences, 33*(2–3), 95–96. http://doi.org/10.1017/S0140525X10000117

Langendorfer, S., & Roberton, M. A. (2002). Individual pathways in the development of forceful throwing. *Research Quarterly for Exercise and Sport, 73*, 245–256.

Marques-Bruna, P., & Grimshaw, P. N. (1997). 3-dimensional kinematics of overarm throwing action of children age 15 to 30 months. *Perceptual and Motor Skills, 84*, 1267–1283.

McLeod, P., & Dienes, Z. (1993). Running to catch the ball. *Nature, 362*, 23.

McLeod, P., & Dienes, Z. (1996). Do fielders know where to go to catch the ball or only how to get there? *Journal of Experimental Psychology, 22*(3), 531–543.

Napier, J. (1956). The prehensile movements of the human hand. *Journal of Bone and Joint Surgery, 38B*, 902–913.

Newell, K. M., Scully, D. M., Tenenbaum, F., & Hardiman, S. (1989). Body scale and the development of prehension. *Developmental Psychobiology, 22*, 11–13.

Roberton, M. A. (1984). Changing motor patterns during childhood. In J. R. Thomas (Ed.), *Motor development during childhood and adolescence* (pp. 48–90). Minneapolis, MN: Burgess.

Roberts, E. M., & Metcalfe, A. (1968). Mechanical analysis of kicking. In *Biomechanics I* (pp. 315–319). New York: Karge.

Shirley, M. M. (1963). The motor sequence. In D. Wayne (Ed.), *Readings in child psychology*. Englewood Cliffs, NJ: Prentice-Hall.

Strohmeyer, H. S., Williams, K., & Schaub-George, D. (1991). Developmental sequences for catching a small ball: A prelongitudinal screening. *Research Quarterly for Exercise and Sport, 62*, 257–266.

Sutherland, D. H. (1997). The development of mature gait. *Gait and Posture, 6*(2), 162–170.

Sutherland, D. H., Olshen, R., Cooper, L., & Woo, S. (1980). The development of mature gait. *Journal of Bone and Joint Surgery, 62-A*, 336–353.

Thelen, E. (1995). Motor development: A new synthesis. *American Psychologist, 50*, 79–95.

Thelen, E., Corbetta, D., Kamm, K., Spencer, J. P., Schneider, K., & Zernicke, R. F. (1993). The transition to reaching: Mapping intention and intrinsic dynamics. *Child Development, 64*, 1058–1098.

Thelen, E., & Ulrich, B. D. (1991). Hidden skills: A dynamic systems analysis of treadmill stepping during the first year. *Monographs of the Society for Research in Child Development, 56*(1), Serial No. 233.

van der Kamp, J., Savelsbergh, G. J. P., & Davis, W. E. (1998). Body-scaled ratio as a control parameter for prehension in 5- to 9-year-old children. *Developmental Psychology, 33*(4), 351–361.

von Hofsten, C. (1980). Predictive reaching for moving objects by human infants. *Journal of Experimental Child Psychology, 30*, 369–382.

von Hofsten, C. (1991). Structuring of early reaching movements: A longitudinal study. *Journal of Motor Behavior, 23*, 280–292.

von Hofsten, C., & Lindhagen, K. (1979). Observations on the development of reaching for moving objects. *Journal of Experimental Child Psychology, 28*, 158–173.

Whitall, J., & Getchell, N. (1995). From walking to running: Using a dynamical systems approach to the development of locomotor skills. *Child Development, 66*, 1541–1553.

Zoia, S., Pezzetta, E., Blason, L., Scabar, A., Carrozzi, M., & Bulgheroni, M. (2006). A comparison of the reach-to-grasp movement between children and adults: A kinematic study. *Developmental Neuorpsychology, 30*, 719–738.

2

DEVELOPMENTAL PROGRESSION IN DCD

Anna L. Barnett, Cara Law and Nichola Stuart

Introduction

Haywood and Getchell (2010, this volume) outline the generally universal progression of motor development trajectories in typically developing children. They provide a clear description of fundamental motor skills, outlining the attainment of 'milestones' as new skills are achieved and progression towards more efficient movement patterns in the three areas of body transport (locomotor skill), object projection (ballistic skill) and object manipulation (manipulative skills). Once fundamental motor skills in these areas are achieved then more specific skills (e.g. different sport skills) are learned. As noted elsewhere in this volume, development and learning can be considered as the same process (see Newell & Pacheco, 2019 this volume). While development is usually considered over longer time scales and related to maturation of the body, learning usually refers to shorter time scales and is related to more specific practice opportunities. However in both development and learning, individual differences in progression are based on unique experiences and interactions between the individual, the task and the environment. This constraints-based approach, within a dynamic systems framework (Thelen & Smith, 1994), is relevant to the understanding of both development and learning in typical and atypical development, supporting the notion that they are characterised by variability and non-linearity of skill acquisition.

The main feature of developmental coordination disorder (DCD) is a significant impairment in the performance of motor skills in the absence of any obvious neurological impairment (e.g., cerebral palsy, muscular dystrophy, degenerative disorder) (APA, 2013). Some of the characteristics of DCD at different ages are provided in the Diagnostic and Statistical Manual of Mental Disorders – 5th Edition,

DSM-5 (see Table 2.1). While these children develop fundamental motor skills in the early years, a range of performance deficits in childhood have been recognised and extensively examined (Wilson et al., 2017).

In this chapter, we consider what is known about the presentation and developmental progression in DCD and how it compares to typically developing individuals. While we recognise the importance of gaining a broad understanding of the individual in all areas of development, here the focus is on development in the motor domain. As outlined in the introduction to this volume (Hill & Barnett, 2019 this volume) DCD often co-occurs with other developmental disorders (including dyslexia, ADHD and ASD) and has a range of 'non-motor' associated features (including anxiety, depression, low self-esteem and other psycho-social difficulties). While we acknowledge that these interact with motor behaviour, they are not the focus of this volume and have been addressed in detail elsewhere (e.g. Cairney, Rigoli, & Piek, 2013; Mancini, Rigoli, Cairney, Roberts, & Piek, 2016). In contrast, there has been surprisingly little specific study of 'motor development' in DCD in terms of investigations of developmental trajectories.

In this chapter we draw on information from a range of different types of studies to explore what is known about the presentation and developmental trajectory of the condition from the early years through to adulthood. We start by looking at studies of infants followed from the neonatal period through to the school years; then we look at studies that have followed the course of DCD across early childhood to late adolescence and finally at studies of young adults with DCD. Before turning to this literature, in the following section we first introduce some of the assessment tools that have been used in research to measure motor performance at different ages. This initial review of assessments is important to help understand the type of information available from the range of methods used. It also helps identify limitations when reviewing and evaluating research in this field.

TABLE 2.1 Excerpts from the DSM-5 description of developmental coordination disorder (APA, 2013, pp. 75–76) outlining the core motor features at different ages

---

"Delayed motor milestones may be the first signs, or the disorder is first recognised when the child attempts tasks such as holding a knife and fork, buttoning clothes, or playing ball games" (p. 76).

"They also may be delayed in developing skills such as negotiating stairs, pedalling, buttoning shirts, completing puzzles, and using zippers. Even when the skill is achieved, movement execution may appear awkward, slow, or less precise than that of peers" (p. 75).

"In middle childhood, there are difficulties with motor aspects of assembling puzzles, building models, playing ball, and handwriting, as well as with organising belongings, when motor sequencing and coordination are required" (p. 76).

"In early adulthood, there is continuing difficulty in learning new tasks involving complex-automatic motor skills, including driving and using tools. Inability to take notes and handwrite quickly may affect performance in the workplace" (p. 76).

Assessment of motor skill through the lifespan

Motor skill can be assessed in various ways, with some techniques more appropriate for particular age groups. Only a few examples are provided here in relation to DCD; for broader reviews see Piek (2006) or Barnett and Peters (2004). In the early months a clinical assessment of body posture, muscle tone, range of movement and involuntary reflex movements are common (e.g. Dubowitz, Dubowitz, & Mercuri, 1999). There have also been attempts to assess and categorise the nature of spontaneous general movements in young infants (Hadders-Algra, 2004). The emergence of new skills can also be observed and recorded, such as the classic 'milestones' of manipulative skill (grasping, manipulating objects, using tools etc.) and postural control/locomotion (lifting the head, rolling the body, crawling, sitting, standing, walking etc.). These can be captured using norm-referenced tools such as the Peabody Developmental Motor Scales-2 (PDMS-2; Folio & Fewell, 2000) or components within more general infant development scales such as the Bayley Scales of Infant Development (Bayley, 2006) and Griffiths Mental Development Scales (Griffiths, 1984). Observational checklists/parent questionnaires about motor milestones can also be used, such as the Ages and Stages Questionnaire (ASQ; Squires, Bricker, & Potter, 1997).

From the age of three to four years, standardised performance tests can be administered to measure general motor competence. Various tools exist, with two of the most popular norm-referenced tests in the field of DCD being the Movement ABC (MABC; Henderson & Sugden, 1992; MABC-2; Henderson, Sugden, & Barnett, 2007 and its precursor, the Test of Motor Impairment, TOMI; Stott, Moyes, & Henderson, 1984) and the Bruininks-Oseretsky Test of Motor Proficiency (BOT; Bruininks, 1978; BOT-2; Bruininks & Bruininks, 2005). The MABC-2 and BOT-2 have norms for children aged three and four years, through to 16 and 21 years respectively. A similar but less widely used test is the McCarron Assessment of Neuromuscular Development (MAND; McCarron, 1997). These three test batteries include a range of tasks requiring balance and locomotion, ballistic and manipulative skill. They also yield a total composite score which is used to identify those with motor difficulties and can further be used to categorise the level of difficulty, for example as 'moderate' or 'severe' in nature.

It is only recently that motor assessments have been specifically developed for adolescents and young adults. Some self-report checklists/questionnaires are available (e.g. Kirby, Edwards, Sugden, & Rosenblum, 2010; Tal Saban, Ornoy, Grotto, & Parush, 2012; Timler, McIntyre, Cantell, Crawford, & Hands, 2016) but standardised general motor performance tests are lacking for this age group. This means that some studies of adolescents and young adults have used tests that only have norms for children and which may include items that are not entirely appropriate for use with this older age group.

The range of assessments outlined above varies in design and content. Even those that seem similar may identify different individuals with motor impairment (Tan, Parker, & Larkin, 2001). However, where these tools have been used in longitudinal studies they can give useful information on the developmental trajectories of motor behaviour over time. An indication of motor impairment is the core feature of DCD, although a broader clinical assessment is required for diagnostic purposes (to apply exclusion criteria). Not all studies that are discussed in this chapter included a full diagnostic assessment. Many studies also used broader assessment tools to examine other domains, however, these are not considered here as the focus is on motor behaviour. The following sections focus on the three areas outlined earlier to chart the developmental progression of DCD from the early years through to young adulthood.

Development of motor skills from birth through early childhood

DCD is included in the DSM-5 category of 'Neurodevelopmental Disorders'. These "typically manifest early in development, often before the child enters school grade" (APA, 2013, p. 31). However, it is recommended that a formal diagnosis is not made before the age of five years (APA, 2013; Blank, Smits-Engelsman, Polata-jko, & Wilson, 2012). This is based on findings from longitudinal studies of motor development, which show considerable variation within individuals across time. For example, Darrah, Senthilselvan, and Magill-Evans (2009) used multi-level models to study data from a performance test, the PDMS-2, on children at nine time points between 9 and 21 months and 4–5½ years. Large variability was found among scores across time both within and between infants, showing non-linear development over time and independent development of fine and gross motor skills. Furthermore, Piek, Dawson, Smith, and Gasson (2008) analysed features of the developmental trajectories obtained from parent report data on the ASQ for 33 children from 4 months to 4 years. They found that neither fine nor gross motor trajectories predicted motor ability at the age of six years. These studies do not focus specifically on children who later have a formal diagnosis, but they do suggest that early developmental trajectories are likely to be as varied in DCD. If, as the studies suggest, an infant's position against a normative sample is unlikely to remain constant over time, then it is clear that attempts to make a diagnosis at a single time point in infancy would not be recommended.

Further insights can be gained from studies which have followed up 'at risk' infants through to the school years, with motor (and often a range of other) assessments conducted after the age of five years. Although these have not all included full diagnostic assessments, they have identified children with motor impairments consistent with what might be considered DCD.

Studies from different countries (including the UK, the Netherlands, Canada, USA, Australia, Malaysia) have followed up cohorts of prematurely born infants to 5 years and beyond, categorised by gestational age and/or birth weight.[1] The primary aim of such studies is to document the outcome of infants with early risk factors and also to identify particular factors predicting outcome across a range of domains (for a review see Piek, 2006). A systematic review has reported that the prevalence of DCD in 5–18 year olds born very preterm (or very low birth weight) is 6–9 times more than in full term controls (Edwards et al., 2011). The prevalence rate increases with decreasing gestational age and birth weight.

Many of the cohort follow up studies on prematurely born infants have used the MABC-2 test or BOT-2 to assess motor performance in early childhood (sometimes as part of a broader test battery) and to identify those with a movement difficulty in the absence of cerebral palsy. For example, one set of studies, the Victorian Infant Brain Studies (VIBeS) in Australia (Anderson, 2017; Griffiths et al., 2017) have followed up very prematurely born children with assessments on the MABC and MABC-2 test. Using the 15th percentile they found the rate of motor impairment decreased from 50% at 5 years, to 30% at 7 years and 28% at 13 years. In terms of the stability of individual cases, they found 50% showed no motor impairment across the three ages, while 13% consistently showed motor impairment from 5 to 13 years. 27% showed improvement over time, shifting from an impaired category at age 5 to a non-impaired category by age 13 and 4% shifted from the non-impaired to the impaired category. The remaining 6% showed unstable trajectories shifting in and out of categories more than once over the time period. The researchers recognise that the lack of stability could be related to several factors, including a change in the assessment tasks (from MABC to MABC-2), intervention between assessment points, as well as other environmental factors (including social support). However, the changes over time could also relate to within-child factors and suggest that for some there is evidence that the motor difficulties persist over time.

The findings from these longitudinal studies are complex, yet have some important implications for our understanding of DCD. Overall, the findings suggest that the trajectories of motor development from the neonatal period through to the school years are varied, both in typically developing children and in those with DCD. For some children, motor difficulties will be a consistent feature through childhood whilst others will show changing patterns over time.

There are also important limitations when considering the cohort study findings in relation to DCD. First and perhaps most important, they do not focus specifically on children with a clinical diagnosis. In some cases satisfactory attempts have been made to identify those with a motor impairment, but not all the diagnostic criteria for DCD have been applied. Second, various motor assessments have been used, making it difficult to compare findings across studies. Finally, results are often based on total test scores, which may mask variation in different components of motor behaviour. In the next section we focus on studies of children who meet the diagnostic criteria for DCD to gain a better understanding of the developmental progression of DCD through childhood and adolescence.

Progression of DCD in childhood and adolescence

There have been a number of studies that have investigated the progression of motor difficulties through childhood and into adolescence (see Table 2.2 for a list of key studies). These are smaller scale studies than those used in the cohort studies

TABLE 2.2 Longitudinal studies of motor difficulties

	Original study	Follow up study	Country	Original sample		Follow up sample(s)		
1	Henderson & Hall, 1982	Losse et al., 1991	UK	5–7y	16 and 16 controls	15–17y	17 and 17 controls	
2	Lyytinen & Ahonen, 1989	Lyytinen & Ahonen, 1989 (1–3) Cantell, Smyth, & Ahonen, 1994 (4) Cantell, Smyth, & Ahonen, 2003 (5)	Finland	5y	115 and 40 controls	1. 7y 2. 9y 3. 11y 4. 15y 5. 17–18y	106 and 40 controls 106 and 40 controls 106 and 40 controls 81 and 34 controls 45 and 20 controls	
3	Rasmussen, Gillberg, Waldenström, & Svenson, 1983	Gillberg, 1985 (1) Gillberg, Gillberg, & Groth, 1989 (2) Hellgren, Gillberg, Gillberg, & Enerskog, 1993 (3)	Sweden	6–8y	82 and 59 controls	1. 10y 2. 12–14y 3. 15–17y	54 and 42 controls 52 and 44 controls 56 and 45 controls	
4	van Dellen, Vaessen, & Schoemaker, 1990	Geuze & Börger, 1993	Netherlands	6–12y	31 and 31 controls	11–17y	12 and 14 controls	
5	Gubbay, 1979	Knuckey & Gubbay, 1983	Australia	8–12y	52 and 51 controls	16–20y	24 and 31 controls	
6	Visser, Geuze, & Kalverboer, 1998	Visser et al., 1998	Netherlands	11y 6m	15 and 16 controls	1. 12y 2. 12y 6m 3. 13y 4. 13y 6m 5. 14y	15 and 16 controls 15 and 16 controls 15 and 16 controls 15 and 16 controls 15 and 16 controls	

outlined in the previous section, and focus on children identified with movement difficulties. Figure 2.1 presents a timeline for the initial and subsequent motor assessments in the six studies listed in Table 2.2, and shows the variation in the frequency and overall length of follow up. There is also considerable variation in how participants were originally selected and the terms used to refer to the children with movement difficulties. For simplicity we refer to them here as the 'target' groups. We focus on results from the motor assessments employed, although for many of the studies these were part of a broader battery assessing other domains of development. In describing and evaluating these studies more information is provided on individual test items than those outlined in the previous section. This allows us to consider in more detail the nature and range of motor difficulties, rather than just results from a total test score. Furthermore, several of the studies have categorised the severity of movement difficulties as 'poor' and 'very poor' (or 'mild', 'moderate' and 'severe').

The tasks used and the group differences in these six original studies and their follow up studies are summarised in Table 2.3. It is not possible to describe all of these studies in detail and so we focus here on an example from the UK, where Losse et al. (1991) followed up on previous work by Henderson and Hall (1982). In the original study, 32 children were assessed for motor difficulties at around 6 years of age. Sixteen participants (13 male) were selected by their teachers as being poorly coordinated, with a further 16 in a control sample. The samples were matched for

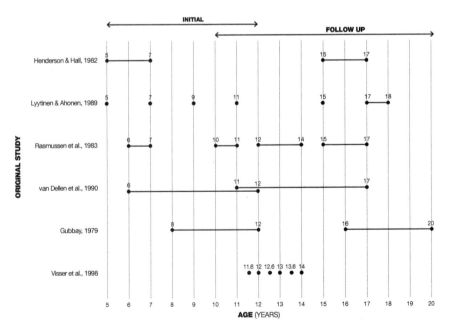

FIGURE 2.1 Age of participants in original and follow up studies described in Table 2.2

age and gender. Significant differences between groups were found on a neurodevelopmental test battery and on a test of general motor competence, the TOMI. Participants were re-assessed after a ten year period by Losse et al. (1991). All sixteen original participants were traced, plus two more who were added in (with data collected during the initial study, but not originally included). Participants were re-assessed at age 15–17 years with a neurodevelopmental test, the TOMI and ratings of reports from their Physical Education teacher at school. Significant group differences were found on all three measures, although closer inspection of performance on the TOMI and neurodevelopmental test revealed differences on some but not all items. However, it is important to note that the TOMI was designed for children up to age 11 years only, so may have underestimated the motor difficulties of these teenagers.

The range of motor tasks employed at follow up by Losse et al. (1991) is shown in Table 2.3, and indicates where there were significant differences between the groups at follow up. Individual results for the target group were categorised as Average, Poor and Very Poor for each assessment, using control group means as a comparison. Based on the TOMI, 73% of the teenagers displayed continuing motor difficulties (being rated as Poor or Very Poor on this test compared to controls). Taking the TOMI results together with the PE teacher reports this increased to 88% who were rated poorly on at least one of these two measures. All 17 (100%) of the target teenagers followed up were judged to have poor motor performance on at least 1 of the 3 measures. In addition, self-perceptions of their physical competence were significantly lower than the controls, with 79% of the target group having 'poor' scores compared to controls on a self-competence scale (Harter, 1985).

In terms of overall outcome, Table 2.4 shows for each set of studies, the number of children (and percentage) in the target group who displayed continuing motor difficulties at follow up, based on performance on motor tasks. This ranges from 35.6% (Hellgren et al., 1993) to 83.3% (Knuckey & Gubbay, 1983). However, it should be noted that there are many challenges in tracking and engaging individuals in longitudinal research across long time periods and this is reflected in considerable data loss during the follow up period in some studies. Thus, the overall rate of 56.4% persistence of motor difficulties (taken across all studies) is based on a total of only 156 individuals from the target groups. In the DSM-5 entry for DCD it is stated that "problems with coordinated movements continue through adolescence in an estimated 50%–70% of children" (APA, 2013, pp. 75–76). We can see from the studies reviewed here that the body of evidence relating to developmental progression is small, but does broadly support this statement.

Table 2.3 shows the different performance tasks employed across the studies displayed in relation to each of the three motor domains described by Haywood and Getchell (2019, this volume) – balance and locomotion, ballistic and manipulation skills. The tasks have been categorised as accurately as possible given the limited detail in some of the papers and it should be noted that not all neatly fit these domains. Most of the studies included tasks across all three domains, with the exception of the Swedish studies, which did not test motor performance as

TABLE 2.3 Motor assessments employed in the original and follow up studies

Study	Authors	Balance and Locomotion		Ballistic	Manipulation		Catching	Graphic
		Static	Dynamic		Uni-manual	Bimanual		
1	**Henderson & Hall, 1982**	Balance – heels raised* Stand on one leg*	Jumping* Hopping*		Post coins* Place objects into open box*	Threading beads*	Bounce and catch (two hands)* Bounce and catch (one hand)*	Drawing trail*
Follow up	Losse et al., 1991	Balance board (tandem)*	Walk backwards* Jump and clap	Aim at target*	Hole piercing	Cut with scissors*	Catch (one hand)*	Pencil control
2	**Lyytinen & Ahonen, 1989**	Stand on one leg[a]	Hopping[a]	–	–	Cut with scissors	–	Draw a person[a] Line quality[a]
Follow up	Cantell et al., 1994	Balance board* Two board balance*	Jump and clap* Walk backwards – heel to toe*	Aim at target*	Purdue pegboard* Dynamic hand coordination*		Catch (one hand)*	Copying geometric figures* Maze tracing*
Follow up	Cantell et al., 2003	–	Walk backwards – heel to toe*	Aim at target*	Purdue pegboard* Dynamic hand coordination*		Catch (one hand)*	Copying geometric figures*
3	**Rasmussen et al., 1983**	Stand on one leg* Stand toe to heel*	Walking and running* Jumping* Hopping* Skip forward* Walk on tiptoe* Walk on heels* Step onto a chair*	Kick a ball*	Purdue pegboard* Pour water*	Thread beads* Cut with scissors*	–	Using a crayon* Figure copying* Draw a circle* Draw a person*
Follow up	Gillberg, 1985	Stand on one leg*	Hopping* Walk on heels*	–	–	–	–	Maze tracing*

Follow up	Gillberg et al., 1989	Stand on one leg*	Hopping Walk on heels*	-	-	-	-	Maze tracing*
Follow up	Hellgren et al., 1993	Stand on one leg*		-	-	-	-	Maze tracing*
4	**van Dellen et al., 1990**	Stand on one leg*	Jump & clap Walk backwards	Aim at target*	Hole piercing*	Cut with scissors*	Catch (one hand)*	Drawing trail*
Follow up	Geuze & Börger, 1993	Stand on one leg	Jump & clap* Walk backwards	Aim at target*	Hole piercing*	Cut with scissors*	Catch (one hand)*	Drawing trail*
5	**Gubbay, 1979** (No data/results given)	-	Skip forwards[a] Roll ball under foot[a]	Throw and catch tennis ball[a]	Hole piercing[a]	Tie shoelaces[a] Thread beads[a] Post objects[a]	-	-
Follow up	Knuckey & Gubbay, 1983	-	Roll ball under foot*		Hole piercing* Post objects into a box*	Thread beads	Throw and catch tennis ball*	-
6	**Visser et al., 1998#**	Two board balance	Jump and clap Walk backwards – heel to toe	Aim at target	Turn pegs	Cut with scissors	Catch (one hand)	Drawing trail

Note: **Bold** denotes original study *Significant differences between groups in at least one category of motor impairment [a] denotes results not reported on individual tasks. Tasks have been categorised as accurately as possible according to domains outlined by Haywood & Getchell (chapter 1, this volume). # Note that Visser et al. (1998) employed the same set of eight motor tasks at each assessment point but do not report group means for each task or the significance of group differences at the initial or any of the subsequent follow up assessments.

TABLE 2.4 Outcomes of follow-up assessments for persistence of motor difficulties through adolescence

Study	Author	Outcome of assessment - number and percentage in parentheses				Age range
		Mild	Moderate	Severe	Overall	
1	**Henderson & Hall, 1982**	–	–	–	*Data not reported*	5–7y
Follow up	Losse et al., 1991	6/15 (40%)	–	5/15 (33.3%)	11/15 (73.3%)★	15–17y
2	**Lyytinen & Ahonen, 1989**	–	–	–	53/106 (50%)	5y–11y
Follow up	Cantell et al., 1994	–	–	–	37/81 (45.7%)	15y
Follow up	Cantell et al., 2003	3/23 (13%)	–	19/22 (86%)	22/45 (48.9%)★	17–18y
3	**Rasmussen et al., 1983**	–	–	–	*Data not reported*	6–8y
Follow up	Gillberg, 1985	–	–	–	27/44 (61.4%)	10y
Follow up	Gillberg et al., 1989	1/5 (20%)	–	11/37 (29.7%)	12/42 (28.6%)	12–14y
Follow up	Hellgren et al. 1993	8/32 (25%)	–	8/13 (61.5%)	16/45 (35.6%) ★	15–17y
4	**van Dellen et al., 1990**	–	–	–	*Data not reported*	6–12y
Follow up	Geuze & Börger, 1993	3/12 (25%)	–	6/12 (50%)	9/12 (75%)★	11–17y
5	**Gubbay, 1979**	–	–	–	*Data not reported*	8–12y
Follow up	Knuckey & Gubbay, 1983	5/24 (20.8%)	8/24 (33.3%)	7/24 (29.2%)	20/24 (83.3%)★	16–20y
6	**Visser et al., 1998**	6/15 (40%)	–	4/15 (26.7%)	10/15 (66.7%)★	11y6m–14y
				Total★	**88/156 (56.4%)**	11–20y

★Final follow-up assessment

extensively as the others. In the following sections we focus on development across the different motor domains. Different tests and motor tasks have been used both across and within the studies listed in Tables 2.2–2.4 and of course results from single test items are not as reliable as those from a full test battery. Nevertheless, a closer examination of performance and group differences gives us the opportunity to describe the motor difficulties characteristic of DCD in childhood and the extent to which performance difficulties extend into adolescence in different areas.

Balance and locomotion skills

Balance and postural control is an important component of motor control and every day functioning. It allows us to keep still (static) and maintain a stable body position when required for some tasks. It is also a critical aspect of locomotor skill, enabling us to keep the body upright in dynamic situations when we move from one position to another. Formal tests to assess static balance include tasks such as standing on one leg or on two legs in various ways. For example, Henderson and Hall (1982) reported significant group differences in their 5–7 year olds for a task involving standing still, with two feet together and heels raised (M = 19.69 seconds (s) for controls vs. M = 11.44s for the target group)[2] and also for standing on one leg (20s for each leg in controls vs. 4.69s (right) and 2.94s (left) for the target group). In the follow up study (Losse et al., 1991) group differences were still apparent on a tandem balance on a raised board (17.1s vs. 9.9s). These findings of continuing difficulties with postural control and balance have been replicated in other follow up assessments (e.g. Gillberg, 1985; Gillberg et al., 1989; Rasmussen et al., 1983). However, not all studies found difficulties in this area at the time of follow up (Geuze & Börger, 1993).

Locomotion involves postural control during active (dynamic) movement of the body in tasks such as walking, running, jumping and hopping. Henderson and Hall (1982) reported significant group differences in jumping with feet together over a knee-high cord, with 15/16 controls able to perform the task compared to only one of the target children. There was also a significant group difference in hopping between two lines over a distance of 15ft (c4.5m). Fifteen out of 16 controls successfully completed the task compared to 6 in the target group. In the follow up study 10 years later, Losse et al. (1991) reported significant group differences for walking backwards (15.0 vs. 12.7 steps) but no group differences on a jump and clap task, although this was designed for much younger children.

Van Dellen et al. (1990) found no group differences on dynamic balance tasks (jump & clap and walking backwards) at ages six to twelve years. The follow up study by Geuze and Börger (1993) however, reported significant group differences on the jump and clap task, but not for walking backwards. This is reflected in other studies where the results vary across the different dynamic balance tasks included at follow up (e.g. Gillberg et al., 1989). However, in four of the five studies that assessed dynamic balance at follow up, significant group differences on at least some tasks are reported. Overall this suggests that difficulties with dynamic balance tasks are evident in adolescents previously identified with movement difficulties.

Ballistic skill

Ballistic skill involves generating and controlling force to project an object to a target. Most assessments of ballistic ability have focused on throwing a ball to a target and studies have reported significant group differences. Henderson and Hall (1982) included a 'Bounce and Catch' task, which involves some element of ballistic skill. They found a significant group difference in the number of successful attempts out of 10 (9.12 vs. 3.13). At follow up (Losse et al., 1991) an aiming task was included and there was a significant group difference in the number of successful throws to a wall target (7.5 vs. 5.6 out of 10 attempts) for the 15–17 year olds. Similarly, significant group differences in an aiming task were reported both in the original van Dellen et al. (1990) study and the follow up study by Geuze and Börger (1993) (7.3 vs. 5.6). This finding of continuing difficulties in throwing is also supported by results from Cantell et al. (2003). Kicking is another type of ballistic skill but has been less well investigated in DCD. Rasmussen et al. (1983) found a significant group difference in kicking a ball at age 6–8 years but this aspect of motor performance was not assessed in the follow up studies.

Manipulation skills

Manipulative skill involves receiving and/or moving items within the hand or hands. A wide range of tasks are included in this category but fall broadly into four groups – tasks which are uni-manual (using predominantly one hand), those that are bimanual (using both hands together), catching[3] and tasks which involve graphic skill (the manipulation of a writing implement). In the set of longitudinal studies considered here, most included tasks from all four categories of manipulative skill and examples of these can be seen in Table 2.3.

Various tasks have been employed in the assessment of uni-manual ability. These include posting coins in a box, inserting pegs in holes and using a pen or pin to pierce holes in paper. Different tasks have sometimes been used at first and follow up assessments. Since each task requires different aspects of control and coordination this means that direct comparisons cannot be made although it is assumed that there are some shared features of control. For example, Henderson and Hall (1982) found significant group differences in the speed of posting coins into a box (right hand 15.82s vs. 20.93s, left hand 17.09s vs. 20.92s) for their 5–7 year olds, although follow up on a different uni-manual task (piercing holes in paper with a pen) showed no group differences in the teenage years. Variations on this latter task have been used in several of the studies, with different outcomes. Some have reported significant group differences both in their original and follow up studies (e.g. van Dellen et al., 1990; Geuze & Börger, 1993). Thus, significant group differences were reported for some but not all uni-manual tasks at follow up.

Table 2.3 illustrates the range of tasks used to assess bimanual ability and the varying results reported. Taking one example, Henderson and Hall (1982) found significant group differences in threading beads (43.53s vs. 68.75s) in the first assessment and in cutting with scissors (0.5 vs. 4.1 errors) at follow up. Geuze and Börger (1993) also report continued difficulties with using scissors at follow up. Various catching tasks have been used across the studies, including catching with one hand and catching with two hands. These tasks require a range of perceptual and timing skills to intercept and receive the ball and close the fingers around it. However, many tasks also involve a ballistic element (first bouncing or throwing the ball against the floor or wall). Poor performance may therefore result from difficulties with throwing, difficulties with catching or both. Henderson and Hall (1982) used a bounce and catch task. As already reported, they found a significant group difference in the number of successful attempts out of 10 (9.12 vs. 3.13) in the original study. These difficulties persisted at follow up (Losse et al., 1991) in a one-hand catching task. There was a significant group difference in the number of successful catches for the 15–17 year olds (9.5 vs. 7.5 for the preferred hand, 9.6 vs. 6.0 for the non-preferred hand, each out of 10 attempts). In all studies that examined group differences in catching, the target group consistently performed more poorly, demonstrating persisting difficulties in this area.

The range of tasks that have been used to assess graphic ability include those involving drawing along a trail/through a maze as well as tasks with a greater perceptual component, such as copying shapes. In the UK studies, Henderson and Hall (1982) found significant group differences on a drawing trail task in the first assessment at 5–7 years but there were no significant group differences on a similar task involving pencil control at follow up (Losse et al., 1991). In contrast there were significant group differences for a drawing trail task at both first and follow up assessments by van Dellen et al. (1990) and Geuze and Börger (1993). The other studies show more mixed results over time and it is notable that a key graphic skill, handwriting, has not been included in these studies.

Taken together, these findings show some evidence of the continuation of movement difficulties from childhood into adolescence across all motor performance areas. For five of the studies this evidence is drawn from an examination of group differences on the motor tasks at each of the follow up points (shown in Table 2.3). However, Visser et al. (1998) employed a different approach to analyse their motor assessment data to examine the developmental trajectory of motor performance from the age of 11 to 14 years. Collapsing across age, they report significantly poorer total and sub-component scores on the MABC test for the target group compared to controls. They also report a main effect for age, showing an improvement over time in all areas (except on the 'Manual Dexterity' component of the test). Importantly, there was a significant interaction between age and group, showing that the difference between the target and control group decreased with age. Although this suggests that the target group 'catches up' over time it was clear that some children in the target group continued to show very poor motor skills at the later ages (see Table 2.4).

Overall our review of these studies shows variation across tasks, with significant differences between the target and control groups evident at follow up on some but not all tasks. The extent to which this is a reflection of true performance profiles or limitations in the tests (for example, inappropriate tasks for the age group tested) is not clear. Furthermore, only group means are available for individual tasks, which will be masking individual differences within the target groups. The study by Visser et al. (1998) was the only one in this set to examine the impact of other factors on motor development in DCD, with a specific focus on physical growth and activity levels. Contrary to their expectations and to previous findings in other groups, they report that for the majority of children with DCD their motor competence was not adversely affected by the growth spurt and in fact their motor skills showed improvement over time. Regarding activity levels (although this was only assessed with a rather basic questionnaire), it was reported that while motor development in the control group seemed to benefit from higher activity levels, this was not the case for the DCD group.

Since our concern in this chapter is the natural progression of DCD, we have excluded from our review longitudinal studies that explicitly included an element of intervention. One such study is that of Sugden and Chambers (2007), in which 31 children identified by their teachers at 7–9 years as having movement difficulties, were tracked over a period of 4 years. After a 16 week programme of intervention delivered by parents and teachers 46% of the sample continued to have significant motor difficulties as assessed on the MABC test. From the studies in Table 2.3 little has been reported about what occurred between initial assessment and follow up(s) but it should be borne in mind that some children are likely to have received intervention, which may have had an impact on the progression of their movement difficulties.

In sum, we have reviewed studies reporting on the motor development of children with DCD through childhood and adolescence. The outcomes from this small set of studies support the view that motor difficulties do persist over time for many but not all children with DCD. However, the conclusions to be drawn from this are hampered by limitations and variation in sample selection, motor assessment, data reporting and data analyses. Future work needs to address these aspects and also explore factors which may help to explain variation in patterns of motor development across different domains, between individuals and the persistence of motor difficulties into adulthood.

Progression of DCD in early adulthood

For the first time in 2013 the DSM-5 recognised the persistence of DCD into adulthood, prior to this there was no formal recognition of DCD beyond childhood. Some of the follow up studies outlined in the previous section extended from childhood into early adulthood. However, there have only recently been studies that focus specifically on the motor difficulties experienced in adolescence and adulthood (see Barnett, Kirby, van Waelvelde, & Weintraub, 2017 for a review).

These include participants across a broad age range, all of whom had motor difficulties consistent with a diagnosis of DCD. Some had a diagnosis of DCD or 'dyspraxia' in childhood, others were diagnosed as adults. There is some confusion around use of the term 'dyspraxia', as it seems to be associated with various definitions. Some use the term interchangeably with DCD, while for others it refers to a much broader constellation of difficulties (Dyspraxia Foundation, 2018). However, on the whole the motor difficulties reported in those with 'dyspraxia' seem to be consistent with DCD and have been included here.

Earlier in this chapter we noted that the study of DCD in adulthood is still hampered by a lack of assessment tools that can be used to formally identify and describe the condition. Since standardised motor performance tests for young adults are lacking, tests designed for a younger age group have been used to select adult participants with DCD for research studies. The MABC-2 (with UK norms up to 16 years) has been used in many studies with adults, as well as an experimental version of the MABC, with tasks extended to be more appropriate for those aged up to 25 years (Cantell, Crawford, & Tish Doyle-Baker, 2008). The BOT-2 (with USA norms up to 21 years) has also been used for selection purposes in some studies, usually alongside the MABC-2. Finally, the MAND (with USA norms for young adults, mean age 25) has been employed in research in Australia (Hyde et al., 2014). Total scores on these tests have been used as selection and inclusion criteria, usually taking a cut-off point below the 5th, 15th or 18th percentile. Such low total scores tend to reflect poor performance across the range of tasks measured. We can conclude that young adults in these studies have difficulties with items measuring speed and coordination, and poor performance in the three main areas of balance and locomotion (e.g. running, hopping), ballistic skill (e.g. throwing) and manipulation skill (e.g. drawing). Although individuals may show differing performance profiles across the range of tasks assessed, such details have not been reported in the adult studies. Even if available, such data are likely to be unreliable, as the tests have not been designed specifically for adults and appropriate norms are not available.

In addition to performance tests, studies have used various self-report questionnaires to identify and select participants. This includes shorter screening measures, such as the Adolescents and Adults Coordination Questionnaire (AAC-Q) (Tal Saban et al., 2012) and an adult version of the DCDQ (DCDQ-A; Cantell et al., 2008). The Adult DCD Questionnaire (ADC; Kirby et al., 2010) is a more comprehensive instrument and has been more widely used in research with adults. The ADC includes 30 items; about half consider a broad range of motor behaviours and the rest focus on behaviours beyond the motor domain (including general organisation, attention and social skills). Results from the self-report measures used in this set of studies illustrate the range of motor difficulties experienced by adults with DCD and suggest that they impact negatively on various aspects of participation in daily life.

In the next section our review of studies on adults with DCD outlines the findings from measures of motor behaviour. The reported impairments in adulthood are considered in relation to each of the three motor domains described by

Haywood and Getchell (2019, this volume) and as used in our description of development through childhood and into adolescence.

Balance and locomotion skills

Balance and postural control continues to be important for many aspects of every day functioning in adulthood, both in static tasks and when moving the whole body. When compared to typically developing age peers it has been reported that on performance measures, adults with DCD show greater body sway during static balance (Cousins & Smyth, 2003) and are slower and make more errors during dynamic balance tasks, such as walking along a line (Cantell et al., 2003). Detailed examinations of walking patterns in adults with DCD have revealed increased variability in foot placement measures (e.g. step width, step length, double support time, stride time and others) compared to a well-coordinated control group (Du, Wilmut, & Barnett, 2015). This reduced ability to produce consistent movement patterns might help explain the increased frequency of trips and bumps reported (Kirby, Edwards, & Sugden, 2011).

Locomotion and navigation of the environment involves not only control of the body but also recognition of and adaptation to obstacles and changes in our surroundings. Some studies have investigated this aspect of performance. For example, Cousins and Smyth (2003) found that adults with DCD walked more slowly than controls when trying to avoid poles in a 'slalom' course. Gentle, Barnett, and Wilmut (2016) examined walking patterns in more detail and found that when walking on an irregular (bumpy) compared to regular (flat) terrain, adults with DCD were more affected than controls. They tended to walk more slowly, with shorter and wider steps and with the head inclined more toward the ground. This is suggestive of an adaptive strategy, to preserve balance and increase visual sampling of the ground. In another study, Wilmut, Du, and Barnett (2015) tracked body movement as adults walked towards and passed through different sized apertures. They found that the adults with DCD tailored their movements to the aperture size more so than the controls, slowing down more in the approach and rotating their shoulders to a greater degree to move through the aperture. Thus it seems that movement difficulties continue into adulthood but that in some situations, adults with DCD are able to take their difficulties into account and use more cautious and adaptive strategies to avoid collisions.

Ballistic skill

In children and adolescents with DCD, poor throwing skills continue into adulthood. Cousins and Smyth (2003) reported lower self-ratings of competence for throwing at a wall target in adults with DCD compared to controls. This was also supported by poorer performance on throwing accuracy (Cantell et al., 2003; Cousins & Smyth, 2003). It could be argued that ballistic skills are less important in adulthood as they are not necessary for most common everyday life activities. However, many adults do participate in games and sports that involve throwing, kicking or using a bat/racket to project an object. Difficulties in this area may impact on participation in such activities and reduce opportunities for social engagement and physical activity. In fact it has been reported that adults with DCD do find it difficult to play sport and that they spend significantly fewer hours in weekly exercise (such as playing football and hockey) (Hill & Brown, 2013).

Manipulation skills

Many everyday work and self-care activities require manual dexterity and manipulative skills. When using the ADC, it has been reported that a greater percentage of those with DCD report 'usually' or 'always' experiencing a range of motor difficulties including with self-care tasks such as shaving and applying make-up (Kirby et al., 2010). Adults with DCD have also reported dropping and spilling things, getting burns at work and home and difficulties performing manual labour jobs (Missiuna, Moll, King, Stewart, & Macdonald, 2008).

Several studies have examined the ability of adults with DCD to reach for and manipulate objects with their hands. In detailed examinations of reaching for an object, Wilmut and colleagues report poor motor planning across different tasks. For example, Wilmut and Byrne (2014) found poor planning in grip selection for 'end state comfort' and less refined discrimination in the movement kinematics of reaches for different onward action intentions (e.g. to simply place or to throw an object) (Wilmut, Byrne, & Barnett, 2013). In terms of manipulating objects, clear group differences have been reported on a range of tasks. This includes slow performance on block construction and various pegboard tasks (inserting, moving and turning pegs) (Cantell et al., 2003; Cousins & Smyth, 2003; Hodgson & Hudson, 2017).

Catching tasks also include manipulative skill (as well as demands on eye-hand coordination). Although not all adults continue with ball sports, most are likely to manage basic catching tasks. However, Cousins and Smyth (2003) report lower self-ratings of competence for catching a tennis ball and Cantell et al. (2003) report poor one-hand catching compared to controls.

As noted earlier, graphic skill is a particular type of manipulative skill involving the accurate control of a pen. Graphic tasks often also have demands on visual perception in copying, drawing and handwriting tasks. Several studies indicate self-reports from adults of difficulties in this area, for example on the ADC (Kirby et al., 2010; Purcell, Scott-Roberts, & Kirby, 2015) and the AAC-Q (Tal-Saban, Zarka et al., 2012). Kirby, Edwards et al. (2011) found that over 70% of their sample reported difficulties with writing neatly and quickly. These self-reported handwriting difficulties are supported by results from actual performance. Cousins and Smith (2003) report poor performance in English handwriting in terms of both speed and errors, while others report significantly poorer performance in speed and legibility of writing in Hebrew compared to controls (Rosenblum, 2013). When examined in finer detail, it is reported that letter strokes take longer, and are taller and wider compared to controls (Rosenblum, 2013).

These findings suggest a persistence of the motor difficulties identified in studies of children with DCD. There is evidence of continued difficulties into adulthood in each of the three main domains. In addition, adulthood requires the learning of new motor skills not required in earlier life. These new challenges have been reported to be a particular problem for adults with DCD (Missiuna et al., 2008). For example, several studies have examined and reported the difficulties associated with learning to drive for adults with DCD. Tal Saban et al. (2014) report lower participation in driving in DCD groups. Kirby and colleagues (e.g. Kirby, Edwards et al., 2011) have also reported lower proportions of adults with DCD learning to drive compared to controls, with adults' comments suggesting that this is related to their coordination difficulties and lack of confidence. They have also reported taking the driving theory and practical test a greater number of times than controls and having more difficulty estimating distance when driving and parking. Adults with DCD also report more bumps and collisions and continuing difficulties with driving (Kirby, Sugden, & Edwards, 2011). Other studies have studied simulated driving behaviour in the laboratory and reported poorer steering control and forward planning compared to controls (de Oliveira & Wann, 2011; 2012).

It can be concluded that there is an emerging literature on DCD in adolescents and young adults. The findings suggest that a similar range of motor difficulties seen in childhood extend into adolescence and adulthood as well as additional challenges learning new skills. All but one of the identified studies described a single 'snapshot' of the condition. (The exception is the 3–4 year follow up study reported by Tal Saban, Ornoy, and Parush (2014), which showed continued impact of motor difficulties on aspects of participation over this time period). One of the major limitations of the set of studies on adults reviewed here is the lack of consistency in selection methods and sometimes limited assessment of motor difficulties. This is in part related to the lack of suitable standardised assessments but also continuing confusion over terminology and definitions of the condition in adulthood.

Summary

In the previous sections we have reviewed work from longitudinal studies on developmental progression from infancy, in DCD beyond early childhood and studies that focus specifically on motor difficulties in young adults. However, the limitations already noted make it hard to draw together findings across these studies and to tease out data relevant to the issue of developmental progression (i.e. changes over time). The contribution of these studies to our understanding of the patterns and mechanisms of motor development in DCD is thus quite limited. Furthermore, in the literature there seems largely to be a focus on deficits in personal capabilities (both motor and non-motor). Only a few studies (Kirby, Sugden, Beveridge, & Edwards, 2008; Missiuna et al., 2008) have reported positive personal and environmental factors that seem to facilitate development (e.g. being determined, finding ways of adapting to difficulties, having practical support from family members). We suggest that a broader approach is needed in research to identify factors that both constrain and facilitate motor development over the lifespan. To better understand the complex nature of motor development it will be important to recognise the dynamic nature of interactions between the individual, task and environment.

Conclusion

Typical motor development has been studied in children since the turn of the last century and as outlined in chapter one of this volume, progression has been well documented, recognising the impact of environmental and personal factors on individual trajectories. Although the motor difficulties of children with DCD are now well documented, with some recognition now also in adults, the way these change over time has been under-studied. While we can distinguish poor motor performance of individuals with DCD from those who are typically developing, this tends to be done as a one-off snapshot and also at the level of general motor competence, rather than the individual task level. Furthermore, there has been a tendency to study at the group level, describing mean performance of groups, rather than an investigation or documentation of individual trajectories over time. Thus we know more about motor *performance* in DCD than we do about motor *development* in DCD. Future work needs to track individual performance in more detail in order to better understand changes over time – and other aspects need to be considered to understand the impact of task, environmental and personal factors on development.

Notes

1 Definitions for prematurity and birth weight vary. According to the World Health Organisation: 'Preterm' 32–37 weeks gestational age, 'Very preterm' 28–32 weeks, 'Extremely preterm' <28 weeks. 'Low Birth Weight' <2500g, 'Very Low Birth Weight' <1500g, 'Extremely Low Birth Weight' <1000g.
2 Throughout this section, raw data means are reported where group differences were statistically significant; we present the mean (M) for the control group first, followed by the target group mean.
3 Our inclusion of catching here is consistent with Haywood and Getchell (2019 this volume). However, we acknowledge that catching is sometimes considered with 'aiming' under a broader category of 'ball skill'.

References

American Psychiatric Association. (2013). *Diagnostic and statistical manual of mental disorders* (5th ed.). Arlington, VA: American Psychiatric Association.

Anderson, P. (2017). Are the brains of very preterm children with developmental coordination disorder different in the neonatal period? *12th International Conference on DCD*, Fremantle, Australia.

Barnett, A. L., Kirby, A., van Waelvelde, H., & Weintraub, N. (2017). Features of DCD in adolescents and adults: A scoping review. *12th International Conference on DCD*, Fremantle, Australia.

Barnett, A. L., & Peters, J. (2004). Motor proficiency assessment batteries. In D. Dewey & D. E. Tupper (Eds.), *Developmental motor disorders: A neuropsychological perspective.* New York: The Guilford Press.

Bayley, N. (2006). *Bayley scales of infant and toddler development* (3rd ed.). Administration Manual. San Antonio, TX: Psychological Corporation.

Blank, R., Smits-Engelsman, B., Polatajko, H., & Wilson, P. (2012). European Academy of Childhood Disability (EACD): Recommendations on the definition, diagnosis and intervention of developmental coordination disorder (long version). *Developmental Medicine and Child Neurology, 54*(11), 54–93.

Bruininks, R. H. (1978). *Bruininks-Oseretsky test of motor proficiency.* Circle Pines, MN: American Guidance Service.

Bruininks, R. H., & Bruininks, B. D. (2005). *Bruininks-Oseretsky test of motor proficiency* (2nd ed.). Manual. Minneapolis, MN: Pearson.

Cantell, M., Crawford, S. G., & Tish Doyle-Baker, P. K. (2008). Physical fitness and health indices in children, adolescents and adults with high or low motor competence. *Human Movement Science, 27,* 344–362.

Cantell, M., Smyth, M. M., & Ahonen, T. P. (1994). Clumsiness in adolescence: Educational, motor and social outcomes of motor delay detected at 5 years. *Adapted Physical Activity Quarterly, 11,* 115–129.

Cantell, M., Smyth, M. M., & Ahonen, T. P. (2003). Two distinct pathways for developmental coordination disorder: Persistence and resolution. *Human Movement Science, 22,* 413–431.

Cairney, J., Rigoli, D., & Piek, J. P. (2013). Developmental coordination disorder and internalizing problems in children: The environmental stress hypothesis elaborated. *Developmental Review, 33*(3), 224–238.

Cousins, M., & Smyth, M. M. (2003). Developmental coordination impairments in adulthood. *Human Movement Science, 22,* 433–459.

Darrah, J., Senthilselvan, A., & Magill-Evans, J. (2009). Trajectories of serial motor scores of typically developing children: Implications for clinical decision making. *Infant Behavior & Development, 32*(1), 72–78.

de Oliveira, R. F., & Wann, J. P. (2011). Driving skills of young adults with developmental coordination disorder: Regulating speed and coping with distraction. *Research in Developmental Disabilities, 32,* 1301–1308.

de Oliveira, R. F., & Wann, J. P. (2012). Driving skills of young adults with developmental coordination disorder: Maintaining control and avoiding hazards. *Human Movement Science, 31,* 721–729.

Du, W., Wilmut, K., & Barnett, A. L. (2015). Level walking in adults with and without developmental coordination disorder: An analysis of movement variability. *Human Movement Science, 43,* 9–14.

Dubowitz, L. M. S., Dubowitz, V., & Mercuri, E. (1999). *The neurological assessment of the preterm & full-term newborn infant* (2nd ed.). Clinics in Developmental Medicine No. 148. London: Mac Keith Press.

Dyspraxia foundation. *What is dyspraxia? Dyspraxia foundation.* (2018). Retrieved from https://dyspraxiafoundation.org.uk/about-dyspraxia/

Edwards, J., Berube, M., Erlandson, K., Haug, S., Johnstone, H., Meagher, M., . . . Zwicker, J. (2011). Developmental coordination disorder in school-aged children born very preterm and/or at very low birth weight: A systematic review. *Journal of Developmental & Behavioral Pediatrics, 32*(9), 678–687.

Folio, M. R., & Fewell, R. R. (2000). *Peabody developmental motor scales* (2nd ed.). (PDMS-2). Austin, TX: Pro-Ed.

Gentle, J., Barnett, A. L., & Wilmut, K. (2016). Adaptations to walking on an uneven terrain for individuals with and without developmental coordination disorder. *Human Movement Science, 49*, 346–353.

Geuze, R., & Börger, H. (1993). Children who are clumsy: Five years later. *Adapted Physical Activity Quarterly, 10*, 10–21.

Gillberg, I. C. (1985). Children with minor neurodevelopmental disorders III: Neurological and neurodevelopmental problems at age 10. *Developmental Medicine & Child Neurology, 27*, 3–16.

Gillberg, I. C., Gillberg, C., & Groth, J. (1989). Children with preschool minor neurodevelopmental disorders. V: Neurodevelopmental profiles at age 13. *Developmental Medicine & Child Neurology, 31*, 14–24.

Griffiths, A., Morgan, P., Anderson, P. J., Doyle, L. W., Lee, K. J., & Spittle, A. J. (2017). Predictive value of the movement assessment battery for children – second edition at 4 years, for motor impairment at 8 years in children born preterm. *Developmental Medicine & Child Neurology, 59*, 490–496.

Griffiths, R. (1984). *The abilities of young children.* Bucks: Association for Research in Infant and Child Development, The Test Agency, Thames.

Gubbay, S. S. (1979). The clumsy child. In F. C. Rose (Ed.), *Paediatric neurology.* Oxford: Blackwell, 145–160.

Hadders-Algra, M. (2004). General movements: A window for early identification of children at high risk for developmental disorders. *The Journal of Pediatrics, 145*(2), Supplement, S12–S18.

Harter, S. (1985). *Manual for the self-perception profile for children.* Denver, CO: University of Denver.

Haywood, K. M., & Getchell, N. (2019). *The synergetic, probabilistic pathways of typical motor development.* Chapter 1, this volume.

Hellgren, L., Gillberg, C., Gillberg, I. C., & Enerskog, I. (1993). Children with Deficits in Attention, Motor Control and Perception (DAMP) almost grown up: General health at 16 years. *Developmental Medicine & Child Neurology, 35*, 881–892.

Henderson, S. E., & Hall, D. (1982). Concomitants of clumsiness in young school children. *Developmental Medicine & Child Neurology, 24*, 448–460.

Henderson, S. E., & Sugden, D. A. (1992). *Movement assessment battery for children: Manual.* London: Psychological Corporation.

Henderson, S. E., Sugden, D. A., & Barnett, A. L. (2007). *Movement assessment battery for children* (2nd ed.). London: Harcourt Assessment.

Hill, E. L., & Barnett, A. L. (2019). *Introduction: Understanding motor behaviour in developmental coordination disorder (DCD)*, this volume.

Hill, E. L., & Brown, D. (2013). Mood impairments in adults previously diagnosed with developmental coordination disorder. *Journal of Mental Health, 22*, 334–340.

Hodgson, J. C., & Hudson, J. M. (2017). Atypical speech lateralization in adults with developmental coordination disorder demonstrated using functional transcranial Doppler ultrasound. *Journal of Neuropsychology, 11*, 1–13.

Hyde, C., Fuelscher, I., Buckthought, K., Enticott, P. G., Gitay, M. A., & Williams, J. (2014). Motor imagery is less efficient in adults with probable developmental coordination disorder: Evidence from the hand rotation task. *Research Developmental Disabilities, 35*, 3062–3070.

Kirby, A., Edwards, L., & Sugden, D. A. (2011). Emerging adulthood in developmental coordination disorder: Parent and young adult perspectives. *Research in Developmental Disabilities, 32*, 1351–1360.

Kirby, A., Sugden, D., Beveridge, S., & Edwards, L. (2008). Developmental Co-Ordination Disorder (DCD) in adolescents and adults in further and higher education. *Journal of Research in Special Educational Needs, 8*, 120–131.

Kirby, A., Sugden, D., & Edwards, L. (2011). Driving behaviour in young adults with developmental co-ordination disorder. *Journal of Adult Development, 18*, 122–129.

Kirby, A., Edwards, L., Sugden, D. A., & Rosenblum, S. (2010). The development and standardization of the Adult Developmental Co-Ordination disorders/dyspraxia checklist (ADC). *Research in Developmental Disabilities, 31*, 131–139.

Knuckey, N. W., & Gubbay, S. S. (1983). Clumsy children: A prognostic study. *Australian Pediatric Journal, 19*, 9–13.

Losse, A., Henderson, S. E., Elliman, D., Hall, D., Knight, E., Jongmans, M. (1991). Clumsiness in children: Do they grow out of it? A ten year follow up study. *Developmental Medicine & Child Neurology, 33*, 55–68.

Lyytinen, H., & Ahonen, T. (1989). Motor precursors of learning disabilities. In D. J. Bakker & D. J. Van Der Vlugt (Eds.), *Learning disabilities: Vol. 1. Neuropsychological correlates*. Amsterdam: Swets & Zeitlinger.

Mancini, V. O., Rigoli, D., Cairney, J., Roberts, L. D., & Piek, J. P. (2016). The elaborated environmental stress hypothesis as a framework for understanding the association between motor skills and internalizing problems: A mini-review. *Frontiers in Psychology, 7*, 239.

McCarron, L. T. (1997). *MAND McCarron assessment of neuro muscular development: Fine and gross motor abilities* (rev. ed.). Dallas, TX: Common Market Press.

Missiuna, C., Moll, S., King, G., Stewart, D., & Macdonald, K. (2008). Life experiences of young adults who have coordination difficulties. *Canadian Journal of Occupational Therapy, 75*, 157–166.

Newell, K. M., & Pacheco, M. M. (2019). *Movement coordination, control and skill development*. Chapter 3, this volume.

Piek, J. P. (2006). *Infant motor development*. Champaign, IL: Human Kinetics.

Piek, J. P., Dawson, L., Smith, L. M., & Gasson, N. (2008). The role of early fine and gross motor development on later motor and cognitive ability. *Human Movement Science, 27*(5), 668–681.

Purcell, C., Scott-Roberts, S., & Kirby, A. (2015). Implications of DSM-5 for recognising adults with Developmental Coordination Disorder (DCD). *British Journal of Occupational Therapy, 78*, 295–302.

Rasmussen, P., Gillberg, C., Waldenström, E., & Svenson, B. (1983). Perceptual, motor and attentional deficits in seven-year-old children: Neurological and neurodevelopmental aspects. *Developmental Medicine & Child Neurology, 25*, 315–333.

Rosenblum, S. (2013). Handwriting measures as reflectors of executive functions among adults with Developmental Coordination Disorders (DCD). *Frontiers in Psychology, 4*, 357.

Stott, D., Moyes, F. A., & Henderson, S. E. (1984). *Test of Motor Impairment (TOMI) – Henderson revision*. San Antonio, TX: The Psychological Corporation.

Squires, J., Bricker, D., & Potter, L. (1997). Revision of a parent-completed developmental screening tool: Ages and stages questionnaires. *Journal of Pediatric Psychology, 22*(3), 313–328.

Sugden, D. A., & Chambers, M. E. (2007). Stability and change in children with developmental coordination disorder. *Child: Care, Health and Development, 33*(5), 520–528.

Tal-Saban, M., Ornoy, A., Grotto, I., & Parush, S. (2012). Adolescents and adults coordination questionnaire: Development and psychometric properties. *The American Journal of Occupational Therapy, 66*(4), 406–413.

Tal-Saban, M., Ornoy, A., & Parush, S. (2014). Young adults with developmental coordination disorder: A longitudinal study. *American Journal of Occupational Therapy*, *68*, 307–316.

Tal-Saban, M., Zarka, S., Grotto, I., Ornoy, A., & Parush, S. (2012). The functional profile of young adults with suspected Developmental Coordination Disorder (DCD). *Research in Developmental Disabilities*, *33*, 2193–2202.

Tan, S. K., Parker, H. E., & Larkin, D. (2001). Concurrent validity of motor tests used to identify children with motor impairment. *Adapted Physical Activity Quarterly*, *18*, 168–182.

Thelen, E., & Smith, L. B. (1994). *A dynamic systems approach to the development of cognition and action*. London: The MIT Press.

Timler, A., McIntyre, F., Cantell, M., Crawford, S., & Hands, B. (2016). Development and evaluation of the psychometric properties of the Adolescent Motor Competence Questionnaire (AMCQ) for Adolescents. *Research in Developmental Disabilities*, *59*, 127–137.

Van Dellen, T., Vaessen, W., & Schoemaker, M. M. (1990). Clumsiness: Definition and selection of subjects. In A. F. Kalverboer (Ed.), *Developmental biopsychology. Experimental and observational studies in children at risk*. Ann Arbor, MI: University of Michigan Press.

Visser, J., Geuze, R. H., & Kalverboer, A. F. (1998). The relationship between physical growth, the level of activity and the development of motor skills in adolescence: Differences between children with DCD and controls. *Human Movement Science, 17*, 573–608.

Wilmut, K., & Byrne, M. (2014). Grip selection for sequential movements in children and adults with and without developmental coordination disorder. *Human Movement Science*, *36*, 272–284.

Wilmut, K., Byrne, M., & Barnett, A. L. (2013). Reaching to throw compared to reaching to place: A comparison across individuals with and without developmental coordination disorder. *Research in Developmental Disabilities*, *34*, 174–182.

Wilmut, K., Du, W., & Barnett, A. L. (2015). How do I fit through that gap? Navigation through apertures in adults with and without developmental coordination disorder. *PLoS One*, *10*, e0124695.

Wilson, P. H., Smits-Engelsman, B. C., Caeyenberghs, K., Steenbergen, B., Sugden, D., Clark, J. . . . Blank, R. (2017). Cognitive and neuroimaging findings in developmental coordination disorder: New insights from a systematic review of recent research. *Developmental Medicine & Child Neurology*, *59*(11), 1117–1129.

3

MOVEMENT COORDINATION, CONTROL AND SKILL DEVELOPMENT

Karl M. Newell and Matheus M. Pacheco

Introduction

The fundamental expressions of movement coordination, control and skill largely emerge through the formative infant (Bayley, 1936; Gesell, 1928; McGraw, 1943; Shirley, 1931; Thelen & Smith, 1994) to late childhood (Henderson, Sugden, & Barnett, 2007; Sugden & Wade, 2013; see Haywood and Getchell, chapter 1, this volume) years. Nevertheless, there is continuous adaptation and generalization of motor skill through to maturity and, indeed, subsequently over the adult years of the lifespan. Collectively, these changes in behavior lead to the large repertoire of movement patterns and outcomes that can be successfully and skillfully engaged by individuals in action. Aging, disease and injury can arrest the acquisition and performance levels of new and established skills and even reduce the range of activities that an individual can perform. Thus, considered over the lifespan, there is elaboration and contraction of the potential repertoire of movement forms in action (Newell & Morrison, 2016), channeled by the confluence of individual, environmental and task constraints (Newell, 1986).

The general focus of this chapter is on dynamical approaches to understanding motor learning and development from birth through late childhood. The central and generic feature to motor learning and development is the change over time in the fundamental properties of movement behavior: namely, coordination, control and skill (Newell, 1985). This change through learning and development up to late childhood is viewed as situated in a continuous and discontinuous flow of the evolving movement behavior over the lifespan (Muchisky, Gershkoff-Stowe, Cole, & Thelen, 1996; Newell & Morrison, 2016; Savelsbergh, van der Maas, & van Geert, 1999).

The theoretical perspective of the chapter draws on the coordinative structure theory (Kugler, 1986; Kugler, Kelso, & Turvey, 1980, 1982) and its related dynamical system's and ecological frameworks for self-organization in movement coordination, control and skill (Kelso, 1995; Turvey, 1990; Newell, Liu, & Mayer-Kress, 2001). This perspective holds that the observed order in behavior is a posteriori emergent feature of the interaction of the subsystems present in the human movement system channeled by constraints of the individual, task and environment. The constraints-perspective of dynamical systems provides a framework that challenges the usefulness of maintaining the maturation – learning emphasis together with the task and age distinctions that have supported the long held position of motor learning and development as separate domains of study. In particular, we focus on common principles to the acquisition of coordination in children's movement patterns and their compatibility with those of the acquisition of coordination in later childhood and adult motor learning (Newell & van Emmerik, 1990; Newell & Liu, 2014).

The acquisition of children's coordination, control and skill is considered here in the context of Bernstein's (1967) proposition that skill acquisition reflects the mastery of the redundant degrees of freedom. Bernstein's (1967, 1996) framework has guided the western literature for some 50 years (including the coordinative structure perspective) and it is instructive to reflect on its contributions and current relevance to motor learning and development. The focus of the chapter is on three related facets of Bernstein's problem, namely: a) the number and nature of the degrees of freedom regulated; b) the pathway of change to the emergent patterns of movement coordination; and c) the redundancy and variability in solutions to coordination and control – all of which change over time as a function of task constraints in the context of motor learning and development. The theoretical framework provides a basis to move beyond the classic descriptions of the emergence of the fundamental movement sequence and its generalization.

The fundamental movement sequence and its generalization

The pathway of change in motor learning and development is nonlinear and discontinuous rather than linear and continuous (Kugler et al., 1980, 1982; Savelsbergh et al., 1999). There are developmental changes in all subsystems of the growing individual that can contribute to the evolving movement behavior expressed through childhood. A striking example and under researched facet of this is the period of adolescence in which the individual passes through rapid changes at many levels of the system and most noticeably in the physical expressions of body scale in the form of height, weight and strength (Newell, 1984).

These changes in the form and function of the body hold challenges for the developing perception-action system and motor development through the lifespan. Thus, a central feature of motor development is the capacity of the system (developmental status) to engage successfully in a broader range of movement forms and task goals. Motor development realizes a growing repertoire of movement patterns and skills that can be organized to adapt to environmental and task demands (see chapter 1).

The introduction of the coordinative structure theory gave emphasis to the construct of self-organization in the formation and emergence of movement patterns (Kugler et al., 1980, 1982). This, in turn, gave renewed impetus to the study of motor development (Kugler, 1986; Newell, 1986; Savelsbergh et al., 1999; Thelen, 1986; Thelen & Smith, 1994) and a way to consider constraints to action and move beyond the limitations of the traditional dichotomy of the maturation versus learning debate (see Sugden & Wade, 2013 for a recent overview of these issues).

Coordination, control and skill as embedded constructs

Bernstein (1967, 1996) considered coordination to reflect an activity that guarantees that a movement has homogeneity, integration and structural unity. It was against this background that Kugler et al. (1980) provided the basis for an embedded nested account of the constructs coordination, control and skill (Newell, 1985). Coordination is the function that constrains the potentially free variables into a behavior unit. Control is the process by which parameter values are mapped in the function. Skill reflects the degree to which optimal values are related to the controlled variables.

In this view, coordination is reflected operationally in the relational variables of the observed movement (Turvey, 1990) whereas control is reflected in the changes to the scalar values of the function. Consider the example of walking. Walking can be identified by an upstanding locomotion that shows opposition in the motion between legs, and contralateral similarity and ipsilateral opposition when considering the relative motion between arms and legs. Additionally, a foot is always in contact with the ground. This description involves the co-occurrence in space and time of all of the body segmental motions – indeed, the coordination of the whole body. Clearly, individuals can walk faster or slower but the qualitative properties of the movement kinematics in the coordination of the act of walking are preserved. The fast/slow scaling characteristic of movement speed could be said to reflect the control of walking coordination. In some cases, it might be necessary to adapt the pace of walking in the context of efficiency and energetics – the acquired configuration of coordination and control is, then, reflecting an expression of skill.

From the coordinative structure theory, the order observed through the relational variables (i.e., the coordination) is assumed to be an *a posteriori* consequence rather than prescribed by higher order structures. Thus, the embedded constructs of coordination, control and skill are emergent properties. It is not that each of the concepts of coordination, control and skill reflects independent processes but rather that the respective constraints of task, individual and environment directly or indirectly give *emphasis to* one or the other facet of movement. This background is relevant to the issues of this chapter because our recent work has shown theoretically and experimentally that the function of learning is *different* for the fixed-point attractor dynamic tasks of movement scaling (Mayer-Kress, Liu, & Newell, 2006; Newell et al., 2001, 2009) than for those that induce transition(s) (Liu, Mayer-Kress, & Newell, 2006, 2010) in the realization of learning a new pattern of coordination. For instance, Langendorfer and Roberton (2002) in the acquisition by children of the overhand throw for distance showed that the movement pattern of the arm has qualitative differences before and after the acquisition of the trunk rotation: the rotation of the trunk seems to add the common observed forward motion of the humerus and forearm lagging – a transition between two patterns. This pattern of change differs from an individual who already presents the "mature" pattern and improves performance slowly and continuously.

Behavioral frames of analysis

Actions are identified in part by the goal to which the movement sequence is directed. This interpretation has led to the outcome score of action being the primary consideration of change in motor learning. In the acquisition of ontogenetic motor skills the emphasis has been on the incremental continuous change in performance outcome as reflected through practice in learning curves (Newell & Rosenbloom, 1981). In phylogenetic activities, measures of discontinuous change and the emergence of new movement forms have been primary with less or even little emphasis on the change of an outcome score in motor development. The distinction of outcome and movement indices to measure the change in motor learning and development has, however, become increasingly less clear-cut through efforts of their integration in contemporary studies of movement and action. Moreover, its relation is a source of the system redundancy and there is increasing evidence that the human movement system in action exploits the many possibilities of movement patterns (e.g., different joint motions) to achieve a given outcome.

There has been a growing theoretical influence of dynamical approaches to motor learning and development and the technical gains in the recording and analysis of movement dynamics, including that of movement forms. On the other hand, these developments in the analysis of movement in action have brought with them the new challenge of rationalizing *what* properties of movement are relevant to the theory of change in motor learning and development. We focus our analysis of change in motor learning and development on the behavioral macroscopic movement and outcome properties of action, though there is currently vigorous investigation of other levels of analysis (brain activity – e.g., EEG, fMRI; muscle activity – EMG, etc.) and their relations to movement.

Table 3.1 shows the primacy of three behavioral frames of emphasis to the analysis of change in motor learning and development (Saltzman & Kelso, 1987). One is the outcome of action that has been emphasized by the traditions of psychology and learning theory in particular (Newell & Rosenbloom, 1981). Another is the movement kinematics and kinetics of the movement trajectories of individual joint and body segment degrees of freedom that has been emphasized by the traditions of the biomechanics of movement (Winter, 2009). Finally, there is the more contemporary interdisciplinary paradigms of coordination dynamics and the ecological approach to perception and action that give emphasis in motor learning and development to the change in the relations of movement of the body segments to themselves and the environment (Jirsa & Kelso, 2004; Kelso, 1995; Turvey, 1990).

TABLE 3.1 Categories of task dynamics

Dynamics of change of movement in action
Task outcome (psychology)
Individual degrees of freedom (biomechanics)
Coordination of the degrees of freedom (coordination dynamics)

The integration of these three categories of emphasis in movement and action is critical for advancing our understanding of motor learning and motor development. This interpretation is relevant because there is not a direct mapping between movement of the individual degrees of freedom, their coordination and outcome in action. Consequently, a variety of movements may be generated to complete any one act (Bernstein, 1967), and, by the same token, a variety of movements may be identified as a particular act (Mischel, 1969).

Bernstein (1967) first articulated the problem directly by referring to motor skill acquisition as the mastery of the redundant degrees of freedom. The redundancy of the movement system in action is a (for some, *the*) central problem in motor control and an understanding of the question of change in motor learning and development. The concept of degrees of freedom is traditionally interpreted as the elements of a system that are free to vary. It is the redundancy[1] of the system that provides flexibility and adaptability of functional equivalence in movement and action across the lifespan. That is, in a broader sense, reflected in the capacity of individuals to realize the same action goal with solutions of different qualitative and/or quantitative properties of movement patterns. The large number of degrees of freedom per se of complex systems is, therefore, not necessarily the negative problem as has generally been interpreted from Bernstein's (1967, 1996) writings in that they contribute to the redundancy of the system and the contextual adaptability and stability of movement in action (Latash, 2012; Lipsitz & Goldberger, 1992; Mayer-Kress et al., 2006).

Bernstein's (1967) degrees of freedom (DF) problem

Physical DF in learning and development

As indicated earlier, Bernstein (1967) viewed motor skill acquisition as the mastery of redundant DF. While the DF can be considered at many levels of analysis of the system (joints, muscles, motor units, neurons and so on) Bernstein gave emphasis to the biomechanical joint motion DF in the coordination mode. This behavioral characterization is consistent with the more descriptive early accounts by developmental researchers of the emergence of motor development sequence.

Recent emphasis has been given to the mapping of information and dynamics of the perceptual-motor workspace (Shaw & Alley, 1985; Turvey, 1990) and the more abstract consideration of the functional or dynamical DF (Haken, 1996; Mitra, Amazeen, & Turvey, 1998). The functional or dynamical DF are the number of independent variables required to describe the dynamics of the system. This framework considers that joints, muscles, etc. of the system are constrained in acting together. The number of physical DF in, for example, joint space will typically be greater than the dynamical DF of their dynamic characterization (Newell & Vaillancourt, 2001; Turvey, Fitch, & Tuller, 1982). Referring to the example of overhand throwing, when characterizing the pattern in terms of joint motions, almost all joint motions must be described (physical DF). Nevertheless, when observing the co-variation in time of these joint motions, one can observe that fewer variables are required to describe the movement pattern (dynamical DF).

Bernstein (1967) proposed a three-stage account of motor learning and the change in the organization of the DF through practice. In the initial stage, the learner freezes the biomechanical DF (limb and torso segments) in movement execution – this, in effect, reduces the number of dynamical DF to a minimum to provide a workable solution to the task demands. In throwing, for instance, one can typically find the beginner by observing which individual relies largely only on movement at the elbow joint of the throwing arm with the trunk and shoulder joints maintaining their initial configuration – working on a single degree-of-freedom basis (see Figure 3.1 – initial pattern). In the second stage, the learner releases the ban on the DF to eventually incorporate all DF into the coordination mode. In throwing, this occurs when the individual starts to perform the movement with added motion at the joints of shoulder and trunk gradually, being able to increase speed of release, eventually adding the participation of the legs (Figure 3.1 – elementary pattern). Stage 3 has the learner utilizing the reactive phenomena (forces) that arise from the freeing of the DF. This advanced stage of utilizing and exploiting the reactive phenomena is essential to the efficient and effective (skilled) production of movement. Following our example, the expert in throwing can increase the velocity at the release by performing the movement with a lagged motion of distal joints in relation to the proximal ones (cf. Roberton & Halverson, 1984). The expert exploits the interactive torques between joints (Putnam, 1993) and the summation principle to have a faster release velocity at the wrist (Figure 3.1 – mature pattern) – the performer then is exploiting the non-muscular forces and reactive phenomena of the environment.

There have been a number of demonstrations of individual aspects of these stages of motor skill acquisition in both the acquisition of the phylogenetic infant movement patterns and a number of ontogenetic movement tasks (Newell & McDonald, 1994; Vereijken, Whiting, & Beek, 1992). However, taken collectively the findings show that the generalizability of Bernstein's (1967) stages of motor learning does not hold across tasks and developmental age (Newell & Vaillancourt, 2001). The freezing of the joint DF depends considerably on the prior experience of the individual learner and its relation to the to-be-learned task constraints. In the same way, the priority and order on the freeing of individual joint motions is related to task constraints. In short, the confluence of constraints to action (environment, individual and task – Newell, 1986) plays a strong role in driving the organization of the action system in a way that we still do not understand.

INITIAL

ELEMENTARY

MATURE

FIGURE 3.1 Three stages on the patterns of overhand throwing

Source: Reprinted by permission from Gallahue & Ozmun, 2006.

The emergence of fetal (Prechtl, 1986) and infant (Gesell, 1928, 1946) movement patterns has shown a directional trend to the progressive freeing of the DF. Gesell observed that infants tended to change the organization of the movement patterns of the fundamental movement skills in cephalo-caudal, proximal-distal, and ulnar-radial directions. And, some subsets of directional trends have been shown in adults learning new movement patterns (Newell & McDonald, 1994).

The anatomically based directional hypothesis of Gesell (1929) for the emergence of the freeing of the DF was one of his core developmental principles. Gesell had an anatomical biological account of the developmental directional effect in movement patterns that was interpreted in the context of the slower rate of the development of the nerve dynamics of the more distal musculature. Empirical investigations of this biological hypothesis for the directional change in movement patterns, however, have still not been forthcoming.

The alternative major hypothesis is due to Bernstein (1967) – a mechanical account of the directional patterns of the emergence of movement patterns in both infancy and through childhood. The mass of the limb segment(s) regulated by the more proximal muscles is larger than that of the segment(s) regulated by the distal muscles. The consequence is that the proximal muscles can overcome more easily the general resistance of the limb and they also provide for a greater range of motion. There is a build up of momentum through the limb segments and the relative velocities as a rule are higher for the distal as opposed to the proximal segments. Bernstein did not rule out the possible influence of the information transmission of the nerve dynamics in the cephalo-caudal and proximal-distal trend but held the importance of the mechanical DF.

The anatomical-physiological and mechanical hypotheses reflect functional and structural constraints on action that are evolving thorough development and learning. It would seem that these are not mutually exclusive hypotheses in that they both contribute to the stability and change of movement in action. An outgrowth of the Bernstein (1967) approach through dynamical systems frameworks has been the consideration of the more abstract dynamical DF of the perceptual-motor workspace (Mitra et al., 1998; Newell & Vaillancourt, 2011; Shaw & Alley, 1985).

Dynamical DF in learning and development

The construct of movement coordination (Turvey, 1990) explicitly requires that the *relations* between the individual DFs are determined to provide an index of the coupling or coordination. In the ecological account of perception and action (Kugler & Turvey, 1987; Shaw & Alley, 1985) the coordination modes are emergent properties of the constraints to action resulting from the mapping of perception and action. The coordination modes are, then, supported by attractive dynamical states to which the system gravitates toward when in action. This perspective provides that the mode is defined over both the information field arising from perception and the kinetic field arising from action (i.e., perceptual-motor workspace). Learning is reflected in the increased coordination of the mapping of the perception and action flow fields (Shaw & Alley, 1985).

The attractor organization of this dynamical interface is viewed as providing the building blocks for the emerging relational properties of the coordination mode. This theorizing has provided a framework for empirical investigations of learning and development of movement coordination at the level of the attractor organization. Several experimental and analytical methods have been used, depending on the question of interest and the nature of the data collected, to characterize properties of the attractor dynamics in movement coordination and control.

Principal component analysis (PCA)

PCA has been used to provide a characterization of the coordination and control of the motions of body joints and segments. PCA is a linear multivariate statistic that uses factor analytic techniques to compress the input of a multivariate data set (e.g., joint motions) into a smaller set of independent components with a weighted combination of the original input variables on each component (Daffertshofer, Lamoth, Meijer, & Beek, 2004). The number of components (PC) derived is taken as an index of the number of dynamical or active degrees of freedom (Haken, 1996) and used as a basis to investigate the acquisition of coordination in motor learning and development.

For example, Bo, Contreras-Vidal, Kagerer, and Clark (2006) and Lee, Bhat, Scholz, and Galloway (2008) have shown that the percent of variance accounted for in the primary PC in arm reaching and drawing tasks was increased with advances in developmental age suggesting a lower dimensional mode of control with motor learning and development. The generality of this proposed changing relation in motor development, however, needs further investigation both within a broader range of reaching tasks and other motor task categories. Moreover, the interpretation of PCA in the movement coordination context is not without its difficulties (Newell & Morrison, 2016).

Correlation dimension

The correlation dimension is a measure of the dimensionality of a dynamical system. It approximates the fractal dimension of the region in state space occupied by the dynamical system (Williams, 1997). A "fractal" dimension, roughly, is a way to describe a geometrical pattern and the characteristics that make it be. For instance, more detailed than a line (1D) but less than a plane (2D) – could give a dimension (D) of, for instance, 1.5 – a non-integer dimension. Specifically, the fractal dimension provides an index of how much detail is gained when the scale of the measurement changes. It is the rule rather than the exception to find fractal dimensions in nature (see Mandelbrot, 1967). The correlation dimension provides an estimate of the dimension of the dynamical system (the dynamic DFs) from a single time series. It fits well to the determination of the dimension of a single time series, such as postural tremor and isometric force.

Newell, van Emmerik, Lee, and Sprague (1993) showed in quiet upright standing posture that the dimension of the center of pressure (COP) in young adults with severe and profound learning difficulties and tardive dyskinesia was of a lower correlation dimension than the age-matched contrast group. Indeed, the dimension of the COP motion was so reduced that the neuroleptic medication changed the quiet standing postural control task into a movement rhythm task the dimension of which approximated a limit cycle with some noise ($D \sim 1.30$).

The attractor dynamics of postural control were investigated in a longitudinal study of postural control of infants learning to sit (Harbourne & Stergiou, 2003). The dimension of the COP decreased in sitting stage 2 when infants began to sit independently briefly but there was an increase from stage 2 to 3 indicating a release of the dynamical DF as independent sitting emerged (see Figure 3.2). This

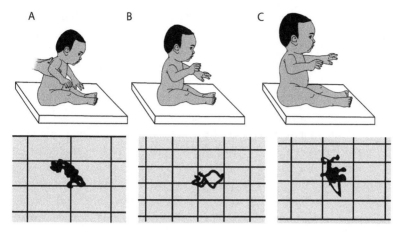

FIGURE 3.2 Infant COP pattern of motion with the developmental stage of sitting

Source: Reprinted by permission from Harbourne & Stergiou, 2003

pattern of findings shows how attractor dynamics can be mapped to the descriptive stages of motor development and gives evidence consistent with Bernstein's (1967) projections on the change of DF but in the frame of analysis of attractor dynamics rather than the physical DF of joint space motions.

There are a number of other methods that determine the attractor dimension but in each case a common limitation is that a large number of data points are needed to accurately calculate dimension. Nevertheless, with continuous movement tasks and longer duration trials these data limitations can be overcome in many experimental situations. On the other hand, the longer the trial duration the more other processes, such as boredom, fatigue and attention drift come into consideration. The correlation dimension is one nonlinear approach to fractal dimension and contrasts to the integer linear solution provided by the number of components in a PCA. Nevertheless, both methods are capturing indices of the qualitative properties of the movement dynamics and can be used to investigate change in motor learning and development. In doing that, one can refer to how the DF organization changes in acquisition of a skill – corroborating or challenging the ideas proposed by Bernstein (1967).

Adaptability and redundancy in motor development

The individual in action needs to accommodate the variability arising from internal (e.g., the so-called noise in the motor system) and external (e.g., changes in task, environment) sources that result in the movement variability of coordination, control and skill. Traditionally, with Bernstein (1967), these many degrees of freedom were viewed as a problem for harnessing motor control but current accounts view them as essential for the system to exploit the redundancy afforded by task and organism and exhibit what has been called redundancy. Redundancy here represents the notion that a given outcome (e.g., resist to a perturbation to avoid letting a mug of coffee turn) can be achieved by many different means (e.g., compensating with the wrist, elbow, shoulder, a combination of them, etc.). A redundant system affords, however, more than only adaptations when a perturbation affects current goals. It also affords more generally creativity and transfer in new environmental and task situations (Edelman, 1987; Sporns & Edelman, 1993).

Adolph (2005) has proposed that the ability to exploit redundancy is acquired in ontogeny. She proposed that this learned phenomenon requires experience on specific problem spaces (i.e., perceptual-motor workspace such as "sitting" or "crawling"), identification of relevant parameters to operate in such space and the acquisition of online adjustment of these parameters. This view matches directly with the coordination, control and skill levels described earlier (Kugler et al., 1980; Newell, 1985). Transfer would occur when the two tasks share the same problem space.

In a number of studies, Adolph's group has shown that when experienced in a given task young children are able to adapt to the situation at hand (in this case, they were able to judge whether they could cross a gap and also to actually perform this task) (e.g., Adolph, 2000). In addition, when tasks differed in terms of the problem space, no transfer was observed between the two situations (cruising over a handrail gap and cruising over a floor gap) (e.g., Adolph, Berger, & Leo, 2011). These studies offer illustrations of how, through development, the individual learns to adapt their actions to the environment.

There are methods that directly measure how much an individual takes advantage of the exploitation of redundancy in the perceptual-motor workspace either when acquiring a new skill or when trying to maintain the performance. These are the Uncontrolled Manifold (UCM, Scholz & Schöner, 1999; Schöner, 1995), the Goal-Equivalent Manifold (GEM, Cusumano & Cesari, 2006) and the Tolerance, Noise and Covariation (TNC, Cohen & Sternad, 2009; Müller & Sternad, 2004). With these methods, one can determine how an individual changes the elemental DF variables (variables assumed to have an effect on the task) to maintain or achieve a given performance.

Figure 3.3.A provides an example of a task space of a bimanual isometric task in which the goal is to maintain the sum of the force output of two fingers. The task space is defined by the relation of the elemental variables (force of the first finger, F_1, and force of the second finger, F_2) and the equation that defines the performance. In this case, for illustrative purposes, we used the following equation, in which E is the error (difference between combined force output performed and the goal of the task) and 10 (N – newtons) is the sum of forces to be produced (the goal). Notice that for the dashed line, all combinations of F_1 and F_2 that are along it maintain an unchanged task-relevant performance. This is usually called the redundant space of the task provided that there are multiple F_1 and F_2 combinations that reflect the same performance. This function shows the aspects under discussion here: a) provided the number of variables (effectors) and the number of equations (task constraints), it presents redundancy – more than one organizational solution will realize the task outcome; and b) provided the function is squared it creates in the space regions that are more tolerant to variation while meeting the task criterion than others (see Figure 3.3).

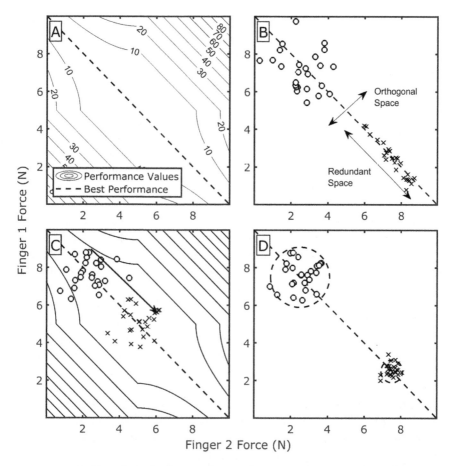

FIGURE 3.3 A. Hypothetical task space (bimanual isometric force, see Lafe, Pacheco and Newell, 2016 for an example) in which the goal is to maintain a constant sum of 10 N. The task space is described as where E is error (or the performance) and F_1 and F_2 are the values of each force exerted by each finger. The task is redundant provided there is a whole line of possible ways of achieving the goal (dashed line). B. Two hypothetical data distributions in the task with 25 trials. The circles are distributed randomly around the line showing similar distributions along redundant and orthogonal spaces. The crosses show a typical distribution of trials after some amount of practice (see text). C. Two hypothetical data distributions in the task with 25 trials. The crosses show the same distribution as the circles but are in a less tolerant region of the task space. D. Two hypothetical data distributions in the task with 25 trials. The circles have a larger distribution than the crosses (see text).

In general, studies that have employed these methods have shown a number of features of how and whether individuals exploit redundant dimensions of the task space. First, individuals show a preference to vary within the redundant space of the task or important variables (e.g., maintaining center of mass static in quiet standing). Second, this effect is not observed for other hypothesized categories of variables (cf. Scholz &

Schöner, 1999). That is, individuals are selective in terms of the space of the task that they allow to vary – reflecting the relevant variables being controlled. Third, this change in distribution is influenced by practice (Latash, 2010) showing, in accordance with Adolph (2005), that one learns how to exploit redundancy of the task.

Figure 3.3.B shows two different hypothetical data sets that illustrate the difference in distribution through learning. The circles show a similar distribution along and orthogonal to the redundant space (typically the beginning of practice) while the crosses have their distribution more pronounced along the redundant space (which occurs after some practice). Note that the distribution change is highly influenced by the nature of the task: simpler tasks usually show a decrease of redundant space variation – interpreted as adjustments to constraints beyond the task performance (e.g., Domkin, Laczko, Jaric, Johansson, & Latash, 2002). These extra constraints have been shown to also lead to changes in how individuals act on a trial-to-trial basis (cf. Cusumano, Mahoney, & Dingwell, 2014).

Another interesting feature is that individuals do not only change the shape of distribution, but also search for regions in the task space in which the performance is less influenced by inherent noise (Sternad, Huber, & Kuznetsov, 2014). Figure 3.3.C provides an example of how this occurs. At the beginning of practice, the individual might start in a region where the inherent variability (e.g., noise) influences the performance to a large degree (circles). Later in practice (crosses) the individual might find regions in which the same variability is not as detrimental as before. That is, individual's search for a more tolerant region to exploit variability (Müller & Sternad, 2004).

In these analyses it has also been shown that individuals decrease the overall amount of variability – the spread or dispersion of the data (Cohen & Sternad, 2009; Müller & Sternad, 2004). Figure 3.3.D shows hypothetical data that reflect the change with practice. At the beginning of practice, the overall variability of the data is more pronounced (circles) than later in practice (crosses).

Although limited in number, studies have shown that these features are observed differentially with advances in age through development. For instance, in two studies that emphasized either control (i.e., pushing a puck to achieve a desired distance, Chu, Sternad, & Sanger, 2013) or coordination tasks (i.e., throwing a hanging ball around a pole to hit a target, Chu, Park, Sanger, & Sternad, 2016), dystonic and typically developing children (5 to 18 and 10 to 16 years of age, respectively) exploited the task space and found more tolerant regions despite their differences in inherent variability. Chu et al. (2013) observed that when variability was externally manipulated (by scaling an added noise in the feedback score), children (as young as 5 years of age) could adapt their movements to maintain a good performance.

Wu, McKay, and Angulo-Barroso (2009) investigated whether the partition of variability in redundant and orthogonal spaces would differ between 6-year-old children, 10-year-old children and young adults provided that a qualitative change in posture is observed through the period from 6 to 10 years of age. In consonance with previous studies (Black, Smith, Wu, & Ulrich, 2007), the redundant space was exploited more by the youngest group in comparison to the other older groups

(10-year-old group was also different from adults). That is, considering that the individuals were trying to maintain the position of center of mass (COM), the motion of the joints occurred in a way that in the majority of cases, the COM position was maintained rather than changed – with this being more pronounced for the youngest group. The interpretation is that the individual not only learns to explore the redundant region of the perceptual-motor workspace but is highly influenced by the constraints that developmental status imposes on it. That is, younger children are less stable and more variable when posture is observed, but they manage to allocate the majority of this variability along the redundant space resulting in a more variable, but still functional task-relevant behavior.

A consequence of these findings is that they support the proposition that through practice individuals learn how to exploit the redundancy present in different tasks. Redundancy affords functional mappings between perception and action even when there is potential for change or improvement in terms of coordination, control and skill. These methods for the decomposition of movement variability offer the possibility to investigate how redundancy develops through the lifespan and might be fruitful in providing new insights on the development of non-typical children (for example, children with DCD).

Concluding remarks

The framework of coordination, control and skill provides the basis for a unified theoretical and experimental approach to the acquisition of both phylogenetic and ontogenetic activities. The role for constraints channeling the organization of the system allows the finessing of the artificial barriers of the traditional dichotomy of maturation and learning in motor development. The coordinative structure theory provides the basis for a theory of motor learning and development that encompasses the lifespan of individuals and the full repertoire of movement tasks.

We have shown that the DF problem of Bernstein (1967) has been elaborated beyond the joint space coordination problem in the fundamental movement patterns to a consideration of the dimension of the attractor dynamics that supports movement coordination, control and skill. A central issue of current interest is the mapping of the task outcome, motion of individual DF and the coordination of DF in the context of the redundancy of the system. Nevertheless, there are many issues here about children's movement coordination that are waiting for a developmental interpretation and perspective for theory and practice.

Finally, it is our view that the coordinative structure theory and the broader ecological approach to perception and action provide a framework for the field of DCD to consider directly through experiments on the central role of coordination in DCD. We have highlighted findings from some of the main paradigms used to consider the DF problem at the physical effector and abstract dynamical frames of reference of the system organization. It is timely that Wade and Kazeck (2018) have outlined the problem of perception-action coupling as a central issue in DCD drawing from the ecological approach to perception and action.

Note

1 The term redundancy here, as in motor control, generally is used in the same way that Edelman and Gally (2001) and Mason (2010) refer to the term degeneracy. In their interpretation, redundancy refers to when a substructure DF has a duplicate that can also perform the same function, while degeneracy refers to different structures that can perform the same function. Degeneracy allows that these structures can also perform new functions and is more robust against perturbations. In biological systems, degeneracy seems to be the preferred term but redundancy prevails in the engineering driven perspectives of motor control.

References

Adolph, K. E. (2000). Specificity of learning: Why infants fall over a veritable cliff. *Psychological Science, 11*, 290–295.

Adolph, K. E. (2005). Learning to learn in the development of action. In J. J. Rieser, J. J. Lockman, & C. A. Nelson (Eds.), *Action as an organizer of learning and development* (pp. 91–122). Mahwah, NJ: Lawrence Erlbaum Associates.

Adolph, K. E., Berger, S. E., & Leo, A. J. (2011). Developmental continuity? Crawling, cruising, and walking. *Developmental Science, 14*(2), 306–318.

Bayley, N. (1936). The development of motor abilities during the first three years: A study of sixty-one infants tested repeatedly. *Monographs of the Society for Research in Child Development, 1*(1), 1–26.

Bernstein, N. A. (1967). *The coordination and regulation of movements.* London: Pergamon Press.

Bernstein, N. A. (1996). On dexterity and its development. In M. Latash & M. T. Turvey (Eds.), *Dexterity and its development* (pp. 3–244). Mahwah, NJ: Lawrence Erlbaum Associates.

Black, D. P., Smith, B. A., Wu, J., & Ulrich, B. D. (2007). Uncontrolled manifold analysis of segmental angle variability during walking: Preadolescents with and without Down syndrome. *Experimental Brain Research, 183*, 511–521.

Bo, J., Contreras-Vidal, J. L., Kagerer, F. A., & Clark, J. E. (2006). Effect of increased complexity of visuo-motor transformations on children's arm movements. *Human Movement Science, 25*, 553–567.

Chu, V. W. T., Park, S. W., Sanger, T. D., & Sternad, D. (2016). Children with dystonia can learn a novel motor skill: Strategies that are tolerant to high variability. *IEEE Transactions on Neural Systems and Rehabilitation Engineering, 24*(8), 847–858.

Chu, V. W. T., Sternad, D., & Sanger, T. D. (2013). Healthy and dystonic children compensate for changes in motor variability. *Journal of Neurophysiology, 109*, 2169–2178.

Cohen, R. G., & Sternad, D. (2009). Variability in motor learning: Relocating, channeling and reducing noise. *Experimental Brain Research, 193*, 69–83.

Cusumano, J. P., & Cesari, P. (2006). Body-goal variability mapping in an aiming task. *Biological Cybernetics, 94*, 367–379.

Cusumano, J. P., & Mahoney, J. M., & Dingwell, J. B. (2014). The dynamical analysis of inter-trial fluctuations near goal equivalent manifolds. In M. F. Levin (Ed.), *Progress in motor control* (pp. 125–145). New York: Springer.

Daffertshofer, A., Lamoth, C. J. C., Meijer, O. G., & Beek, P. J. (2004). PCA in studying coordination and variability: A tutorial. *Clinical Biomechanics, 19*, 415–428.

Domkin, D., Laczko, J., Jaric, S., Johansson, H., & Latash, M. L. (2002). Structure of joint variability in bimanual pointing tasks. *Experimental Brain Research, 143*, 11–23.

Edelman, G. M. (1987). *Neural Darwinism: The theory of neuronal group selection.* New York: Basic Books.

Edelman, G. M., & Gally, J. A. (2001). Degeneracy and complexity in biological systems. *PNAS, 98*(24), 13463–13768.

Gallahue, D. L., & Ozmun, J. C. (2006). *Understanding motor development: Infants, children, adolescents, adults.* New York: McGraw-Hill.

Gesell, A. (1928). *Infancy and human growth.* New York: Macmillan.

Gesell, A. (1929). Maturation and infant behavior pattern. *Psychological Review, 36*(4), 307–319.

Gesell, A. (1946). The ontogenesis of infant behavior. In L. Charmichael (Ed.), *Manual of child psychology* (pp. 295–331). New York: Wiley.

Haken, H. (1996). *Principles of brain functioning: A synergetic approach to brain activity, behavior and cognition.* Berlin: Springer.

Harbourne, R. T., & Stergiou, N. (2003). Nonlinear analysis of the development of sitting postural control. *Developmental Psychobiology, 42*, 368–377.

Henderson, S. E., Sugden, D. A., & Barnett, A. L. (2007). *Movement assessment battery for children-2, Second Edition [Movement ABC-2].* London: The Psychological Corporation.

Jirsa, V. K., & Kelso, J. A. S. (2004). *Coordination dynamics: Issues and trends.* Berlin: Springer.

Kelso, J. A. S. (1995). *Dynamic patterns: The self-organization of brain and behavior.* Cambridge, MA: MIT Press – Bradford Books.

Kugler, P. N. (1986). A morphological perspective on the origin and evolution of movement patterns. In M. G. Wade and & H. T. A. Whiting (Eds.), *Motor development in children: Aspects of coordination and control* (pp. 459–525). Boston, MA: Martinus Nijhoff Publishers.

Kugler, P. N., & Turvey, M. T. (1987). *Information, natural law, and the self-assembly of rhythmic movement.* Hillsdale, NJ: Lawrence Erlbaum Associates.

Kugler, P. N., Kelso, J. A. S., & Turvey, M. T. (1980). On the concept of coordinative structures as dissipative structures: I. Theoretical lines of convergence. In G. E. Stelmach & J. Requin (Eds.), *Tutorials in motor behavior* (pp. 1–49). New York: North – Holland.

Kugler, P. N., Kelso, J. A. S., & Turvey, M. T. (1982). On the control and coordination of naturally developing systems. In J. A. S. Kelso & J. E. Clark (Eds.), *The development of movement control and co-ordination* (pp. 5–78). New York: Wiley.

Lafe, C. W., Pacheco, M. M., & Newell, K. M. (2016). Bimanual coordination and the intermittency of visual information in isometric force tracking. *Experimental Brain Research, 234*, 2025–2034.

Langendorfer, S. J., & Roberton, M. A. (2002). Individual pathways in the development of forceful throwing. *Research Quarterly for Exercise and Sport, 73*, 245–256.

Latash, M. L. (2010). Stages in learning motor synergies: A view based on the equilibrium-point hypothesis. *Human Movement Science, 29*, 642–654.

Latash, M. L. (2012). The bliss (not the problem) of motor abundance (not redundancy). *Experimental Brain Research, 217*, 1–5.

Lee, H. M., Bhat, A., Scholz, J. P., & Galloway, J. C. (2008). Toy-oriented changes during early arm movements IV: Shoulder-elbow coordination. *Infant Behavior & Development, 31*, 447–469.

Lipsitz, L. A., & Goldberger, A. L. (1992). Loss of "complexity" and aging: Potential applications of fractals and chaos theory to senescence. *Journal of American Medical Association, 267*, 1806–1809.

Liu, Y.- T., Mayer-Kress, G., & Newell, K. M. (2006). Qualitative and quantitative change in the dynamics of motor learning. *Journal of Experimental Psychology: Human Perception and Performance, 32*, 380–393.

Liu, Y-. T., Mayer-Kress, G., & Newell, K. M. (2010). Bi-stability of movement coordination as a function of skill level and task difficulty. *Journal of Experimental Psychology: Human Perception and Performance, 36*, 1515–1524.

Mandelbrot, B. (1967). How long is the coast of Britain? Statistical self-similarity and fractional dimension. *Science, 156* (3775), 636–638.

Mason, P. H. (2010). Degeneracy at multiple levels of complexity. *Biological Theory*, 5, 277–288.

Mayer-Kress, G., Liu, Y.-. T., & Newell, K. M. (2006). Complex systems and human movement. *Complexity, 12*, 40–51.

McGraw, M. B. (1943). *The neuromuscular maturation of the human infant*. New York: Columbia University Press.

Mischel, T. (1969). Scientific and philosophical psychology: A historical introduction. In T. Mischel (Ed.), *Human action*. New York: Academic Press.

Mitra, S., Amazeen, P. G., & Turvey, M. T. (1998). Intermediate motor learning as decreasing active (dynamical) degrees of freedom. *Human Movement Science, 17*, 17–65.

Muchisky, M., Gershkoff-Stowe, L., Cole, E., & Thelen, E. (1996). The epigenetic landscape revisited: A dynamic interpretation. In C. Rovee-Collier (Ed.), *Advances in infancy research* (Vol. 10, pp. 121–159). Norwood, NJ: Ablex.

Müller, H., & Sternad, D. (2004). Decomposition of variability in the execution of goal-oriented tasks: Three components of skill improvement. *Journal of Experimental Psychology: Human Perception and Performance, 30*(1), 212–233.

Newell, A., & Rosenbloom, P. S. (1981). Mechanisms of skill acquisition and the law of practice. In J. R. Anderson (Ed.), *Cognitive skills and their acquisition* (pp. 1–55). Hillsdale, NJ: Lawrence Erlbaum Associates.

Newell, K. M. (1984). Physical constraints to development of motor skills. In J. R. Thomas (Ed.), *Motor development during childhood and adolescence* (pp. 105–120). Minneapolis, MN: Burgess.

Newell, K. M. (1985). Coordination, control and skill. In D. Goodman, I. Franks, & R. Wilberg (Eds.), *Differing perspectives in motor learning, memory and control* (pp. 295–317). Amsterdam: North-Holland.

Newell, K. M. (1986). Constraints on the development of coordination. In M. G. Wade & H. T. A. Whiting (Eds.), *Motor skill acquisition in children: Aspects of coordination and control* (pp. 341–360). Amsterdam, Netherlands: Martinies NIJHOS.

Newell, K. M., & Liu, Y-. T. (2014). Dynamics of motor learning and development across the lifespan. In P. C. M. Molenaar, R. Lerner, & K. M. Newell (Eds.), *Handbook of developmental systems theory and methodology* (pp. 316–342). New York: Guilford Publications.

Newell, K. M., & McDonald, P. V. (1994). Learning to coordinate redundant biomechanical degrees of freedom. In S. Swinnen, H. Heuer, J. Massion, & P. Casaer (Eds.), *The control and modulation of patterns of inter-limb coordination: A multidisciplinary perspective* (pp. 515–536). New York: Academic Press.

Newell, K. M., & Morrison, S. (2016). The evolving dynamical landscape of movement forms: A degrees of freedom perspective. *Kinesiology Review, 5*, 4–14.

Newell, K. M., & Vaillancourt, D. E. (2001). Dimensional change in motor learning. *Human Movement Science, 20*, 695–715.

Newell, K. M., & van Emmerik, R. E. A. (1990). Are Gesell's developmental principles general principles for the acquisition of coordination. In J. E. Clark & J. H. Humphrey (Eds.), *Advances in motor development research* (Vol. 3, pp. 143–164). New York: AMS Press.

Newell, K. M., Liu, Y-. T., & Mayer-Kress, G. (2001). Time scales in motor learning and development. *Psychological Review, 108*, 57–82.

Newell, K. M., Mayer-Kress, G., Hong, S. L., & Liu, Y-. T. (2009). Adaptation and learning: Characteristic time scales of performance dynamics. *Human Movement Science, 28*, 655–687.

Newell, K. M., van Emmerik, R. E. A., Lee, D., & Sprague, R. L. (1993). On postural stability and variability. *Gait & Posture, 4*, 225–230.

Prechtl, H. F. R. (1986). Prenatal motor development. In M. G. Wade & H. T. A. Whiting (Eds.), *Motor development in children: Aspects of coordination and control* (pp. 53–64). Dordrecht: Martinus Nijhoff Publishers.

Putnam, C. A. (1993). Sequential motion of body segments in striking and throwing skills: Descriptions and explanations. *Journal of Biomechanics, 26*, 125–135.

Roberton, M. A., & Halverson, L. E. (1984). *Developing children – their changing movement: A guide for teachers*. Philadelphia, PA: Lea & Febiger.

Saltzman, E., & Kelso, J. A. S. (1987). Skilled actions: A task dynamic approach. *Psychological Review, 94*, 84–106.

Savelsbergh, G., van der Maas, H., & van Geert, P. (Eds.) (1999). *Non-linear developmental processes*. Amsterdam, Netherlands: Royal Netherlands Academy of Arts and Sciences.

Scholz, J. P., & Schöner, G. (1999). The uncontrolled manifold concept: Identifying control variables for a functional task. *Experimental Brain Research, 126*, 289–306.

Schöner, G. (1995). Recent developments and problems in human movement science and their conceptual implications. *Ecological Psychology, 7*(1), 291–314.

Shaw, R. E., & Alley, T. R. (1985). How to draw learning curves: Their use and justification. In T. D. Johnson, & A. T. Pietrewicz (Eds.), *Issues in the ecological study of learning* (pp. 275–304). Hillsdale, NJ: Lawrence Erlbaum Associates.

Shirley, M. M. (1931). *The first two years: A study of twenty-five babies. Vol 1. Postural and locomotor development*. Minneapolis, MN: University of Minnesota Press.

Sporns, O., & Edelman, G. M. (1993). Solving Bernstein's problem: A proposal for the development of coordinated movement by selection. *Child Development, 64*(4), 960–981.

Sternad, D., Huber, M. E., & Kuznetsov, N. (2014). Acquisition of novel and complex motor skills: Stable solutions where intrinsic noise matter less. In M. F. Levin (Ed.), *Progress in motor control* (pp. 101–124). New York: Springer.

Sugden, D., & Wade, M. (2013). *Typical and atypical motor development*. London: Mac Keith Press.

Thelen, E. (1986). Treadmill-elicited stepping in seven-month-old infants. *Child Development, 57*, 1498–1506.

Thelen, E., & Smith, L. B. (1994). *A dynamic systems approach to the development of cognition and action*. Cambridge, MA: MIT Press.

Turvey, M. T. (1990). Coordination. *American Psychologist, 45*, 938–953.

Turvey, M. T., Fitch, H. L., & Tuller, B. (1982). The Bernstein perspective: I. The problems of degrees of freedom and context-conditioned variability. In J. A. S. Kelso (Ed.), *Human motor control* (pp. 239–252). Hillsdale, NJ: Lawrence Erlbaum Associates.

Vereijken, B., Whiting, H. T. A., & Beek, W. J. (1992). A dynamical systems approach to skill acquisition. *The Quarterly Journal of Experimental Psychology Section A: Human Experimental Psychology, 45*(2), 323–344.

Wade, M. G., & Kazeck, M. (2018). Developmental coordination disorder and its cause: The road less travelled. *Human Movement Science, 57*, 489–500. http://dx.doi.org/10.1016/j.humov.2016.08.004.

Williams, G. P. (1997). *Chaos theory tamed*. Washington, DC: Joseph Henry Press.

Winter, D. A. (2009). *Biomechanics and motor control of human movement*. Hoboken, NJ: Wiley.

Wu, J., McKay, S., & Angulo-Barroso, R. (2009). Center of mass control and multi-segment coordination in children during quiet stance. *Experimental Brain Research, 196*, 329–339.

4

MOVEMENT COORDINATION, CONTROL AND SKILL ACQUISITION IN DCD

Kate Wilmut and Anna L. Barnett

Introduction

Motor development reflects how an infant or child learns and acquires skill through spontaneous practice. Given that children with developmental coordination disorder (DCD) do not spontaneously acquire motor skill in the same way as we see in typical development, it is clear why DCD is often referred to as a motor learning disorder (Biotteau, Chaix, & Albaret, 2016; Ferguson, Jelsma, Jelsma, & Smits-Engelsman, 2013; Magallón, Crespo-Eguílaz, & Narbona, 2015; Schoemaker & Smits-Engelsman, 2015). It also explains the motivation for the definition of the first criterion for DCD in the Diagnostic and Statistical Manual of Mental Disorders which in fact states *'the acquisition and execution of coordinated motor skills are substantially below that expected given the individual's chronological age and opportunity for skill learning and use'* (American Psychiatric Association, 2013). However, surprisingly few studies have specifically examined motor learning in this group and so although we may describe DCD as a disorder of motor learning, exactly what this means is unclear. This chapter will describe the handful of studies which *have* focused on motor learning in this population and will contextualise this within the constraints-based-approach to motor control. We will then consider aspects of motor control and skill acquisition raised by Newell and Pacheco, which have not yet been studied in children with DCD.

Constraints-based approach to motor control

The 'constraints-based' approach to understanding motor behaviour has been adopted as a clear way to describe and understand the motor behaviour seen in children with DCD (Sugden & Wade, 2013). Newell (1986) first proposed the idea of constraints as variables which limit movement and can be broken down into three categories; organismic, which relate to the individual; environmental, which relate to features of the environment such as physical and social elements (ambient light, social groups etc.); and task, which include task goals, tools needed, specific rules of the task, etc. The constraints-based approach suggests that these three factors interact to constrain or promote learning and the resulting movement is unique to that *individual* at that given *time* (Davids, Button, & Bennett, 2008). The way in which these factors constrain movement is constantly changing and so can go from enhancing to suppressing learning over consecutive sessions (Davids et al., 2008). One of the strengths of the constraints-based approach is that it can be used to conceptualise the constraints when learning a skill over a short period (a few practice trials) and when learning over a much longer time frame (i.e. during development). This approach provides a useful context for motor control in children with DCD as it encompasses all of the factors involved in movement and allows us to consider these together rather than focusing on a single element (Sugden & Wade, 2013). In addition, Anson, Elliott, and Davids (2005) have argued that this approach sits well with Bernstein's theoretical perspective of coordination and regulation of movement including the control of degrees of freedom (Bernstein, 1967) which is clearly defined by Newell and Pacheco in this volume (also see Bongaardt & Meijer, 2000 for a detailed description of Bernstein's work).

Motor skill acquisition in DCD

Therapeutic intervention

A body of work relevant to the understanding of skill acquisition in children with DCD is therapeutic intervention, where practice is provided in a therapeutic setting to improve skill where there is a known difficulty in learning that specific motor skill. There is not always a clear distinction between these therapeutic studies and those designed to evaluate learning per se. In the field of DCD there are some well-established approaches to intervention used by allied health professionals. These can broadly be divided into 'task-oriented' and 'process-oriented' approaches (Kennedy-Behr & Rodger, this volume; Polatajko & Cantin, 2007). Evaluations of these typically involve measurement of performance before and after an intervention period and sometimes include a control group not receiving the intervention and/or a follow up test of skill retention. Generally these studies show pre to post-intervention improvements in performance in the range of skills investigated, with studies focusing on recognised task-oriented approaches on skills such as handwriting (Farhat et al., 2013; Jongmans, Linthorst-Bakker, Westenberg, & Smits-Engelsman, 2003), balance (Ferguson et al., 2013) and catching (Miles, Wood, Vine, Vickers, & Wilson, 2015). (For more detail regarding intervention, both in general and those specific to DCD, we refer the reader to chapters 9 and 10.) These studies demonstrate the capacity for learning in children with DCD when practice is highly structured and supported by expert practitioners. However, far fewer studies have focused on how children with DCD actually learn new motor skills and whether repeated practice is sufficient to enable skill acquisition in this population. In the previous chapter Newell and Pacheco discuss the categories in which change following training can be considered. They outline three categories: task outcome; individual degrees of freedom (kinematics and kinetics of a single degree of freedom); and coordination of the degrees of freedom (coordination dynamics). Research which has considered motor learning in DCD has focused very much on change in task outcome or change in movement kinematics and kinetics rather than a focus on change in coordination dynamics of movement (these categories of change are discussed in more detail in chapter 3 and will be returned to later in the current chapter). This research is described next.

Perceptual-motor adaptation tasks and sequence learning tasks

Most commonly, motor skill learning has been assessed via: perceptual-motor adaptation; and sequence learning. Perceptual-motor adaptation tasks require a child to learn a new association between the movements they make and the visual outcome of those movements. This can be achieved by asking a child to make simple discrete aiming movements using a mouse or stylus. Visual feedback from the hand is removed and instead feedback is provided via the cursor or stylus point; this feedback is rotated to the right or left causing a mismatch between perception and action. Using such a task Kagerer, Bo, Contreras-Vidal, and Clark (2004) and Kagerer, Contreras-Vidal, and Clark (2006) found children were as able to adapt to the new perceptual-motor map as typically developing children. Using a similar paradigm, Lejeune, Wansard, Geurten, and Meulemans (2016) found similar rates of learning, consolidation and transfer across their participants with and without DCD. However, asymptotic performance level reached by the children with DCD was lower than that reached by their typical counterparts. Studies have also found a similar adaptation rate across a typically developing group and a DCD group when using a 'throwing prism adaptation test', whereby throwing is performed whilst wearing prism goggles that displace the field of view (Cantin, Polatajko, Thach, & Jaglal, 2007). All of these studies demonstrate that children with DCD can and do adapt to these types of distortion. However, as these studies impose error on movement through external manipulation, the extent to which they inform us about learning everyday movement patterns is limited. Given that a certain degree of error is inherent in all movement that we make, a more naturalistic way to consider motor learning is to measure how individuals minimise error over repeated trials using tasks which do not artificially impose error into movement.

In a bid to do just that a number of studies have focused on sequence learning using finger tapping tasks (Gheysen, van Waelvelde, & Fias, 2011; Lejeune, Catale, Willems, & Meulemans, 2013; Wilson, Maruff, & Lum, 2003). The idea is that this type of sequence learning is important in naturalistic motor tasks as all movements are composed of a sequence of action and the order of that sequence is key in smooth controlled movement. Studies using the serial reaction task (Nissen & Bullemer,

1987), where targets appear in one of four locations in a repeating sequence and reductions in reaction time denote sequence learning, have shown that children with DCD showed sequence learning in line with their peers (Lejeune et al., 2013). Furthermore, a study involving a finger tapping task (requiring the individual to learn and tap out a short sequence) similarly found a clear effect of repeated practice in both a group of children with DCD and a group of children with DCD and Developmental Dyslexia (Biotteau, Chaix, & Albaret, 2015).

This collection of studies focusing on perceptual-motor adaptation and sequence learning provides a really clear insight into motor learning in children with DCD and we can see very common themes regarding apparently unimpaired motor learning in children with DCD. However, where studies have not imposed error into movement they have measured motor learning in very simple motor tasks (finger press). Therefore, it is not clear whether repeated practice would result in motor learning when the constraints of the task are changed.

The effects of repeated practice

There are only a handful of studies which have investigated the effects of repeated practice on more complex motor tasks in this population and each varies in terms of the type of task, extent of practice and the extent and frequency of measures over time. Zwicker, Missiuna, Harris, & Boyd (2011) used a tracing task in an fMRI study to explore the brain mechanisms underlying learning in DCD. Children with DCD showed no improvement in the accuracy of a tracing task over three days of practice while the typically developing children did show an improvement (Zwicker et al., 2011). The method used to determine accuracy in this study may have precluded learning in the children with DCD, since the authors counted the number of times the children went out of bounds when tracing. While it is possible the children with DCD did improve (crossing the line for less time or deviating from it to a lesser extent), these changes would not have been measured using this assessment of accuracy. Furthermore, the practice sessions were performed in a seated position, whereas the measures were taken while supine in the scanner, this change in orientation may have been more difficult for the children with DCD to accommodate to than the typically developing children, thus occluding any improvement. In a smaller scale study, involving just two 'physically awkward' children, a stationary hockey slap shot was practiced over a six-week period (Marchiori, Wall, & Bedingfield, 1987). The quality of their shots was poor and very variable compared to controls and they showed no improvement. However, a task such as this would rarely be learnt through repetitive practice but would need specific teaching and feedback. Given the methodological limitations of these two studies, the null results cannot be taken to infer that children with DCD are unable to learn through repeated practice.

In contrast, other studies do provide some evidence that children with DCD can improve with repeated practice. Missiuna (1994) investigated skill acquisition in children with DCD using a discrete aiming task. The size and position of targets varied randomly during practice which continued until movement time reached a plateau. The children with DCD showed similar rates of learning to typically developing controls, showing reductions in both movement time and reaction time. However, even though it took the groups a similar amount of time to reach asymptote in movement time, the final performance in the children with DCD at this point was still poorer compared to the typically developing group. Candler and Meeuwsen (2002) also considered repeated practice on a computer-based task which required participants to 'catch' a descending ball using a paddle that could be moved to the left and right. In addition to considering whether children with DCD could improve at this task with repeated exposure, Candler and Meeuwsen (2002) considered whether they could utilise 'cues' to improve their performance. These cues were not explicitly explained to the participants and as such utilisation would demonstrate implicit learning. Essentially the findings demonstrated that both children with DCD and typically developing children could improve their performance with practice and could utilise the cue by making anticipatory adjustments when it appeared. Finally, Magallón et al. (2015) considered skill acquisition after repeated practice on an assembly learning task (Purdue pegboard task) and on a mirror drawing task. The focus of this study was on the different rate of learning across groups of children with different patterns of co-occurring conditions. All of the groups improved on the two tasks following a short period of repeated practice demonstrating once again that children with DCD (and other co-occurring conditions) can improve with repeated practice. However, this study also demonstrated that for some of the measures the children without DCD (but with other developmental disorders) outperformed the children with DCD (and other co-occurring conditions) in terms of rate of learning. It would seem, therefore, that although children with DCD can improve with repeated practice, the rate at which they do this is suppressed in a way which is unique to DCD rather than being a characteristic of a developmental disorder more generally.

The role of active video games in motor learning

The studies discussed have provided children with DCD with direct practice of motor tasks and then measured improvement in motor competence on that skill. Recently there has been a growth of studies considering whether active video games can improve general motor performance in children with DCD. The Nintendo Wii Fit system and Playstation eye toy have both been used in such studies, with improvements seen on standard measures of motor competence using the Movement Assessment Battery for children and the Bruininks-Oseretsky Test of Motor Proficiency (Hammond, Jones, Hill, Green, & Male, 2014; Jelsma, Geuze, Mombarg, & Smits-Engelsman, 2014), in other related areas such as functional strength and anaerobic fitness (Ferguson et al., 2013) and in terms of the children's perception of their motor abilities (Hammond et al., 2014; Straker et al., 2015). Although these studies suggest that merely offering the opportunity to practice motor skills using active video games can lead to improved motor performance (Schoemaker & Smits-Engelsman, 2015), not all studies have found changes in motor skill following the use of these technologies. For example, Straker et al. (2015) compared changes in motor competence following training with active video games (Playstation eye toy and XBox Kinetic) versus non-active video games. This was a home-based intervention study and training was unsupervised. No difference was seen in terms of the change in motor competence across the two groups suggesting that active videos games did not promote motor learning in this group any more than the non-active video games. A follow up study demonstrated that this null effect may have been due to an inadequate quality of play with children being reluctant to play games which were 'hard' either in terms of task difficulty or intensity level (Howie, Campbell, Abbott, & Straker, 2017). Further detail regarding these studies can be found in a recent review, which discusses the use of virtual reality technology with children with neuro-developmental disorders, including DCD (Wilson, Green, Caeyenberghs, Steenbergen, & Duckworth, 2016). This provides a comprehensive overview with a particular focus on the potential for technological innovation in rehabilitation, or in a learning context, for promoting learning in this, and other populations.

Although informative, the studies discussed do not focus on motor learning per se as they use the active video games to determine improvements in general motor skill rather than learning of the practice task. Smits-Engelsman, Jelsma, Ferguson, & Geuze (2015) examined learning using a ski-slalom simulator game (Wii Fit) in children with DCD. During practice children alternated between an easy and hard version. Children with DCD showed similar rates of learning to typically developing controls and after training no difference was seen between the children with DCD and the typically developing children in terms of their ski-slalom score. The two groups also demonstrated similar retention rates and similar transfer effects to other tasks requiring static and dynamic balance. Therefore, this study demonstrates very little difference between a group of children with and without DCD in terms of motor learning. Jelsma, Ferguson, Smits-Engelsman, and Geuze (2015) extended the findings described earlier to consider whether the beneficial effects of the ski-slalom game could be realised following a much shorter training period. They used the same ski-slalom simulator as Smits-Engelsman et al. (2015) and found that even though the children with DCD improved over time, the rate and performance of children with DCD was reduced compared to the typically developing children (the learning curves were distinctly different across these groups). Furthermore, as expected the typically developing children showed an efficient speed accuracy trade off (as they learnt they slowed down slightly to reduce error) while the children with DCD did not. Comparing these studies we see that although both found similar retention rates across children with and without DCD, one found a depressed rate of learning and distinctly different strategies in children with DCD while the other did not. It would seem, therefore, that although children with DCD can learn over short periods, a prolonged training period is needed in order to see similar rates of learning.

Our current understanding of motor skill acquisition in DCD

It would seem that there are some characteristics of motor skill learning in children with DCD that are seen across the majority of these studies. Repeated practice alone can allow these children to learn new skills. Studies have demonstrated that this is the case for perceptual-motor adaptation tasks, for sequence learning, for motor tasks where repeated practice is given and for motor skills learnt via active video games. Rate of learning for many of these tasks is at a typical level (where it is not we have highlighted clear methodological reasons for the disparity) and so although the children with DCD may still perform below the level of their typically developing counterparts, after practice they do learn and change their movements at the same rate. Studies which have included measurements of transfer, retention and automatisation have also failed to find any clear deficits in children with DCD. Given that the research discussed here demonstrates that children with DCD can learn through repeated practice it raises the question as to why they do not naturally do this in the same way as typically developing children. The activity-deficit hypothesis (Green et al., 2011; Schoemaker & Smits-Engelsman, 2015) may provide one explanation. Green et al. (2011) suggested that as children with DCD are well aware of their poor motor skills, they may reduce their motor occupations and adopt a much more sedentary lifestyle. This is supported by evidence demonstrating that self-perception is an important mediator in physical activity (Cairney et al., 2005) and that children with DCD generally show a lower engagement with this type of activity (Cairney, Hay, Veldhuizen, Missiuna, & Faught, 2010). This then becomes a vicious cycle whereby motor skills are poor, engagement in motor activity (including play, activities of daily living, etc.) declines and so skills remain poor. Over time the gap between these individuals and their peers widens, thus highlighting those poor motor skills further. A word of caution is needed here, although the account given here is an appealing one the studies described in this chapter have used relatively simple tasks measuring task outcome and change in a single degree of freedom. As elegantly described in Newell and Pacheco (in chapter 3) a single outcome can be achieved using many different coordination patterns and therefore, a similar task outcome or similar kinematics for a single degree of freedom does not necessarily indicate the same level of control or skill. Newell and Pacheco describe Bernstein's three-stage account of motor learning using the example of throwing. One can see from this that considering control and skill across the coordination of the entire body, and how this changes as one learns, is needed in order to fully understanding motor skill acquisition.

Where is the coordination?

Looking back to the three categories for which change can be measured during skill acquisition (task outcome, individual degrees of freedom and coordination of the degrees of freedom), Newell and Pacheco highlight the importance of considering change across all of these levels given that there is no direct mapping between movement of individual degrees of freedom, their coordination and the outcome. In other words, any one outcome can emerge as a result of many different coordination patterns, for example, successfully catching a ball can be achieved in many different ways. The research described here in terms of motor skill acquisition in DCD has focused only on the first two of these three categories and to date no studies have considered change in coordination following motor training. However, studies that have looked at coordination skills in children with DCD demonstrate that they generally show deficits when asked to produce rhythmic coordination patterns in tasks requiring self-paced uni- and bi-manual finger tapping movements (Volman & Geuze, 1998), bimanual finger tapping to an auditory beat (Whitall et al., 2008) and clapping while marching to an auditory beat (Whitall et al., 2006). Furthermore, removal of external cues, such as visual and auditory cues do not alter performance in children with DCD (Mackenzie et al., 2008; Roche, Wilms-Floet, Clark, & Whitall, 2011) suggesting that this deficit is not due to a difficulty integrating external information but rather is a difficulty with coupling multiple body segments. Elders et al. (2010) considered the coupling of the head, torso and hand in a pointing task and found that the general coordination pattern was the same across groups but that the children with DCD failed to reliably couple body segments. Astill and Utley (2006) also considered the coupling of multiple limb segments but in a catching rather than a pointing task. Children with DCD showed a 'freezing' of the degrees of freedom in the upper limbs which was not apparent in the age matched controls, thus demonstrating a difference in coordination across these groups. These latter findings demonstrate that it is not only a difficulty with rhythmic coordination but coordination generally that these children face. The research emphasises the importance of coordination dynamics and we would advocate the importance of considering changes following motor learning across coordination dynamics rather than single outcomes.

Usually when we think about coordination we think about the coordination of different limbs or muscles. However, Newell and Pacheco introduce the idea of coordination of perception and action, citing Shaw and Alley (1985) who state that skill improvement occurs as perception and action become more coordinated. Research which has considered the mapping between perception and action outside a learning context has demonstrated a difference in how perception and action are coordinated in children with DCD as compared to typically developing peers (Wilmut, Du, & Barnett, 2017), therefore, improving the coordination between perception and action in DCD may change the way in which movements are acquired and then controlled. Although this is purely speculative at the moment it is an avenue which we believe requires further consideration given that it is impossible to separate perception from action.

Variability of movement

All movements are subject to variability whereby even when a movement is repeated under the same constraints it will differ from previous executions (exactly how it differs can be very subtle and not always apparent through simple observation). This variability tends to be greater in children with DCD compared to their typically developing peers (Wade & Kazeck, 2018), yet we know from experimental studies that children with DCD can account for their increased movement variability when generating coordinative movements (Wilmut, Du, & Barnett, 2015; Wilmut et al., 2017). However, Wade and Kazeck (2018) distinguish between two types of variability. The first is a measure of performance variability which is often referred to as 'error' or 'noise'. The second is the variability we see in coordination and represents the performer's capability for response flexibility. Newell and Pacheco discuss this in terms of exploiting the redundancy of a task; that is learning that a task outcome may be achieved through a number of different coordinative actions and that having the flexibility to perform a task in many different ways while still achieving the desired goal is an indication of optimal motor control.

The concept that variability represents noise has received a greater focus of attention in DCD research as compared to variability representing flexibility. It has been suggested that the motor learning difficulties in DCD may relate to the commonly reported variability of motor performance, which represents 'noise' in the motor system. This 'noise' makes it hard for these individuals to develop accurate motor plans that represent the control of specific movement skills (Smits-Engelsman, Westenberg, & Duysens, 2008). Studies advocating 'assisted' motor learning in children with DCD have suggested that if this 'noise' can be reduced, then learning may be enhanced (Snapp-Childs, Mon-Williams, & Bingham, 2013). Snapp-Childs et al. (2013) report improvements in children with DCD in both spatial and temporal elements of a 3D tracking task while using a robotic arm to provide graded assistance to movement. During practice children progressed through the levels of difficulty; only moving onto the next stage when they had successfully completed the previous stage. Both the children with and without DCD improved as a result of the training, but interestingly, in this study the children with DCD demonstrated a higher rate of learning which allowed them to attain the same level of performance as typically developing children by the end of the training (Snapp-Childs et al., 2013). In a follow up study, Snapp-Childs, Shire, Hill, Mon-Williams, and Bingham (2016) used a cross-over design to consider learning and transfer in children with DCD using the same task as described earlier. Their findings replicated that of Snapp-Childs et al. (2013) but also demonstrated a clear transfer effect to a 2D shape copying task. Although this provides an interesting insight into learning in this population and also strengthens the idea of error or noise in the motor system, it may be that the gradually increased difficulty of the task (as assistance was reduced) actually promoted skill learning rather than the assistance per se. This sits within the 'challenge point framework' (Guadagnoli & Lee, 2004) which states that in order for an individual to acquire a skill there needs to be a balance between the difficulty of the task and the initial skill level of an individual. If the task is too difficult and the skill level too low then skill acquisition is unlikely, similarly if task difficulty is low and skill level high no skill improvement will be seen. Therefore, as skill improves, task difficulty needs to increase in order to see an increase in skill level. In studies described here, which have found clear motor learning in children with DCD there has been a manipulation of task difficulty: Missiuna (1994) used a variety of target sizes and distances, Candler and Meeuwsen (2002) had the 'falling ball' change direction and Smits-Engelsman et al. (2015) and Jelsma et al. (2015) used an easy and a hard version of their task. Furthermore, Howie et al. (2017) cite the children with DCD not challenging themselves enough when playing active video games as key in the null results of the Straker et al. (2015) study. All of these studies fit with the challenge point framework in terms of how we can promote learning. This makes it difficult to determine whether Snapp-Childs et al. (2013) and Snapp-Childs et al. (2016) found a higher rate of learning in children with DCD because of the assisted support inherent in the task or whether it was simply due to the manipulation surrounding level of difficulty.

The description provided by Wade and Kazeck (2018) calls into question what we mean when we refer to variability and indeed whether it is a 'good' or a 'bad' construct (also see Wilson, Dewey, Smits-Engelsman, & Steenbergen, 2017, for a debate on this issue). Clearly, in the context of the studies described here, variability was described as error and noise and was deemed disruptive to motor control. However, the concept that variability could also demonstrate flexibility of skill is an important one to consider. Thinking about variability in this context in DCD may provide a framework in which coordinative tasks can be considered. Research is needed to focus on whether children with DCD can learn to exploit the redundancy of a task when faced with complex coordinative actions. If they cannot do this it may explain why they are not showing optimal movement control and why they show deficits with motor skill.

Concluding remarks

In their chapter, Newell and Pacheco outline some key aspects of motor learning that need attention in the DCD community. The studies focusing on motor learning in this population have provided an important insight with some evidence clearly demonstrating that motor learning can follow a typical pattern in DCD. However, the constraints-based approach advocates consideration of *all* factors which may constrain or suppress learning and one which is clearly missing from the DCD literature is the measurement of coordination dynamics. Therefore, the question as to whether these children can learn complex *coordinative* tasks remains unclear. These studies showing a change in outcome following training demonstrate an ability to learn at one level, but whether this 'learning' is in line with that seen in typical development and results in releasing of degrees of freedom or a change in coordination of movement is also unclear. Until we fully explore learning in complex tasks requiring multiple degrees of freedom, we will not be able to determine the full nature of Developmental *Coordination* Disorder.

References

American Psychiatric Association. (Ed.). (2013). *Diagnostic and statistical manual of mental disorders* (5th ed.). Washington, DC: American Psychiatric Association.

Anson, G., Elliott, D., & Davids, K. (2005). Information processing and constraints-based views of skill acquisition: Divergent or complementary? *Motor Control, 9,* 217–241.

Astill, S., & Utley, A. (2006). Two-handed catch in children with developmental coordination disorder. *Motor Control, 10*(2), 109–124.

Bernstein, N. (1967). *The coordination and regulation of movements.* Oxford: Pergamon Press.

Biotteau, M., Chaix, Y., & Albaret, J. M. (2015). Procedural learning and automatization process in children with developmental coordination disorder and/or developmental dyslexia. *Human Movement Science, 43,* 78–89. doi:10. 1016/j.humov.2015.07.005

Biotteau, M., Chaix, Y., & Albaret, J. M. (2016). What do we really know about motor learning in children with developmental coordination disorder? *Current Developmental Disorders Reports, 3*(2), 152–160.

Bongaardt, R., & Meijer, O. G. (2000). Bernstein's theory of movement behavior: Historical development and contemporary relevance. *Journal of Motor Behavior, 32*(1), 57–71.

Cairney, J., Hay, J. A., Faught, B. E., Wade, T. J., Corna, L., & Flouris, A. (2005). Developmental coordination disorder, generalized self-efficacy toward physical activity, and participation in organized and free play activities. *Journal of Pediatrics, 147*(4), 515–520.

Cairney, J., Hay, J. A., Veldhuizen, S., Missiuna, C., & Faught, B. E. (2010). Developmental coordination disorder, sex, and activity deficit over time: A longitudinal analysis o fparticipation trajectories in children with and without coordination difficulties. *Developmental Medicine and Child Neurology, 52*(3), e67–e72. doi:10.1111/j.1469-8749.2009.03520.x

Candler, C., & Meeuwsen, H. (2002). Implicit learning in children with and without developmental coordination disorder. *American Journal of Occupational Therapy, 56,* 429–435.

Cantin, N., Polatajko, H. J., Thach, W. T., & Jaglal, S. (2007). Developmental coordination disorder: Exploration of a cerebellar hypothesis. *Human Movement Science, 26*(3), 491–509.

Davids, K., Button, C., & Bennett, S. (Eds.). (2008). *Dynamics of skill acquisition: A constraints-led approach.* Champaign, IL: Human Kinetics.

Elders, V., Sheehan, S., Wilson, A. D., Levesley, M., Bhakta, B., & Mon-Williams, M. (2010). Head – torso – hand coordination in children with and without developmental coordination disorder. *Developmental Medicine and Child Neurology, 52,* 238–243.

Farhat, R., Hsairi, I., Baati, H., Smits-Engelsman, B. C. M., Masmoudi, K., Mchirgui, R., . . . Moalla, W. (2013). The effect of a motor skills training program in the improvement of practiced and non-practiced tasks performance in children with Developmental Coordination Disorder (DCD). *Human Movement Science, 46,* 10–22.

Ferguson, G. D., Jelsma, D., Jelsma, J., & Smits-Engelsman, B. C. (2013). The efficacy of two task-orientated interventions for children with developmental coordination disorder: Neuromotor task training and Nintendo Wii Fit training. *Research in Developmental Disabilities, 34,* 2449–2461.

Gheysen, F., van Waelvelde, H., & Fias, W. (2011). Imparied visual-motor sequence learning in developmental coordination disorder. *Research in Developmental Disabilities, 32,* 749–756.

Green, D., Lingam, R., Mattocks, C., Riddoch, C., Ness, A., & Emond, A. (2011). The risk of reduced physical activity in children with probable developmental coordination disorder: A prospective longitudinal study. *Research in Developmental Disabilities, 32*(4), 1332–1342.

Guadagnoli, M. A., & Lee, T. D. (2004). Challenge point: A framework for conceptualizing the effects of various practice conditions in motor learning. *Journal of Motor Behavior, 36*(2), 212–224.

Hammond, J., Jones, V., Hill, E. L., Green, D., & Male, I. (2014). An investigation of the impact of regular use of the Wii Fit to improve motor and psychosocial outcomes in children with movement difficulties: A pilot study. *Child Care Health Development, 40*(2), 165–175.

Howie, E. K., Campbell, A. C., Abbott, R. A., & Straker, L. M. (2017). Understanding why an active video game intervention didnot improve motor skill and physical activity in children withdevelopmental coordination disorder: A quantity or quality issue? *Research in Developmental Disabilities, 60,* 1–12.

Jelsma, D., Ferguson, G. D., Smits-Engelsman, B., & Geuze, R. (2015). Short-term motor learning of dynamic balance control in children with probably developmental coordination disorder. *Research in Developmental Disabilities, 38,* 213–222.

Jelsma, D., Geuze, R. H., Mombarg, R., & Smits-Engelsman, B. (2014). The impact of Wii Fit intervention of dynamic balance control in children with probable developmental coordination disorder and balance problems. *Human Movement Science, 33,* 404–418.

Jongmans, M. J., Linthorst-Bakker, E., Westenberg, Y., & Smits-Engelsman, B. C. (2003). Use of a task-oriented self-instruction method to support children in primary school with poor handwriting quality and speed. *Human Movement Science, 22,* 549–566.

Kagerer, F. A., Bo, J., Contreras-Vidal, J. L., & Clark, J. E. (2004). Visuomotor adaptation in children with developmental coordination disorder. *Motor Control, 8*(4), 450–460.

Kagerer, F. A., Contreras-Vidal, J. L., & Clark, J. E. (2006). Abrupt, but not gradual visuomotor distortion facilitates adaptation in children with developmental coordination disorder. *Human Movement Science, 25*(4–5), 622–633.

Lejeune, C., Catale, C., Willems, S., & Meulemans, T. (2013). Intact procedural motor sequence learning in developmental coordination disorder. *Research in Developmental Disabilities, 34*(6), 1974–1981. doi:10.1016/j.ridd.2013.03.017

Lejeune, C., Wansard, M., Geurten, M., & Meulemans, T. (2016). Procedural learning, consolidation, and transfer of a new skill in developmental coordination disorder. *Child Neuropsychology, 22*(2), 143–154. doi:10.1080/09297049.2014.988608

Mackenzie, S. J., Getchell, N., Deutsch, K., Wilms-Floet, A., Clark, J. E., & Whitall, J. (2008). Multi-limb coordination and rhythmic variability under varying sensory availability conditions in children with DCD. *Human Movement Science, 27,* 256–269.

Magallón, S., Crespo-Eguílaz, N., & Narbona, J. (2015). Procedural learning in children with developmental coordination, reading, and attention disorders. *Journal of Child Neurology, 30*(11), 1496–1506. doi:10.1177/0883073815572227

Marchiori, G. E., Wall, A. E., & Bedingfield, E. W. (1987). Kinematic analysis of skill acquisition in physically awkward boys. *Adapted Physical Activity Quarterly, 4,* 305–315.

Miles, C. A. L., Wood, G., Vine, S. J., Vickers, J. N., & Wilson, M. R. (2015). Quiet eye training facilitates visuomotor coordination in children with developmental coordination disorder. *Research in Developmental Disabilities, 40,* 31–41.

Missiuna, C. (1994). Motor skill acquisition in children with developmental coordination disorder. *Adapted Physical Quarterly, 11*(2), 214–235.

Newell, K. M. (1986). Constraints on the development of coordination. In M. G. Wade & H. T. A. Whiting (Eds.), *Motor development in children: Aspects of coordination and control* (pp. 341–361). Amsterdam: Martinus Nijhoff Publishers.

Nissen, M. J., & Bullemer, P. (1987). Attentional requirements of learning: Evidence from performance measures. *Cognitive Psychology, 19*, 1–32.

Polatajko, H. J., & Cantin, N. (2007). Review of interventions for children with developmental coordination disorder: The approaches and the evidence. In R. H. Geuze (Ed.), *Developmental coordination disorder: A review of current approaches* (pp. 139–181). Marseille: Solal.

Roche, R., Wilms-Floet, A., Clark, J. E., & Whitall, J. (2011). Auditory and visual information do not affect self-paced bilateral finger tapping in children with DCD. *Human Movement Science, 30*, 658–671.

Schoemaker, M., & Smits-Engelsman, B. (2015). Is treating motor problems in DCD just a matter of practice ad more practice? *Current Developmental Disorders Reports, 2*, 150–156.

Shaw, R., & Alley, T. (1985). How to draw learning curves: Their use and justification. In T. Johnston & A. Pietrewicz (Eds.), *Issues in the ecological study of learning* (pp. 275–304). Hillsdale, NJ: Lawrence Erlbaum Associates.

Smits-Engelsman, B. C. M., Jelsma, L. D., Ferguson, G. D., & Geuze, R. H. (2015). Motor learning: An analysis of 100 trials of a Ski Slalom game in children with and without developmental coordination disorder. *PLoS One, 10*(10), e0140470. doi:10.1371/journal.pone.0140470

Smits-Engelsman, B. C. M., Westenberg, Y., & Duysens, J. (2008). Children with developmental coordination disorder are equally able to generate force but show more variability than typically developing children. *Human Movement Science, 27*, 296–309.

Snapp-Childs, W., Mon-Williams, M., & Bingham, G. P. (2013). A sensorimotor approach to the training of manual actions in children with developmental coordination disorder. *Journal of Child Neurology, 28*(2), 204–212.

Snapp-Childs, W., Shire, K., Hill, L., Mon-Williams, M., & Bingham, G. P. (2016). Training compliance control yields improved drawing in 5–11 year old children with motor difficulties. *Human Movement Science, 48*, 171–183.

Straker, L., Howie, E., Smith, A., Jensen, L., Piek, J., & Campbell, A. (2015). A crossover randomised and controlled trial of the impact of active video games on motor coordination and perceptions of physical ability in children at risk of developmental coordination disorder. *Human Movement Science, 42*, 146–160.

Sugden, D., & Wade, M. G. (2013). *Typical and atypical motor development.* Hoboken, NJ: Wiley.

Volman, M. J. M., & Geuze, R. H. (1998). Stability of rhythmic finger movements in children with a developmental coordination disorder. *Motor Control, 2*, 34–60.

Wade, M. G., & Kazeck, M. (2018). Developmental coordination disorder and its cause: The road less travelled. *Human Movement Science, 57*, 489–500. http://dx.doi.org/10.1016/j.humov.2016.08.004

Whitall, J., Chang, T., Horn, C., Jung-Potter, J., McMenamin, S., Wilms-Floet, A., & Clark, J. E. (2008). Auditory-motor coupling of bilateral finger tapping in children with and without DCD compared to adults. *Human Movement Science, 27*, 914–931.

Whitall, J., Getchell, N., McMenamin, S., Horn, C., Wilms-Floet, A., & Clark, J. E. (2006). Perception-action coupling in children with and without DCD: Frequency locking between task-relevant auditory signals and motor responses in a dual-motor task. *Child Care, Health and Development, 32*, 679–692.

Wilmut, K., Du, W., & Barnett, A. L. (2015). How do I fit through that gap? Navigation through apertures in adults with developmental coordination disorder. *PLoS One, 10*(4), e124695. doi:10.1371/journal.pone.0124695

Wilmut, K., Du, W., & Barnett, A. L. (2017). Navigating through apertures: Perceptual judgements and actions of children with developmental coordination disorder. *Developmental Science, 20*, e12462. doi:10.1111/desc.12462

Wilson, P. H., Dewey, D., Smits-Engelsman, B., & Steenbergen, B. (2017). Hybrid is not a dirty word: Commentary on Wade and Kazeck. *Human Movement Science, 57*, 510–515.

Wilson, P. H., Green, D., Caeyenberghs, K., Steenbergen, B., & Duckworth, J. (2016). Integrating new technologies into the treatment of CP and DCD. *Current Developmental Disorders Reports, 3*, 138–151.

Wilson, P. H., Maruff, P., & Lum, J. (2003). Procedural learning in children with developmental coordination disorder. *Human Movement Science, 22*, 515–526.

Zwicker, J. G., Missiuna, C., Harris, S. R., & Boyd, L. A. (2011). Brain activation associated with motor skill practice in children with developmental coordination disorder: An fMRI study. *International Journal of Developmental Neuroscience, 29*(2), 145–152.

SECTION II
Biological aspects of development

5

GENETIC CONTRIBUTIONS TO NEURODEVELOPMENTAL DISORDERS

Dianne F. Newbury

The Human Genome Project

The human genome consists of a string of 3 billion chemical letters (nucleotide bases) stuck onto a sugar-phosphate backbone. This string is found inside almost every cell in your body and contains all the instructions you will ever need to grow from a single cell to a fully functioning human. These instructions are contained within genes which encode proteins. Each cell inside you carries the same complement of genes but individual genes can be switched on and off, turned up and down to allow the cell to respond to environmental cues in a very dynamic way.

In 2001, the first sequence of the human genome was published (McPherson et al., 2001; Venter et al., 2001). This project involved hundreds of scientists across the world and generated a human reference sequence that indicated the order of 3-billion bases of DNA, from the start of chromosome 1 through to the end of the Y chromosome (Lander et al., 2001). This information was made publically available and catalysed a rapid period of discovery in the world of genetics.

The human genome is smaller than we thought . . . but more complex

Within any genome, the start and end of protein-coding units (genes) are marked by characteristic sequence motifs. The Human Genome Project therefore enabled the positioning of all human genes. Twenty to twenty-five thousand genes were found; a much lower number than expected; just double the number found in flies and worms (International Human Genome Sequencing Consortium, 2004). The distribution of genes varies across chromosomes but the position of any given gene is fixed between individuals. For example, the first gene seen on chromosome 1 is always found at the 11874th base-pair (relative to the human reference sequence)

(UCSC, 2016). Genes do not occur as single blocks in the DNA. Instead they are split into modules of coding sequences (exons), that are separated by non-coding spacer sequences (introns). The entire gene unit (exons and introns) is copied during the protein-making process. This primary transcript is then processed to allow the mix and match of different exon modules in the final protein. This enables a single gene to encode multiple different protein forms (isoforms) with subtly different jobs in different tissue and cell types (Lander et al., 2001). The use of introns is not human specific; they are found in most species. However, it is believed that humans exploit modular processing to a greater degree than other species. This allows a high level of flexibility and the ability to produce numerous proteins while maintaining a modest genome size.

Another surprise finding from the Human Genome Project was the fact that the exonic coding modules make up only 1–2% of the genome. Intronic sequences make up an additional 25%. The remainder is accounted for by "gene deserts" which contain regulatory sequences, repeat elements and encode functional molecules that do not take a protein form (Lander et al., 2001).

Sequencing across populations has built a picture of human variation

The sequencing of the first human genome took over ten years and cost billions of pounds but today, we can sequence a genome for under £2000 in a day or two. Such shifts have allowed the sequencing of over half a million human genomes and exomes (i.e. all exon sequences) to date. These include samples from around the world from healthy controls and individuals affected by disease (Lek et al., 2016). Arguably, these have provided a greater advancement in understanding than the first human genome. The average human genome contains considerable variation, at the sequence level and in terms of structure and chemical modification of the DNA molecule (Figure 5.1).

When a given genome is compared against the reference human sequence, it varies at about 4 million positions (International Human Genome Sequencing Consortium, 2004). Although this is large in absolute numbers, consider that it represents only 0.01% of the genome. The majority of these differences involve only a single base of sequence (termed a single nucleotide polymorphism – SNP, Figure 5.1.iii) but the typical human genome also contains around 2000 structural variants (deletions and duplications – Figure 5.1.ii) (Sudmant et al., 2015). The majority of catalogued variation is rare; of the 84 million SNPs documented across the human genome, 76% have a population frequency of less than 0.05% (1000 Genomes Project et al., 2015). However, at the individual level, the majority of variation (>99%) is made up of common SNPs (1000 Genomes Project et al., 2015). The typical genome contains 150 sequence changes that result in truncated proteins (Figure 5.1.iv.b) and 10,000 changes that alter protein sequences (Figure 5.1.iv.c). Each genome carries around 2,000 variants that have been associated with common disease and 25 mutations that have been reported to be causative of rare disease

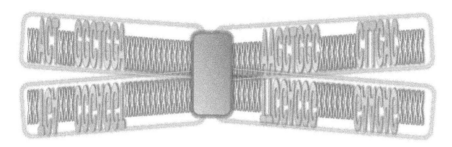

FIGURE 5.1 Types of genetic variation

(i)   Humans have 23 pairs of chromosomes. Each chromosome consists of gene units, represented here by capital letters (Note that, for simplicity, exons and introns are not depicted in this figure). Each gene unit carries the code for a given protein.

Genes are spread unevenly across chromosomes and are interspersed with regulatory and non-coding DNA, represented here by Xs.

(ii.a) Sometimes, small segments of chromosomes become deleted and duplicated. These may include genes (shown as numbered boxes. Note that exons and introns are not depicted here) and/or intervening non-coding sequences (shown as Xs). Deletions and duplications are known as structural rearrangements or copy number variants (CNVs).

(ii.b) When a region is deleted, genetic sequence is removed. This can result in a reduced copy number of a given gene (in this case, gene 2) and changes the absolute position of the surrounding genes and the overall length of the chromosome

(ii.c) When a region is duplicated, genetic sequence is repeated. This can result in an increased copy number of a given gene (in this case, gene 2) and changes the absolute position of the surrounding genes and the overall length of the chromosome

(iii.a) The genetic sequence can also vary at the single base level. This is known as a Single Nucleotide Polymorphism (SNP).

(iii.b) Some changes occur outside of gene regions (in this case, the black C base, which was a G in the original sequence in (iii.a)). These alter the genetic sequence but do not affect the protein code and are known as non-coding variants.

(iii.c) Some changes occur inside gene regions (in this case, the black T base, which was a G in the original sequence in (iii.a)). These alter the genetic sequence and may also affect the protein code and are known as coding variants.

(iv.a) Coding variants can alter protein sequences and structures. The exact effect of a coding variant will depend on its location in the gene and its effect upon the resultant protein (depicted here as a black line under the gene)

(iv.b) Some variants create signals which stop protein production (in this case, the dark grey T base, which was a G in the original sequence in (iv.a)) leading to truncated proteins.

(iv.c) Some variants alter just a small part of the protein code (in this case, the dark grey T base, which was a C in the original sequence in (iv.a)). These are known as non-synonymous variants.

(iv.d) Some variants occur with gene regions but do not alter the protein code (in this case, the dark grey A base, which was a C in the original sequence in (iv.a)). These are known as synonymous variants.

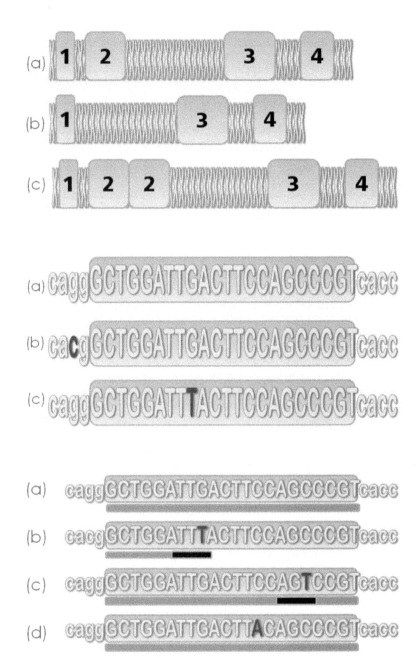

FIGURE 5.1 (Continued)

(1000 Genomes Project et al., 2015). To distinguish between different types of variation, the term "mutation" is now only applied to changes in the sequence that have been definitively demonstrated to cause, or contribute to, disease. In contrast, the term "variant" refers to changes that alter the sequence but have not been unequivocally linked to disease. Most common variants are shared across populations but rare variants and mutations tend to be restricted to specific sub-populations reflecting the genetic history of those people (1000 Genomes Project et al., 2015).

Gene mapping

These numbers illustrate the complexity of gene identification in relation to disease; every genome represents a huge dataset with an extremely high level of variation both within and between individuals and in terms of sequence and structure. The traditional means of identifying links between genes and disorders (gene mapping) is to compare variations within families. If we compare the sequences of a pair of siblings, both of whom are affected by a given disorder, we would expect to find 2.5 million shared variants between them, any of which might underlie the disorder. Under a particularly optimistic, fully informative scenario, the number of shared variants would halve with each additional sibling investigated. In order to reduce our dataset from the entire genome to 1 or 2 candidate variants, we would need to sequence 33 siblings from the same family. Add to this the fact that mutations are often found in the genomes of healthy individuals, then the magnitude of the challenge becomes clear. For a disorder like Developmental Coordination Disorder (DCD), where do we start gene mapping? The following sections describe approaches to mapping in neurodevelopmental disorders. Each technique targets a particular type of variant and disease model. It is therefore important to consider what kind of genetic changes might underlie your disorder before you start looking for them. In this chapter, we use a broad base of neurodevelopmental disorders to illustrate different concepts. The next chapter goes on to discuss genetic influences and neural mechanisms that are particularly relevant to DCD.

Mendelian traits and gene dosage

Observations of the way that traits and disorders are inherited can provide evidence of a Mendelian mechanism; when changes in a single gene account for the majority of genetic liability. If a single mutation is necessary and sufficient to cause disease (Mendelian dominant trait) then if a child is affected, one of their parents and 50% of their immediate family members will also be affected. If both copies of the gene need to be non-functional for disease to develop (Mendelian recessive trait), then the disease can skip generations as parents can carry only a single mutation. These mutation events can then combine in the child to cause disease. If an affected individual has children then they only pass on a single mutated copy of the gene and their children are unlikely to be affected (unless their partner also carries a mutation).

Such clear inheritance patterns are rarely seen in conditions like DCD but are sometimes observed in rare and distinct forms of neurodevelopmental disorder. For example, in the 1990s, scientists described a family in which three generations were affected by severe developmental verbal dyspraxia (difficulty with speech but not with other aspects of motor control and coordination) inherited in a Mendelian dominant fashion (Hurst, Baraitser, Auger, Graham, & Norell, 1990). In such cases, gene mapping typically involves a search for variants that are shared by affected family members but not unaffected individuals. Luckily, the reported family was extensive and this approach led to the identification of a mutation in a gene known as *FOXP2* (short for Forkhead-box-protein-P2) (Fisher, Vargha-Khadem, Watkins, Monaco, & Pembrey, 1998; Lai et al., 2000; Lai, Fisher, Hurst, Vargha-Khadem, & Monaco, 2001). The mutation only led to a small change in the protein coded by this gene (a non-synonymous mutation, as in Figure 5.1.iv.c) but this small change occurred in a critical region (Lai et al., 2001). The change obliterated the DNA-binding functionality of the protein. Subsequent studies have identified additional individuals with *FOXP2* mutations, all of whom present with a disorder of motor control that restricts their speech production (Estruch, Graham, Chinnappa, Deriziotis, & Fisher, 2016; Morgan et al., 2015).

FOXP2 is an example of a "dosage sensitive gene". The amount of FOXP2 protein is strictly regulated during development and genetic changes that alter its level appear to be particularly problematic. In mice, a complete lack of Foxp2 protein leads to motor impairment and premature death. Disruption of a single copy of the gene (as described in humans) results in developmental delay but is not lethal (Fujita et al., 2008; Shu et al., 2005). Thus FOXP2 is critical for survival and reduced levels lead to disorder. Does this mean that all changes in *FOXP2* will result in verbal dyspraxia? DNA databases show that changes in *FOXP2* occur less often than expected (Exome Aggregation Consortium, 2016) indicating that the gene sequence is highly constrained.

It is estimated that only 10% of genes are sensitive to loss of function (Lek et al., 2016). These tend to encode proteins that function in essential cell processes and usually cause severe disease when mutated (Lek et al., 2016). It is therefore interesting to note that many of these genes have not been assigned to a disorder. If changes in the protein levels encoded by these genes are not lethal, then they represent excellent candidate genes for human disease.

Not all sequence changes are equal

Even in highly constrained genes, we do observe changes to the coding sequence within healthy individuals demonstrating that all changes are not equal. While some drastically alter protein function, others may have a minimal effect. Ten years ago, the standard experimental procedure upon discovering a candidate sequence change was to sequence the base in 100 population controls. If we did not see the variant in these controls, we would infer that it was a causative mutation. We are now able to recognise that such changes may actually represent rare variation.

While population frequency can act as a good indicator of variant effect; rare variants are either very new in the population or are highly constrained indicating that they have a disruptive effect upon protein function, additional functional information is always needed to infer causality, is now widely accepted, especially if the change was only observed in a single case.

The same gene can contribute to distinct disorders

It is possible for the same gene to underlie several clinical classifications (Zhu, Need, Petrovski, & Goldstein, 2014). For example, mutations and variations in the *DCDC2* gene have been linked to dyslexia (Meng et al., 2005; Schumacher et al., 2006), the liver disease neonatal sclerosing cholangitis (Girard et al., 2016; Grammatikopoulos et al., 2016) and deafness (Grati et al., 2015). Although they appear clinically disparate, it is hypothesised that these disorders are functionally linked at the cellular level. DCDC2 functions in cilia maintenance and is argued that this basic cellular function may play a role in multiple diseases. Interestingly, the clinical patients with neonatal sclerosing cholangitis all carry mutations that completely knock out *DCDC2* function (Girard et al., 2016; Grammatikopoulos et al., 2016) while the changes associated with deafness alter recognised protein motifs but do not completely obliterate function (Grati et al., 2015). Variants associated with dyslexia occur in less important protein motifs or in non-coding regions. These presumably conserve protein function, but affect its efficacy (Meng et al., 2011). Reports of single genes being linked to variable outcomes are becoming more common but it is unusual to observe such clear relationships between mutation type and consequence. For example, disruptions of the *CNTNAP2* gene, which encodes a neuronal protein regulated by FOXP2, have been associated with a wide range of neurodevelopmental disorders including Tourettes syndrome, epilepsy, autism, intellectual disability, speech and language disorders, dyslexia and schizophrenia (Rodenas-Cuadrado, Ho, & Vernes, 2014). It has been suggested that the complete loss of CNTNAP2 function may be related to profound effects on cognitive function, while other changes may instead lead to less severe disorders (Rodenas-Cuadrado et al., 2014). Because the CNTNAP2 protein interacts with many different neuronal partners, the exact manifestation of a given change will depend upon many inter-related factors. The accurate prediction of outcome therefore requires the consideration of variation across the entire genome and in combination with environmental factors, rather than a single mutation or change in isolation.

Missing heritability

Beyond genetic variation gene-gene interactions and changes outside of the DNA may represent important mechanisms underlying disease. These influences provide alternative explanations for so called "missing heritability"; the idea that changes at single bases only account for a proportion of genetic contributions to a given trait (Manolio et al., 2009). A single change may have a moderate effect upon the end point of a genetic pathway. When combined with a "second-hit", in the same pathway, the effect at the end-point may be amplified (Girirajan et al., 2010). For example, individuals who carry a deletion in a particular region of chromosome 16, show considerable disparity in terms of outcomes. While some are affected by intellectual disability and/or autism, other have apparently typical development. It has been suggested that the risk associated with this deletion is increased when individuals carry a second large deletion or duplication elsewhere in their genome (Girirajan et al., 2010). The two-hit model has also been applied to variants at single bases; O'Roak described an individual affected by autism who carried a truncating mutation in the *FOXP1* gene, which encodes a binding partner of FOXP2, and a non-synonymous change in *CNTNAP2* (O'Roak et al., 2011). Since both these proteins have known interactions with FOXP2, these authors hypothesised that this case epitomised the two-hit model. Of course, the "two"-hit model does not have to stop at bipartite interactions. It is likely that any single genetic change will affect multiple interacting proteins, which themselves are subject to mutations and variations. These interactions may additionally be influenced by non-genetic factors such as environmental stressors and chemical modifications of DNA (epigenetic changes). A single variant only represents a small part of the risk matrix even when its effect size is relatively large.

Common disease, common variant

This newfound knowledge regarding the diverse effects of genetic variation upon disease has caused many researchers to revisit the way in which genetic disorders are modelled. Prior to the Human Genome Project, it was largely thought that most genetic diseases could be modelled as Mendelian traits in which high impact changes in one (dominant) or two (recessive) copies of a given gene were necessary and sufficient to cause disease. These diseases tend to be rare in populations as the mutations that cause them are subject to negative selective pressure. In contrast, common disorders, were considered to be the extreme of normal distributions (e.g. hypertension, language impairment) and were modelled to involve interactions between 3 and 10 common genetic variants and environmental factors. In these genetically complex disorders, the variants themselves do not cause disease but instead act as risk factors that increase the chances of impairment. Independently, each variant has only a small effect upon disorder risk and so is less constrained and relatively common in a given population; the common disease, common variant hypothesis (Lander, 1996; Reich & Lander, 2001).

Genome Wide Association studies (GWAs)

If common variants underlie common disorders then there is no need to sequence every single base within a genome to map the genes underlying them. Instead we can sample sites of known common genetic variation. The Genome Wide Association study (GWAs) approach uses "arrays" to interrogate sites of known common variation. The "array" is a solid surface onto which millions of probes are fixed. Each probe is a short fragment of artificially produced DNA that corresponds to a known SNP. Each SNP is represented by many copies of a given probe. The DNA of an individual is fragmented and attached to the probes. Fluorescent methods capture whether the DNA of the individual carries a given variant (Ragoussis, 2009). Array technologies allow us to characterise (or genotype) a million sites of common variation in a single experiment. Because genetic variants that occur in close proximity tend to be related in terms of their sequence, the interrogation of a million variants allows us to capture the majority of common variation within a given genome.

By genotyping common variants in unrelated cases, who are affected by the disorder of interest, and controls, who are unaffected, we can identify variants that occur more commonly in cases than controls (genetic association). These variants are assumed to either directly contribute to the disorder or represent proxies for the contributory variants. It is important to note that arrays only genotype pre-specified sites of variation and do not sequence every base. Thus, a GWAs cannot discover rare or new variants within a genome. GWAs have been performed for many neurodevelopmental disorders, although not yet for DCD. A number of GWAs have been published for attention deficit hyperactivity disorder (ADHD) and attention-related traits (reviewed by (Hawi et al., 2015). Across these studies, only one gene (a regulator of axon growth known as *CDH13*) has repeatedly shown significance (Lasky-Su et al., 2008; Neale et al., 2010). This lack of replication is typical of GWAs and, especially in neurodevelopmental disorders, is likely to reflect small sample sizes (Munafo, 2010). Because a GWAs involves so many test-points, the p-value required to declare significant association is very small (5×10^{-8}). In general, GWAs indicate that hundreds or thousands of genetic variants contribute to any given complex genetic disorder (Schizophrenia Working Group of the Psychiatric Genomics, 2014). The effect size of each variant will therefore be very low and extremely large sample sizes will be needed to identify them. These trends generalise across disorders; early GWAs of schizophrenia proved unfruitful but more recent investigations that included more than 30,000 cases identified 105 associated SNPs (Schizophrenia Working Group of the Psychiatric Genomics, 2014). Sites of association were enriched among brain-expressed genes and particularly those genes that function in neurotransmission (Schizophrenia Working Group of the Psychiatric Genomics, 2014). Interestingly, the top ADHD GWAs hits highlight similar pathways (synaptic transmission, neuronal signalling and cell migration)(Alemany et al., 2015; Cristino et al., 2014), supporting the idea that the same gene may contribute to clinically distinct disorders (as discussed earlier).

Common disease, rare variant

The findings of GWAs and the shift in genetic technologies have driven researchers to propose the "common disease, rare variant" hypothesis in which rare variants may also contribute to the risk of common disease (Schork, Murray, Frazer, & Topol, 2009). This hypothesis offers an alternative explanation for missing heritability since rare variants will not be detected by GWAs studies. Rare variant models fall intermediate to Mendelian and common variant hypotheses; the rare variants are not suggested to be necessary or sufficient to cause disorder but will carry an increased risk over common variants. Accordingly, sequencing studies demonstrate that disorders such as autism are associated with an increased burden of rare variants across the genome (Iossifov et al., 2014). The common disease, rare variant hypothesis has driven a new conceptual model in gene mapping – the *de novo* paradigm (Vissers et al., 2010). This method targets a particular subset of rare variants – changes that have occurred within the last generation (*de novo* changes) (Vissers et al., 2010). An average newborn accumulates 50–100 *de novo* changes that were not inherited. Because genes make up 1% of the genome, only one or two of these *de novo* variants will affect gene coding sequences. These *de novo* coding variants therefore offer a manageable subset on which to focus gene mapping efforts. Since *de novo* mutations are not inherited, they escape selective pressure and this may explain why devastating disorders, such as autism and schizophrenia, persist, if the number of candidate genes is high enough. *De novo* mutations in autism have been found to cluster within genes that encode synaptic proteins indicating that similar pathways modulate risk at the level of common and rare variation (De Rubeis et al., 2014).

Copy Number Variants (CNVs)

Another kind of variation that is often overlooked by GWAs is the deletion and duplication of genetic material (Copy Number Variants, CNVs). It has long been appreciated that the large-scale rearrangement of genetic material can lead to neurodevelopmental disorder (e.g. Williams–Beuren Syndrome is caused by the deletion of ~1.5 million base pairs on chromosome 7) (Morris, 1993). However, healthy individuals also carry deletions and duplications of their genetic material and these form part of normal variation. Structural variants are less common than sequence variants but perhaps have a higher likelihood of causing problems because they each affect many bases of DNA. An increased burden of large copy number variants is associated with intellectual disability, schizophrenia and autism (Girirajan et al., 2011; Schizophrenia Working Groups of the Psychiatric Genomics & Psychosis Endophenotypes International, 2016). In particular, regions on chromosomes 1, 3, 15, 16 and 22 have been identified as hotspots for structural variants that contribute to an increased risk of neurodevelopmental disorder (Torres, Barbosa, & Maciel, 2016). In contrast, the frequency of large CNVs in individuals with dyslexia and developmental language disorder has been reported to be comparable to population controls (Gialluisi et al., 2016; Girirajan et al., 2011; Simpson et al., 2015) leading some to suggest that there may be a correlation between CNV burden and the severity of disorder. There is some evidence that smaller, inherited CNVs may contribute to the risk of developmental language disorder (Simpson et al., 2015) suggesting that combinations of CNVs within pathways may contribute to disorder risk in much the same way as sequence variants. In schizophrenia and autism, CNV burden is enriched for genes associated with synaptic function, again reinforcing the importance of pathways implicated by studies of sequence variants (Pinto et al., 2010; Schizophrenia Working Groups of the Psychiatric Genomics & Psychosis Endophenotypes International, 2016).

The "perfect storm"

It is likely that each of these mechanisms play a role in neurodevelopmental disorders. Complex combinations of distinct variables, both genetic and environmental, across multiple pathways may come together to modulate the overall risk of disorder. These risk variables are likely to overlap between disorders and the exact outcome of an individual will depend on the combination of variables they are exposed to (Zhu et al., 2014). This model has been called the "perfect storm" (Virgin & Todd, 2011). The idea of a perfect storm emphasises the complexity and sometimes random nature of the contributions to neurodevelopmental disorder. However, it also has important implications for the validity of gene mapping approaches. If you expect common variation to account for the majority of disorder risk, then a GWAs approach will be optimal and extremely large samples will be necessary. If rare variants are thought to be important, then sequencing technologies are more applicable and large family studies may offer more power. Genome sequencing will capture both rare and common variants as well as CNVs. This approach therefore represents the gold standard but it remains comparatively expensive (~£2000 per genome, £1-million will allow 500 genomes) when compared to arrays (~£75 per array, £1-million will allow 13333 arrays) or exome sequencing (~£500 per genome, £1-million will allow 2000 exomes). In addition, genome sequencing generates large amounts of data that require secure storage (~90GB of computer space per genome). The analysis of these data is computationally and intellectually demanding and in practise, we often disregard information for sequences outside of genes. Lastly, we must remember that there are many effects that even genome sequencing does not capture, for example, epigenetic effects.

All these factors should be considered when contemplating the application of genetic studies to DCD. A baseline understanding of the comorbidities and biological and environmental influences in DCD (as outlined in the next chapter) will allow a directed approach to the genetic study of this disorder, maximising the likelihood of successful gene mapping.

References

1000 Genomes Project, Consortium, Auton, A., Brooks, L. D., Durbin, R. M., Garrison, E. P., Kang, H. M., . . . Abecasis, G. R. (2015). A global reference for human genetic variation. *Nature, 526*(7571), 68–74. doi:10.1038/nature15393

Alemany, S., Ribases, M., Vilor-Tejedor, N., Bustamante, M., Sanchez-Mora, C., Bosch, R., . . . Sunyer, J. (2015). New suggestive genetic loci and biological pathways for attention function in adult attention-deficit/hyperactivity disorder. *American Journal of Medical Genetics Part B: Neuropsychiatric Genetics.* doi:10.1002/ajmg.b.32341

Cristino, A. S., Williams, S. M., Hawi, Z., An, J. Y., Bellgrove, M. A., Schwartz, C. E., . . . Claudianos, C. (2014). Neurodevelopmental and neuropsychiatric disorders represent an interconnected molecular system. *Molecular Psychiatry, 19*(3), 294–301. doi:10.1038/mp.2013.16

De Rubeis, S., He, X., Goldberg, A. P., Poultney, C. S., Samocha, K., Cicek, A. E., . . . Buxbaum, J. D. (2014). Synaptic, transcriptional and chromatin genes disrupted in autism. *Nature, 515*(7526), 209–215. doi:10.1038/nature13772

Estruch, S. B., Graham, S. A., Chinnappa, S. M., Deriziotis, P., & Fisher, S. E. (2016). Functional characterization of rare FOXP2 variants in neurodevelopmental disorder. *Journal of Neurodevelopmental Disorders, 8*, 44. doi:10.1186/s11689-016-9177-2

Exome Aggregation Consortium, The. (2016). *ExAC*. Retrieved December 12, 2016, from http://exac.broadinstitute.org/

Fisher, S. E., Vargha-Khadem, F., Watkins, K. E., Monaco, A. P., & Pembrey, M. E. (1998). Localisation of a gene implicated in a severe speech and language disorder. *Nature Genetics, 18*(2), 168–170. doi:10.1038/ng0298-168

Fujita, E., Tanabe, Y., Shiota, A., Ueda, M., Suwa, K., Momoi, M. Y., & Momoi, T. (2008). Ultrasonic vocalization impairment of Foxp2 (R552H) knockin mice related to speech-language disorder and abnormality of Purkinje cells. *Proceedings of the National Academy of Sciences of the United States of America, 105*(8), 3117–3122. doi:10.1073/pnas.0712298105

Gialluisi, A., Visconti, A., Willcutt, E. G., Smith, S. D., Pennington, B. F., Falchi, M., . . . Fisher, S. E. (2016). Investigating the effects of copy number variants on reading and language performance. *Journal of Neurodevelopmental Disorders, 8*, 17. doi:10.1186/s11689-016-9147-8

Girard, M., Bizet, A. A., Lachaux, A., Gonzales, E., Filhol, E., Collardeau-Frachon, S., . . . Saunier, S. (2016). DCDC2 mutations cause neonatal sclerosing cholangitis. *Human Mutation, 37*(10), 1025–1029. doi:10.1002/humu.23031

Girirajan, S., Brkanac, Z., Coe, B. P., Baker, C., Vives, L., Vu, T. H., . . . Eichler, E. E. (2011). Relative burden of large CNVs on a range of neurodevelopmental phenotypes. *PLoS Genetics, 7*(11), e1002334. doi:10.1371/journal.pgen.1002334

Girirajan, S., Rosenfeld, J. A., Cooper, G. M., Antonacci, F., Siswara, P., Itsara, A., . . . Eichler, E. E. (2010). A recurrent 16p12.1 microdeletion supports a two-hit model for severe developmental delay. *Nature Genetics, 42*(3), 203–209. doi:10.1038/ng.534

Grammatikopoulos, T., Sambrotta, M., Strautnieks, S., Foskett, P., Knisely, A. S., Wagner, B., . . . Thompson, R. J. (2016). Mutations in DCDC2 (doublecortin domain containing protein 2) in neonatal sclerosing cholangitis. *Journal of Hepatology, 65*(6), 1179–1187. doi:10.1016/j.jhep.2016.07.017

Grati, M., Chakchouk, I., Ma, Q., Bensaid, M., Desmidt, A., Turki, N., . . . Masmoudi, S. (2015). A missense mutation in DCDC2 causes human recessive deafness DFNB66, likely by interfering with sensory hair cell and supporting cell cilia length regulation. *Human Molecular Genetics, 24*(9), 2482–2491. doi:10.1093/hmg/ddv009

Hawi, Z., Cummins, T. D., Tong, J., Johnson, B., Lau, R., Samarrai, W., & Bellgrove, M. A. (2015). The molecular genetic architecture of attention deficit hyperactivity disorder. *Molecular Psychiatry, 20*(3), 289–297. doi:10.1038/mp.2014.183

Hurst, J. A., Baraitser, M., Auger, E., Graham, F., & Norell, S. (1990). An extended family with a dominantly inherited speech disorder. *Developmental Medicine Child Neurology, 32*(4), 352–355.

International Human Genome Sequencing Consortium, The. (2004). Finishing the euchromatic sequence of the human genome. *Nature, 431*(7011), 931–945. doi:10.1038/nature03001

Iossifov, I., O'Roak, B. J., Sanders, S. J., Ronemus, M., Krumm, N., Levy, D., . . . Wigler, M. (2014). The contribution of de novo coding mutations to autism spectrum disorder. *Nature, 515*(7526), 216–221. doi:10.1038/nature13908

Lai, C. S., Fisher, S. E., Hurst, J. A., Levy, E. R., Hodgson, S., Fox, M., . . . Monaco, A. P. (2000). The SPCH1 region on human 7q31: Genomic characterization of the critical interval and localization of translocations associated with speech and language disorder. *American Journal of Human Genetics*, *67*(2), 357–368. doi:10.1086/303011

Lai, C. S., Fisher, S. E., Hurst, J. A., Vargha-Khadem, F., & Monaco, A. P. (2001). A forkhead-domain gene is mutated in a severe speech and language disorder. *Nature*, *413*(6855), 519–523. doi:10.1038/35097076

Lander, E. S. (1996). The new genomics: Global views of biology. *Science*, *274*(5287), 536–539.

Lander, E. S., Linton, L. M., Birren, B., Nusbaum, C., Zody, M. C., Baldwin, J., . . . Chen, Y. J. (2001). Initial sequencing and analysis of the human genome. *Nature*, *409*(6822), 860–921. doi:10.1038/35057062

Lasky-Su, J., Neale, B. M., Franke, B., Anney, R. J., Zhou, K., Maller, J. B., . . . Faraone, S. V. (2008). Genome-wide association scan of quantitative traits for attention deficit hyperactivity disorder identifies novel associations and confirms candidate gene associations. *American Journal of Medical Genetics Part B: Neuropsychiatric Genetics*, *147B*(8), 1345–1354. doi:10.1002/ajmg.b.30867

Lek, M., Karczewski, K. J., Minikel, E. V., Samocha, K. E., Banks, E., Fennell, T., . . . Exome Aggregation, Consortium. (2016). Analysis of protein-coding genetic variation in 60,706 humans. *Nature*, *536*(7616), 285–291. doi:10.1038/nature19057

McPherson, J. D., Marra, M., Hillier, L., Waterston, R. H., Chinwalla, A., Wallis, J., . . . International Human Genome Mapping, Consortium. (2001). A physical map of the human genome. *Nature*, *409*(6822), 934–941. doi:10.1038/35057157

Manolio, T. A., Collins, F. S., Cox, N. J., Goldstein, D. B., Hindorff, L. A., Hunter, D. J., . . . Visscher, P. M. (2009). Finding the missing heritability of complex diseases. *Nature*, *461*(7265), 747–753. doi:10.1038/nature08494

Meng, H., Powers, N. R., Tang, L., Cope, N. A., Zhang, P. X., Fuleihan, R., . . . Gruen, J. R. (2011). A dyslexia-associated variant in DCDC2 changes gene expression. *Behavior Genetics*, *41*(1), 58–66. doi:10.1007/s10519-010-9408-3

Meng, H., Smith, S. D., Hager, K., Held, M., Liu, J., Olson, R. K., . . . Gruen, J. R. (2005). DCDC2 is associated with reading disability and modulates neuronal development in the brain. *Proceedings of the National Academy of Sciences of the United States of America*, *102*(47), 17053–17058. doi:10.1073/pnas.0508591102

Morgan, A. T., Mei, C., Da Costa, A., Fifer, J., Lederer, D., Benoit, V., . . . White, S. M. (2015). Speech and language in a genotyped cohort of individuals with Kabuki syndrome. *American Journal of Medical Genetics Part A*, *167*(7), 1483–1492. doi:10.1002/ajmg.a.37026

Morris, C. A. (1993). Williams syndrome. In R. A. Pagon, M. P. Adam, H. H. Ardinger, S. E. Wallace, A. Amemiya, L. J. H. Bean, . . . K. Stephens (Eds.), *GeneReviews(R)*. Seattle, WA, NCBI bookshelf. Online publisher – see https://www.ncbi.nlm.nih.gov/books/NBK1116/See online.

Munafo, M. R. (2010). Credible genetic associations? *International Journal of Molecular Epidemiology and Genetics*, *1*(1), 31–34.

Neale, B. M., Medland, S., Ripke, S., Anney, R. J., Asherson, P., Buitelaar, J., . . . Group, Image Ii Consortium. (2010). Case-control genome-wide association study of attention-deficit/hyperactivity disorder. *Journal of American Academy of Child Adolescent Psychiatry*, *49*(9), 906–920. doi:10.1016/j.jaac.2010.06.007

O'Roak, B. J., Deriziotis, P., Lee, C., Vives, L., Schwartz, J. J., Girirajan, S., . . . Eichler, E. E. (2011). Exome sequencing in sporadic autism spectrum disorders identifies severe de novo mutations. *Nature Genetics*, *43*(6), 585–589. doi:10.1038/ng.835

Pinto, D., Pagnamenta, A. T., Klei, L., Anney, R., Merico, D., Regan, R., . . . Betancur, C. (2010). Functional impact of global rare copy number variation in autism spectrum disorders. *Nature*, *466*(7304), 368–372. doi:10.1038/nature09146

Ragoussis, J. (2009). Genotyping technologies for genetic research. *Annual Review of Genomics and Human Genetics, 10*, 117–133. doi:10.1146/annurev-genom-082908-150116

Reich, D. E., & Lander, E. S. (2001). On the allelic spectrum of human disease. *Trends in Genetics, 17*(9), 502–510.

Rodenas-Cuadrado, P., Ho, J., & Vernes, S. C. (2014). Shining a light on CNTNAP2: Complex functions to complex disorders. *European Journal of Human Genetics, 22*(2), 171–178. doi:10.1038/ejhg.2013.100

Schizophrenia Working Group of the Psychiatric Genomics, Consortium. (2014). Biological insights from 108 schizophrenia-associated genetic loci. *Nature, 511*(7510), 421–427. doi:10.1038/nature13595

Schizophrenia Working Groups of the Psychiatric Genomics, Consortium, & Psychosis Endophenotypes International, Consortium. (2016). Contribution of copy number variants to schizophrenia from a genome-wide study of 41,321 subjects. *Nature Genetics, 49*(1), 27–35. doi:10.1038/ng.3725

Schork, N. J., Murray, S. S., Frazer, K. A., & Topol, E. J. (2009). Common vs. rare allele hypotheses for complex diseases. *Current Opinion Genetics & Development, 19*(3), 212–219. doi:10.1016/j.gde.2009.04.010

Schumacher, J., Anthoni, H., Dahdouh, F., Konig, I. R., Hillmer, A. M., Kluck, N., . . . Kere, J. (2006). Strong genetic evidence of DCDC2 as a susceptibility gene for dyslexia. *American Journal of Human Genetics, 78*(1), 52–62. doi:10.1086/498992

Shu, W., Cho, J. Y., Jiang, Y., Zhang, M., Weisz, D., Elder, G. A., . . . Buxbaum, J. D. (2005). Altered ultrasonic vocalization in mice with a disruption in the Foxp2 gene. *Proceedings of the National Academy of Sciences of the United States of America, 102*(27), 9643–9648.

Simpson, N. H., Ceroni, F., Reader, R. H., Covill, L. E., Knight, J. C., Consortium, S. L. I., . . . Newbury, D. F. (2015). Genome-wide analysis identifies a role for common copy number variants in specific language impairment. *European Journal of Human Genetics, 23*(10), 1370–1377. doi:10.1038/ejhg.2014.296

Sudmant, P. H., Rausch, T., Gardner, E. J., Handsaker, R. E., Abyzov, A., Huddleston, J., . . . Korbel, J. O. (2015). An integrated map of structural variation in 2,504 human genomes. *Nature, 526*(7571), 75–81. doi:10.1038/nature15394

Torres, F., Barbosa, M., & Maciel, P. (2016). Recurrent copy number variations as risk factors for neurodevelopmental disorders: Critical overview and analysis of clinical implications. *Journal of Medical Genetics, 53*(2), 73–90. doi:10.1136/jmedgenet-2015-103366

UCSC. (2016). *Genome browser*. Retrieved December 12, 2016, from www.genome.ucsc.edu/

Venter, J. C., Adams, M. D., Myers, E. W., Li, P. W., Mural, R. J., Sutton, G. G., . . . Zhu, X. (2001). The sequence of the human genome. *Science, 291*(5507), 1304–1351. doi:10.1126/science.1058040

Virgin, H. W., & Todd, J. A. (2011). Metagenomics and personalized medicine. *Cell, 147*(1), 44–56. doi:10.1016/j.cell.2011.09.009

Vissers, L. E., de Ligt, J., Gilissen, C., Janssen, I., Steehouwer, M., de Vries, P., . . . Veltman, J. A. (2010). A de novo paradigm for mental retardation. *Nature Genetics, 42*(12), 1109–1112. doi:10.1038/ng.712

Zhu, X., Need, A. C., Petrovski, S., & Goldstein, D. B. (2014). One gene, many neuropsychiatric disorders: Lessons from Mendelian diseases. *Nature Neuroscience, 17*(6), 773–781. doi:10.1038/nn.3713

6

BIOLOGICAL AND GENETIC FACTORS IN DCD

Melissa K. Licari, Daniela Rigoli and Jan P. Piek

Introduction

The previous chapter outlined the considerable complexity involved in identifying genetic mechanisms responsible for particular disorders. It also highlighted the importance of considering both biological and environmental influences in order to understand aetiology. This is no different for developmental coordination disorder (DCD), and similar principles apply in determining any genetic origins of the disorder. This chapter will outline the evidence to date in relation to the genetics of DCD and possible neural mechanisms that may be affected.

In addition, as outlined in the previous chapter, co-occurrence is an important issue to consider with genetic overlap between different, even disparate, disorders. Many developmental disorders have been linked to motor deficits although often this has not been associated with DCD but attributed to the disorder itself. This has led to confusion in terms of understanding the biological basis of DCD and determining the underlying processes affected in those with DCD, hence impacting targeted interventions for DCD and other developmental disorders.

Co-occurrence in DCD

Perhaps the most researched area in regards to co-occurrence in DCD is its relationship with attention deficit hyperactivity disorder (ADHD). Earlier studies identified up to 50% of children with ADHD also having DCD (Pitcher, Piek, & Hay, 2003; Rasmussen & Gillberg, 2000). A recent review (Goulardins et al., 2015) examined both the overlap between these disorders as well as their distinct features, and concluded that they should be considered as separate disorders. One area receiving interest is that of attention, identified as a key deficit in ADHD (e.g., Barkley, Edwards, Laneri, Fletcher, & Metevia, 2001) and also in DCD (e.g., Tsai, Pan, Cherng, Hsu, & Chiu, 2009). However, attention mechanisms are complex and further research is needed to tease out the different processes responsible for attentional problems in DCD and ADHD. This has been a focus of several neuroimaging studies in recent years.

Another area gaining considerable interest in recent years is the link between DCD and autism spectrum disorders (ASD). Green et al. (2009) and Whyatt and Craig (2012) identified significant general motor impairment in children with ASD. However, further analysis of the movement sub-components, particularly ball catching and static balance, demonstrated substantial deficits in children with ASD. That is, children with ASD appeared to have a "profile of motor ability *specific* to autism" (Whyatt & Craig, 2012, p. 1808), suggesting unique motor deficits that should not be considered as a separate diagnosis of DCD. However, others have argued that if the criteria for DCD are met in children with ASD then it should be diagnosed as a co-occurring disorder (e.g., Miyahara, 2013; Piek & Dyck, 2004). In his meta-review, Miyahara (2013) argued that movement difficulties cannot be considered a core symptom of ASD as previously suggested, primarily because not all individuals with ASD have motor deficits. This view was supported by Caeyenberghs et al. (2016) who identified groups of children with ASD, DCD and ASD+DCD. They found that both the DCD and the DCD+ASD groups scored more poorly than the ASD and typically developing groups on movement and visuomotor tests. In addition, their examination of the topological architecture of brain networks identified distinct differences in the ASD groups compared with the DCD and control groups, while the DCD+ASD group produced a topological pattern different to either the DCD or ASD patterns.

Several studies have identified a link between specific language impairment (SLI) and DCD (Archibald & Alloway, 2008; Hill, 2001). A recent study by Flapper and Schoemaker (2013) diagnosed DCD in over 32% of children with SLI. Those children with the more severe motor difficulties were more likely to have problems with receptive (75%) or receptive-expressive (88%) subtypes compared with the expressive subtype (44%). Other learning difficulties have been identified in children with DCD, such as spelling, writing and reading (Dewey, Kaplan, Crawford, & Wilson, 2002; Tseng, Howe, Chuang, & Hsieh, 2007), and arithmetic and working memory (Alloway, 2007). Furthermore, Rigoli, Piek, Kane, and Oosterlaan (2012) found a relationship between aiming and catching skills, working memory and academic achievement (reading, spelling and numerical operations) in adolescents.

Similar complex relationships have been described when considering internalising problems (e.g., anxiety and depression) identified in children with DCD (e.g., Skinner & Piek, 2001; Missiuna et al., 2014). Cairney, Rigoli, and Piek (2013) describe a model (the environmental stress hypothesis) that attributes comorbid internalising problems in individuals with DCD in part to numerous interacting psychosocial variables including perceived competence, peer problems, and peer and parental social support. However, biological factors are also recognised as playing an important role in these complex relationships, and the interplay between biological and environmental factors must also be considered when understanding the aetiology of DCD.

Environmental influences

Accumulating studies investigating risk factors for DCD have suggested an important role for early environmental experiences, specifically pre- and peri-natal influences, in the aetiology of DCD. For example, in their birth cohort of approximately 7,000 7 year old children, Lingam and colleagues (2009) found an increased risk of DCD with lower gestation (<37 weeks) and lower birthweight (<2500g). In another large birth cohort study, Faebo Larsen, Hvas Mortensen, Martinussen, and Nybo Andersen (2013) examined those born pre-term separately to those children born at term, using the Developmental Coordination Disorder Questionnaire (DCDQ; Wilson, Kaplan, Crawford, Campbell, & Dewey, 2000); at seven years of age. The percentage of children born very pre-term (23–31 weeks) with DCD was 18.3%, 6.4% in children born moderately pre-term (32–36), and 2.9% in children born at term (37–41). Faebo Larsen and colleagues also found that being small for gestational age presented as a strong risk factor for DCD for both term and pre-term infants. For term-born children, younger maternal age (<25 years) and increased maternal smoking were risk factors, although these may be confounded by other factors such as socioeconomic status.

Another recent study involving a population-based birth cohort found gender differences (Grace, Bulsara, Robinson, & Hands, 2016). Smoking during early pregnancy and stress during later pregnancy were associated with poorer motor development outcomes for females, while lower percentage of optimal birthweight was related to motor outcomes for males. It was suggested that this may represent differences in the development of underlying neurological systems between males and females. Maternal pre-eclampsia, caesarian section, and low income were negatively associated with motor outcomes in both genders (Grace et al., 2016).

Pearsall-Jones and colleagues (2008) used a co-twin control design of monozygotic twins discordant and concordant for DCD in order to investigate possible aetiological factors. Oxygen perfusion complications were greater in those twins with DCD versus those without DCD. Such complications have been related to cerebral palsy and thus, these two movement disorders may fall on a continuum of severity with similar aetiology (Pearsall-Jones et al., 2008). However, neuroimaging and experimental research is required in order to draw further conclusion regarding this potential continuum (Williams, Hyde, & Spittle, 2014).

Finally, it is important to note the new exclusion criterion of DCD listed in the DSM-5, that is, lack of opportunity for skill learning and use. A recent population-based study of approximately 4,000 preschool children in China provided further support for the role of the environment in delayed motor development (Hua et al., 2016). While controlling for confounds such as age, sex, obesity and socioeconomic status, it was found that toys promoting motor development in the family home and access to sufficient space and furnishing in classrooms, impacted motor performance. Although the study points to the potential importance of home and educational factors in motor development, the cross-sectional relationships cannot imply causality. However, the findings highlight the need to consider an individual's movement experience when interpreting motor assessment results. While DCD may be misdiagnosed if children's opportunities are not taken into account and enriching one's environment may not be suffice to prevent DCD, the results support the importance of movement experiences for all children including those children with DCD (Van Waelvelde & Miyahara, 2016).

Heritability and twin studies

Although DCD is considered to be a multifactorial disorder in which both genetic and environmental factors play a role, investigations into the heritability of DCD are still very limited. For example, Gaines and colleagues' (2008) study appears to be the only one that has reported on the familial clustering of DCD and the presence of comorbid conditions. They examined a large family, in which mother and five of the six children who were measured met diagnostic criteria for DCD. It was suggested that the familial clustering provides evidence for both genetic and environmental contributions to DCD (Gaines et al., 2008).

In their population-based twin study of 1,245 Australian children and adolescents, Martin and colleagues (2006) presented the first genetic study of DCD. The aim of the study was to investigate the comorbidity of ADHD and DCD in order to examine their shared genetic heritability, while also teasing apart the genetic versus environmental contributions of these disorders. Using the parent-rated DCDQ (Wilson et al., 2000), Martin et al. (2006) found a common family environment component of 20% across all DCDQ subscales except for general coordination for which a common environmental component was not found. Potential contributions from shared peri-natal experiences (e.g., pre-term birth) of the twins and other possibilities such as nutrition or shared patterns of exercise were hypothesised (Martin et al., 2006). In their study, the remaining variance explained by non-shared environmental influences ranged from .07 to .16 (Martin et al., 2006). Conversely, others have found non-shared environmental influences ranging from .30 (Lichtenstein et al., 2010) to .56 (Moruzzi et al., 2010). In a recent twin/ sibling study of 858 adults, approximately half of the variance in coordination difficulty was explained by non-shared environmental influences (Waszcuk, Leonard, Hill, Rowe, & Gregory, 2016). Martin et al. (2006) noted that non-shared environment by definition also includes any error of measurement. Regardless, it has been argued that future studies focus on identifying these environmental factors, including the potential impact of epigenetic mechanisms, in order to inform interventions (Waszcuk et al. 2016).

Martin and colleagues (2006) found a high heritable component for the DCDQ Full Scale (.69) and across subscales (.64 to .85), which appears to be consistent with a more recent, large population-based study of 16,858 Swedish twins aged 9 to 12 years (Lichtenstein, Carlström, Råstam, Gillberg, & Anckarsäter, 2010). In their study, Lichtenstein et al., found a heritability estimate of 70% for DCD using a validated parent telephone interview assessing various child neuropsychiatric problems. Higher DCD concordance rates for monozygotic twins compared to dizygotic twins were also found (Lichtenstein et al., 2010). Conversely, Moruzzi and colleagues (2010) presented a lower heritability estimate of .44 for 'clumsiness' in 398 Italian twins (8 to 17 years old) from the general population. However, it is important to note that a limitation of this study was the use of three items from the Child Behavior Checklist (CBCL) ('Gets hurt a lot, accident prone', 'Poorly coordinated or clumsy', 'Underactive, slow moving, or lacks energy'; Achenbach & Rescorla, 2001) that were selected to tap the construct of 'clumsiness', limiting the conclusions that can be drawn. Piek, Barrett, Dyck, and Reiersen (2010) examined the validity of the CBCL as a screening tool for identifying motor impairment by employing a validated motor performance test as a criterion measure. The results did not support the use of the CBCL to identify mild to moderate motor impairment in non-clinical populations.

In regards to the comorbid relationship between ADHD and DCD examined by Martin et al. (2006), shared genetic contributions were small to moderate depending on which DCDQ subscale was analysed and with which ADHD questionnaire measure. Martin et al. (2006) noted that while it may be preferable to determine diagnoses using clinical interview and performance measures rather than questionnaire measures, this is particularly difficult given the large samples needed for genetic analysis. It is also argued that the questionnaire tools used in their study demonstrate good psychometric data for their use, including comparable prevalence estimates compared to previous studies.

Fliers et al. (2009) also highlighted methodological issues when the importance of considering the impact of different informants was emphasised. They demonstrated the influence of parent versus teacher assessment of motor performance when estimating familial contributions. In their study involving a clinical sample of 275 children with ADHD (aged 5–19 years) and their siblings, it was revealed that familial influences (combined genetic and shared environmental influences) differed according to rater, with .47 for parent and .22 teacher ratings, with the remainder explained by non-shared environmental influences on motor performance. Fliers et al., noted that while the same parent assessed motor performance for each twin pair, different teachers per twin pair completed the teacher rated questionnaire, which may have inflated the environmental contribution when examining this measure.

DNA genetic studies

Despite the high heritability of DCD, with estimates around 70% (Lichtenstein et al., 2010; Martin et al., 2006), and its relationship to other neurodevelopmental disorders with known genetic origins (e.g. ADHD and ASD), it is somewhat surprising that very little research has explored DNA genetics of DCD. As demonstrated in the previous chapter, there certainly is a lot we can learn surrounding the genetics of DCD through studies in other neurodevelopmental disorders, which have been more heavily researched in relation to genetic and epigenetics. Some of this research has even explored the genetic profiles of motor impairment within their cohort, providing some insight into potential genetic links to poor motor coordination.

One such study is that of Fliers and colleagues (2012) who conducted a genome-wide association study (GWAS) to identify genes associated with coordination difficulties in children with ADHD (N = 890). In a GWAS, single nucleotide polymorphisms (SNPs) are tested for their association with particular traits which, in this particular study, was parental report of coordination difficulties. Using the Parental Account of Children's Symptoms questionnaire (PACS, Taylor, 1986), 22.4% of the sample was reported to have definite movement difficulties and 25.3% with possible movement difficulties. Even though findings did not reach genome-wide significance, 174 SNPs located in 97 genes were associated with PACS. Bioinformatics analysis identified that 45 out of the 97 genes were significantly enriched in five categories of neurological disease; including neurodegenerative disorders, progressive motor neuropathy, amyotrophic lateral sclerosis, bipolar disorder and schizophrenia. Genes involved in neurite outgrowth and muscle functioning were also found to be enriched. While the study provided evidence linking neuropathology to poor motor coordination, the authors also highlighted that disruption may extend beyond the neurological level and be evident at the muscular level too, raising the question of whether DCD is more than a disorder of the brain.

Morris and colleagues (2015) studied the clinical phenotype of individuals presenting with 7q11.23 duplication syndrome (Dup7), the genes deleted in Williams syndrome. Thirty-one children with Dup7 were assessed for DCD using the DSM-5 criteria, with 23 (74.2%) confirmed with movement difficulties consistent with DCD. A variety of motor features were evaluated, with 82.6% presenting with a speech disorder, 62.3% with atypical walking gait, 58.5% with hypotonia, and abundant motor overflow was also reported. While there were some distinct clinical features of Dup7, including a recognisable facial phenotype (e.g. broad forehead, straight eyebrows and broader nasal tip) and macrocephaly, it demonstrates how broad the DCD diagnosis could extend.

Hanson et al. (2015) conducted a similar study to Morris et al. (2015) by examining the cognitive and behavioural phenotype of 16p.11.2 deletion. Of the 85 participants with 16p11.2 deletion, >90% presented with psychiatric and developmental disorders, with the most commonly diagnosed conditions including DCD (58%), phonologic processing disorder (56%), language disorders (46%), ASD (25%) and ADHD (19%). Even though the focus of this study was on autism-related characteristics, the finding of a broad range of developmental issues across the cohort studied, implicates this deletion across several developmental disorders, including DCD.

A recent study by Mosca et al. (2016) was the first to specifically concentrate on the genetic origins of DCD. The study examined copy number variations (CNVs) and structural variation of base pairs within DNA in 82 children with DCD, with and without co-occurring ADHD and reading disorder. The study found greater genomic variation, with 26% of the DCD cohort displaying rare de novo CNVs, and 64% inherited CNVs from a parent who also had a neurodevelopmental disorder. The study also found an enrichment of duplications for brain expressed genes, along with an overlap in duplications and deletions in genes previously implicated in other neurological and neurodevelopmental disorders, including FHIT, GAP43, RBFOX1, PTPRN2, SHANK3, 16p11.2 and 22q11.2 seen in ADHD, ASD, epilepsy, schizophrenia and Tourette's syndrome. While a number of the variations were seen in children with co-occurring disorders, there was also presence of variations in children with isolated cases of DCD, providing significant evidence to support that this disorder has a genetic basis that is heritable.

Given that 4.8–9.5% of the human genome can be classified as a CNV (Zarrei, MacDonald, Merico, & Scherer, 2015), one of the challenges facing researchers is whether identified variations are causative. Many of the CNVs identified within neurodevelopmental disorders are variants of unknown significance, and those having clinical significance, may not necessarily result in phenotypes associated with the disorder. Therefore, there is a need for ongoing research to not only identify overlapping genes and pathways across neurodevelopmental disorders to improve our understanding of shared aetiology, but also how these genes may ultimately result in neuropathology and specific behavioural phenotypes.

Studying the functional impact of genetic variation is challenging, but animal models have the potential to contribute to our understanding of the neurobiology of neurodevelopmental disorders. Among the most frequently used are mouse models, which can be engineered to study the genotype of interest. For instance, 16p11.2 duplication and deletion CNVs have been replicated and shown to impact synaptic function, chromatin modification and transcriptional regulation (Blumenthal et al., 2014), with mice displaying hyperactivity, difficulty adapting to change, repetitive and restricted behaviour, recognition memory deficits and sleep disturbances (Arbogast et al., 2016; Hippolyte et al., 2016). 22q11.2 deletion mouse models have been shown to present with alterations in prefrontal synaptic plasticity and connectivity (Drew et al., 2011), along with abnormalities in neuronal dendrites across a variety of cortical pathways (Ellegood et al., 2014), behaviourally showing poor working memory, impaired social interaction and anxiety-like traits (Hiroi et al., 2012). Whilst developing mouse models to evaluate motor impairment could be considered quite challenging, especially when one considers the first year of human development is equivalent to 12 days in a mouse (Vinay et al., 2005), research certainly emphasises a need for it.

Research in relation to genetic pathways contributing to movement dysfunction is just at its tipping point. Researchers are acknowledging the need for thorough phenotyping of participants they are recruiting for genetic studies so that clearer connections can be made between specific genotypes and certain disorders. Equally important are studies recruiting participants with distinct genetic variations, like the studies by Morris et al. (2015) and Hanson et al. (2015), thoroughly exploring the behavioural phenotypes across these individuals. This will enable researchers to start disentangling genetics, determining how over-expression and under-expression of genes may impact on brain development and function, and ultimately result in the observable symptoms we see across so many disorders.

Brain structure and function: evidence from neuroimaging research

Modern in vivo neuroimaging and neurophysiological techniques are able to elucidate the pattern of neuronal activity both at rest and during the performance of various tasks, providing an unprecedented opportunity to study the assumption that impaired movement is the result of atypical brain development in DCD (Brown-Lum & Zwicker, 2015).

Studies using MRI to examine DCD at a structural level have utilised a variety of techniques, including measures of cortical thickness and cortical volume, and water molecule anisotropy and diffusion. Results from these studies have been variable, with reduced grey matter thickness in the temporal pole (Langevin, MacMaster, & Dewey, 2015), and reduced right-lateralised grey matter volume in the medial and middle frontal, and superior frontal gyri reported (Reynolds et al., 2017). While diffusion studies have revealed reduced fractional anisotrophy and/or diffusivity in the corticospinal tract, internal capsule, superior longitudinal fasciculus and posterior corpus callosum (Debrabant et al., 2016; Langevin, MacMaster, Crawford, Lebel, & Dewey, 2014; Kashuk, Williams, Thorpe, Wilson, & Egan, 2017; Zwicker, Missiuna, Harris, & Boyd, 2012). These areas are involved in a variety of neurological processes, including motor planning and execution, attention, working memory and other components of executive function, along with sensory function.

Whilst many of the studies share some similarities to the ADHD and ASD literature, the alterations in white matter structure reported by Zwicker et al. (2012) and Debrabant et al. (2016) also overlap with studies in cerebral palsy (Nagae et al., 2007; Rai et al., 2013; Yoshida et al., 2010). Cerebral palsy may be considered as quite distinct from other neurodevelopmental disorders. However, children who have pre- and neonatal risk factors (e.g. pre-term birth, traumatic birth) can easily be diagnosed with DCD when they do not present with the 'typical' clinical features of cerebral palsy.

Like the structural studies, the results of functional studies have also been quite variable, but this is not surprising given the variety of paradigms (i.e. tasks) that have been used across these studies. Interestingly, aside from the work of Zwicker and colleagues (2010, 2011), only small differences in brain activation (often at an uncorrected level) have been reported in studies of DCD (Debrabant, Gheysen, Caeyenberghs, Van Waelvelde, & Vingerhoets, 2013; Kashiwagi, Iwaki, Narumi, Tamai, & Suzuki, 2009; Licari et al., 2015; Reynolds et al., 2015).

One of the more consistent findings across studies is varying patterns of activation in the frontal lobe (Kashiwagi et al., 2009; Licari et al., 2015; Reynolds et al., 2015; Zwicker et al., 2010, 2011), a region involved in the planning and execution of movement, along with the higher order processes. Altered activity in the dorsolateral prefrontal cortex has been reported across studies utilising tasks with higher visuomotor demands (Debrabant et al., 2013; Querne et al., 2008; Zwicker et al., 2011), indicating issues with attentional control, which may also impact on motor planning. The inferior frontal gyrus is another cortical region reported more than once (Debrabant et al., 2013; Licari et al., 2015; Reynolds et al., 2015), involved in our ability to observe and imitate movement, forming part of the parietal-premotor network.

Differential functioning of the parietal lobe has also been found across fMRI studies (Kashiwagi et al., 2009; Licari et al., 2015; Querne et al., 2008; Zwicker et al., 2010, 2011). Areas of the parietal lobe that have been implicated include regions involved in the processing of somatic sensation (e.g. postcentral gyrus; Licari et al., 2015; Zwicker et al., 2010), along with regions involved in spatial and motor attention (e.g. inferior parietal lobe; Kashiwagi et al., 2009; Reynolds et al., 2015). Deficits in somatosensory function have long been reported in behavioural studies of children with DCD (Hoare & Larkin, 1991; Piek & Coleman-Carman, 1995), however, evidence in relation to spatial and motor attention is unclear. Studies of patients with damage to the parietal lobe (Gréa et al., 2002) highlight the important role this lobe plays in attention, with patients experiencing reduced ability to direct attention in space, along with difficulties making online adjustments. Similar difficulties are reported in studies examining reaching/grasping movements and visuomotor tasks in DCD (Hyde & Wilson, 2011, 2013; Johnston, Burns Brauer, & Richardson, 2002), but there is a combination of other factors that might contribute to decrements in performance, such as timing issues potentially related to cerebellar dysfunction (e.g., Piek & Skinner, 1999).

Studies examining patterns of activation in the cerebellum within DCD are quite limited, with researchers often electing to exclude it from the scan volume to minimise scan time. Of the studies that have included the cerebellum, differential activation has been reported (Debrabant et al., 2013; Zwicker et al., 2010), providing evidence to support the cerebellar dysfunction hypothesis of DCD (Cantin, Polatajko Thach, & Jaglal, 2007; O'Hare & Khalid, 2002), along with extensive behavioural studies reporting deficits in timing and postural control. Given that the cerebellum is part of extensive networks, including frontocerebellar and parietocerebellar networks, its dysfunction has the potential to disturb the function of so many cortical regions. Further research to explore this neurological region, particularly at a network level, is warranted.

In recent years there has been a shift towards studying brain connectivity. Querne et al. (2008) were the first to explore connectivity, reporting differential effective connectivity (using structural equation modelling from fMRI) in frontoparietal networks, along with the right striatum and parietal cortex. Debrabant et al. (2016) have also looked at connectivity (diffusion-based) within DCD, and reported reduced clustering coefficients, as well as global and local efficiency, suggestive of weaker structural networks.

Other connectivity studies have examined network differences between different neurodevelopmental disorders, which have included groups with DCD. Caeyenberghs et al. (2016) found a low degree of overlap in connectivity abnormalities between children with DCD and ASD, with children with ASD displaying more connectivity alterations. Children with DCD only displayed clustering increases in the right lateral orbitofrontal cortex, part of the limbic network and involved in switching or reversing stimulus-response associations.

Functional connectivity studies by McLeod and colleagues (2014, 2016) have revealed atypical motor connections, both within- and between-hemispheres, in children with DCD and/or ADHD. Some of the altered connections were common between disorders, while some disruptions were specific to DCD. Interestingly, one of the findings from their 2016 study was a lack of hemispheric dominance of functional connections between the putamen and motor cortex in those with DCD only (n=6). This finding is consistent with another recent research study that reported reduced leftwards lateralisation of speech in adults with DCD (Hodgson & Hudson, 2016), potentially providing a new direction of research surrounding a deficit in hemispheric specialisation.

There has been a considerable amount of research utilising EEG to examine brain activation in the DCD cohort over the years. Reduced activity in frontal regions has been reported during eye-gaze cuing (Wang et al., 2015), processing of auditory stimuli (Holeckova, Cepicka, Mautner, Stepanek, & Moucek, 2014), and functional motor tasks (Fong et al. 2016), which have been attributed to deficits in attentional function. Parietal regions have also been implicated, with reduced activation on visuospatial attention shifting (Tsai et al., 2009) and spatial working memory tasks (Tsai, Chang, Hung, Tseng, & Chen, 2012). Like studies using fMRI, the tasks utilised across studies have varied, but there are some consistencies in findings.

Even though we have learnt a lot about the neural correlates of DCD through neuroimaging, there are also many question marks surrounding this research given how variable the findings have been. A lot of this variability is likely to come from the paradigms employed (i.e. motor tasks used), differences in acquisition protocols and different analysis procedures. Whilst very powerful, results obtained from imaging software can be easily misinterpreted and have advanced features which are often misused. Also important to consider, is the varying phenotypic profiles of participants across these studies, with some not measuring criteria for other neurodevelopmental disorders, potentially resulting in a mixed sample. Others have taken co-occurrence into consideration, but then collapsed children with movement difficulties into one sample. Small sample sizes, broad age ranges, gender and pre- and peri-natal history are all variables that have been shown to impact on neurological findings, which have not been particularly well controlled across neuroimaging studies to date and should be considered in this field moving forward.

Summary and conclusions

Given the rapid growth of genetic and neuroimaging research, it will certainly be exciting to see the expansion of research in these areas as time passes and more techniques are developed. Equally exciting is the greater awareness of motor abnormalities across neurodevelopmental disorders, which will ultimately result in more research attempting to unravel the genetic influences and neurological mechanisms contributing to impaired movement. Even though the knowledge gained from such research moves us one step closer to understanding the complex mechanisms involved in DCD and motor difficulties in neurodevelopmental disorders in general, the next step will be finding rehabilitation approaches that may improve the way in which the brain operates leading to improved motor outcomes.

References

Achenbach, T. M., & Rescorla, L. A. (2001). *Manual for ASEBA school-age forms and profiles.* Burlington, VT: University of Vermont, ASEBA.

Alloway, T. P. (2007). Working memory, reading, and mathematical skills in children with developmental coordination disorder. *Journal of Experimental Child Psychology, 96*(1), 20–36. doi:10.1016/j.jecp.2006.07.002

Arbogast, T., Ouagazzal, A. M., Chevalier, C., Kopanitsa, M., Afinowi, N., Migliavacca, E., . . . Herault, Y. (2016). Reciprocal effects on neurocognitive and metabolic phenotypes in mouse models of 16p11.2 deletion and duplication syndromes. *PLoS Genetics, 12*(2), e1005709. doi:10.1371/journal.pgen.1005709

Archibald, L. M., & Alloway, T. P. (2008). Comparing language profiles: Children with specific language impairment and developmental coordination disorder. *International Journal of Language & Communication Disorders, 43*(2), 165–180. doi:10.1080/13682820701422809

Barkley, R. A., Edwards, G., Laneri, M., Fletcher, K., & Metevia, L. (2001). Executive functioning, temporal discounting, and sense of time in adolescents with attention deficit hyperactivity disorder (ADHD) and oppositional defiant disorder (ODD). *Journal of Abnormal Child Psychology, 29*(6), 541–556.

Blumenthal, I., Ragavendran, A., Erdin, S., Klei, L., Sugathan, A., Guide, J. R., . . . Ernst, C. (2014). Transcriptional consequences of 16p11.2 deletion and duplication in mouse cortex and multiplex autism families. *The American Journal of Human Genetics, 94*(6), 870–883. doi:10.1016/j.ajhg.2014.05.004

Brown-Lum, M., & Zwicker, J. G. (2015). Brain imaging increases our understanding of developmental coordination disorder: A review of literature and future directions. *Current Developmental Disorders Reports, 2*(2), 131–140. doi:10.1007/s40474-015-0046-6

Caeyenberghs, K., Taymans, T., Wilson, P. H., Vanderstraeten, G., Hosseini, H., & Waelvelde, H. (2016). Neural signature of developmental coordination disorder in the structural connectome independent of comorbid autism. *Developmental Science, 19*(4), 599–612. doi:10.1111/desc.12424

Cairney, J., Rigoli, D., & Piek, J. (2013). Developmental coordination disorder and internalizing problems in children: The environmental stress hypothesis Elaborated. *Developmental Review, 33*, 224–238. doi:10.3389/fpsyg.2016.00239

Cantin, N., Polatajko, H. J., Thach, W. T., & Jaglal, S. (2007). Developmental coordination disorder: Exploration of a cerebellar hypothesis. *Human Movement Science, 26*(3), 491–509. doi:10.1016/j.humov.2007.03.004

Debrabant, J., Gheysen, F., Caeyenberghs, K., Van Waelvelde, H., & Vingerhoets, G. (2013). Neural underpinnings of impaired predictive motor timing in children with developmental coordination disorder. *Research in Developmental Disabilities, 34*(5), 1478–1487. doi:10.1016/j.ridd.2013.02.008

Debrabant, J., Vingerhoets, G., Van Waelvelde, H., Leemans, A., Taymans, T., & Caeyenberghs, K. (2016). Brain connectomics of visual-motor deficits in children with developmental coordination disorder. *The Journal of Pediatrics, 169*, 21–27. doi:10.1016/j.jpeds.2015.09.069

Dewey, D., Kaplan, B. J., Crawford, S. G., & Wilson, B. N. (2002). Developmental coordination disorder: Associated problems in attention, learning, and psychosocial adjustment. *Human Movement Science, 21*(5), 905–918. doi:10.1016/S0167-9457(02)00163-X

Drew, L. J., Crabtree, G. W., Markx, S., Stark, K. L., Chaverneff, F., Xu, B., . . . Karayiorgou, M. (2011). The 22q11.2 microdeletion: Fifteen years of insights into the genetic and neural complexity of psychiatric disorders. *International Journal of Developmental Neuroscience, 29*(3), 259–281. doi:10.1016/j.ijdevneu.2010.09.007

Ellegood, J., Markx, S., Lerch, J. P., Steadman, P. E., Genç, C., Provenzano, F., . . . Gogos, J. A. (2014). Neuroanatomical phenotypes in a mouse model of the 22q11. 2 microdeletion. *Molecular Psychiatry, 19*(1), 99–107. doi:10.1038/mp.2013.112

Faebo Larsen, R., Hvas Mortensen, L., Martinussen, T., & Nybo Andersen, A. M. (2013). Determinants of developmental coordination disorder in 7-year-old children: A study of children in the Danish national birth cohort. *Developmental Medicine & Child Neurology, 55*(11), 1016–1022. doi:10.1111/dmcn.12223

Flapper, B. C., & Schoemaker, M. M. (2013). Developmental coordination disorder in children with specific language impairment: Co-morbidity and impact on quality of life. *Research in Developmental Disabilities, 34*(2), 756–763. doi:10.1016/j.ridd.2012.10.014

Fliers, E. A., Vasquez, A. A., Poelmans, G., Rommelse, N., Altink, M., Buschgens, C., . . . Miranda, A. (2012). Genome-wide association study of motor coordination problems in ADHD identifies genes for brain and muscle function. *The World Journal of Biological Psychiatry, 13*(3), 211–222. doi:10.3109/15622975.2011.560279

Fliers, E., Vermeulen, S., Rijsdijk, F., Altink, M., Buschgens, C., Rommelse, N., . . . Franke, B. (2009). ADHD and poor motor performance from a family genetic perspective. *Journal of the American Academy of Child & Adolescent Psychiatry, 48*(1), 25–34. doi:10.1097/CHI.0b013e31818b1ca2

Fong, S. S., Chung, J. W., Cheng, Y. T., Yam, T. T., Chiu, H. C., Fong, D. Y., . . . Macfarlane, D. J. (2016). Attention during functional tasks is associated with motor performance in children with developmental coordination disorder: A cross-sectional study. *Medicine, 95*(37), e4935. doi:10.1097/MD.0000000000004935

Gaines, R., Collins, D., Boycott, K., Missiuna, C., DeLaat, D., & Soucie, H. (2008). Clinical expression of developmental coordination disorder in a large Canadian family. *Paediatrics & Child Health, 13*(9), 763. doi:10.1093/pch/13.9.763

Goulardins, J. B., Rigoli, D., Licari, M., Piek, J. P., Hasue, R. H., Oosterlaan, J., & Oliveira, J. A. (2015). Attention deficit hyperactivity disorder and developmental coordination disorder: Two separate disorders or do they share a common aetiology? *Behavioural Brain Research, 292*, 484–492. doi:10.1016/j.bbr.2015.07.009

Grace, T., Bulsara, M., Robinson, M., & Hands, B. (2016). Early life events and motor development in childhood and adolescence: A longitudinal study. *Acta Paediatrica, 105*, e219–e227. doi:10.1111/apa.13302

Gréa, H., Pisella, L., Rossetti, Y., Desmurget, M., Tilikete, C., Grafton, S., Prablanc, C., & Vighetto, A. (2002). A lesion of the posterior parietal cortex disrupts on-line adjustments during aiming movements. *Neuropsychologia, 40*, 2471–2480. doi:10.1016/S0028-3932(02)00009-X

Green, D., Charman, T., Pickles, A., Chandler, S., Loucas, T., Simonoff, E., & Baird, G. (2009). Impairment in movement skills of children with autistic spectrum disorders. *Developmental Medicine & Child Neurology, 51*(4), 311–316. doi:10.1111/j.1469-8749.2008.03242.x

Hanson, E., Bernier, R., Porche, K., Jackson, F. I., Goin-Kochel, R. P., Snyder, L. G., . . . Chen, Q. (2015). The cognitive and behavioral phenotype of the 16p11. 2 deletion in a clinically ascertained population. *Biological Psychiatry, 77*(9), 785–793. doi:10.1016/j.biopsych.2014.04.021

Hill, E. L. (2001). Non-specific nature of specific language impairment: A review of the literature with regard to concomitant motor impairments. *International Journal of Language & Communication Disorders, 36*(2), 149–171. doi:10.1080/13682820010019874

Hippolyte, L., Maillard, A. M., Rodriguez-Herreros, B., Pain, A., Martin-Brevet, S., Ferrari, C., . . . Reigo, A. (2016). The number of genomic copies at the 16p11. 2 locus modulates language, verbal memory, and inhibition. *Biological Psychiatry, 80*(2), 129–139. doi:10.1016/j.biopsych.2015.10.02

Hiroi, N., Hiramoto, T., Harper, K. M., Suzuki, G., & Boku, S. (2012). Mouse models of 22q11. 2-associated autism spectrum disorder. *Autism Open Access*, 001. doi:10.4172/2165-7890. S1-001

Hoare, D., & Larkin, D. (1991). Kinaesthetic abilities of clumsy children. *Developmental Medicine & Child Neurology, 33*(8), 671–678. doi:10.1111/j.1469-8749.1991.tb14944.x

Hodgson, J. C., & Hudson, J. M. (2016). Atypical speech lateralization in adults with developmental coordination disorder demonstrated using functional transcranial Doppler ultrasound. *Journal of Neuropsychology, 11*(1), 1–13. doi:10.1111/jnp.12102

Holeckova, I., Cepicka, L., Mautner, P., Stepanek, D., & Moucek, R. (2014). Auditory ERPs in children with developmental coordination disorder. *Activitas Nervosa Superior, 56*(1/2), 37–44. doi:10.1007/BF03379606

Hua, J., Duan, T., Gu, G., Wo, D., Zhu, Q., Liu, J. Q., . . . Meng, W. (2016). Effects of home and education environments on children's motor performance in China. *Developmental Medicine & Child Neurology, 58*(8), 868–876. doi:10.1111/dmcn.13073

Hyde, C. E., & Wilson, P. H. (2013). Impaired online control in children with developmental coordination disorder reflects developmental immaturity. *Developmental Neuropsychology, 38*(2), 81–97. doi:10.1080/87565641.2012.718820

Hyde, C., & Wilson, P. H. (2011). Dissecting online control in developmental coordination disorder: A kinematic analysis of double-step reaching. *Brain and Cognition, 75*(3), 232–241. doi:10.1016/j.bandc.2010.12.004

Johnston, L. M., Burns, Y. R., Brauer, S. G., & Richardson, C. A. (2002). Differences in postural control and movement performance during goal directed reaching in children with developmental coordination disorder. *Human Movement Science, 21*(5), 583–601. doi:10.1016/S0167-9457(02)00153-7

Kashiwagi, M., Iwaki, S., Narumi, Y., Tamai, H., & Suzuki, S. (2009). Parietal dysfunction in developmental coordination disorder: A functional MRI study. *Neuroreport, 20*(15), 1319–1324. doi:10.1097/WNR.0b013e32832f4d87

Kashuk, S. R., Williams, J., Thorpe, G., Wilson, P. H., & Egan, G. F. (2017). Diminished motor imagery capability in adults with motor impairment: An fMRI mental rotation study. *Behavioural Brain Research, 334*, 86–96. doi:10.1016/j.bbr.2017.06.042.

Langevin, L. M., MacMaster, F. P., & Dewey, D. (2015). Distinct patterns of cortical thinning in concurrent motor and attention disorders. *Developmental Medicine & Child Neurology, 57*(3), 257–264. doi:10.1111/dmcn.12561

Langevin, L. M., MacMaster, F. P., Crawford, S., Lebel, C., & Dewey, D. (2014). Common white matter microstructure alterations in pediatric motor and attention disorders. *The Journal of Pediatrics, 164*(5), 1157–1164. doi:1 0.1016/j.jpeds.2014.01.018

Licari, M. K., Billington, J., Reid, S. L., Wann, J. P., Elliott, C. M., Winsor, A. M., . . . Bynevelt, M. (2015). Cortical functioning in children with developmental coordination disorder: A motor overflow study. *Experimental Brain Research, 233*(6), 1703–1710. doi:10.1007/s00221-015-4243-7

Lichtenstein, P., Carlström, E., Råstam, M., Gillberg, C., & Anckarsäter, H. (2010). The genetics of autism spectrum disorders and related neuropsychiatric disorders in childhood. *American Journal of Psychiatry, 167*(11), 1357–1363. doi:10.1176/appi.ajp.2010.10020223

Lingam, R., Hunt, L., Golding, J., Jongmans, M., & Emond, A. (2009). Prevalence of developmental coordination disorder using the DSM-IV at 7 years of age: A UK population – based study. *Pediatrics, 123*(4), e693–e700. doi:10.1542/peds.2008-1770

Martin, N. C., Piek, J. P., & Hay, D. (2006). DCD and ADHD: A genetic study of their shared aetiology. *Human Movement Science, 25*(1), 110–124. doi:10.1016/j.humov.2005.10.006

McLeod, K. R., Langevin, L. M., Dewey, D., & Goodyear, B. G. (2016). Atypical within-and between-hemisphere motor network functional connections in children with developmental coordination disorder and attention-deficit/hyperactivity disorder. *NeuroImage: Clinical, 12*, 157–164. doi:10.1016/j.nicl.2016.06.019

McLeod, K. R., Langevin, L. M., Goodyear, B. G., & Dewey, D. (2014). Functional connectivity of neural motor networks is disrupted in children with developmental coordination disorder and attention-deficit/hyperactivity disorder. *NeuroImage: Clinical, 4*, 566–575. doi:10.1016/j.nicl.2014.03.010

Missiuna, C., Cairney, J., Pollock, N., Campbell, W., Russell, D. J., Macdonald, K., . . . Cousins, M. (2014). Psychological distress in children with developmental coordination disorder and attention-deficit hyperactivity disorder. *Research in Developmental Disabilities, 35*(5), 1198–1207. doi:10.1016/j.ridd.2014.01.007

Miyahara, M. (2013). Meta review of systematic and meta analytic reviews on movement differences, effect of movement based interventions, and the underlying neural mechanisms in autism spectrum disorder. *Frontiers in Integrative Neuroscience, 7*, 16. doi:10.3389/fnint.2013.00016

Morris, C. A., Mervis, C. B., Paciorkowski, A. P., Abdul-Rahman, O., Dugan, S. L., Rope, A. F., . . . Osborne, L. R. (2015). 7q11. 23 Duplication syndrome: Physical characteristics and natural history. *American Journal of Medical Genetics Part A, 167*(12), 2916–2935. doi:10.1002/ajmg.a.37340

Moruzzi, S., Pesenti-Gritti, P., Brescianini, S., Salemi, M., Battaglia, M., & Ogliari, A. (2010). Clumsiness and psychopathology: Causation or shared etiology? A twin study with the CBCL 6–18 questionnaire in a general school-age population sample. *Human Movement Science, 29*(2), 326–338. doi:10.1016/j.humov.2010.01.005

Mosca, S. J., Langevin, L. M., Dewey, D., Innes, A. M., Lionel, A. C., Marshall, C. C., . . . Bernier, F. P. (2016). Copy-number variations are enriched for neurodevelopmental genes in children with developmental coordination disorder. *Journal of Medical Genetics, 53*(12), 812–819. doi:10.1136/jmedgenet-2016-103818

Nagae, L. M., Hoon, A. H., Stashinko, E., Lin, D., Zhang, W., Levey, E., . . . Van Zijl, P. C. M. (2007). Diffusion tensor imaging in children with periventricular leukomalacia: Variability of injuries to white matter tracts. *American Journal of Neuroradiology, 28*(7), 1213–1222. doi:10.3174/ajnr.A0534

O'Hare, A., & Khalid, S. (2002). The association of abnormal cerebellar function in children with developmental coordination disorder and reading difficulties. *Dyslexia, 8*(4), 234–248. doi:10.1002/dys.230

Pearsall-Jones, J. G., Piek, J. P., Martin, N. C., Rigoli, D., Levy, F., & Hay, D. A. (2008). A monozygotic twin design to investigate etiological factors for DCD and ADHD. *Journal of Pediatric Neurology, 6*(3), 209–219. doi:10.1375/twin.12.4.381

Piek, J. P., & Coleman-Carman, R. (1995). Kinaesthetic sensitivity and motor performance of children with developmental co-ordination disorder. *Developmental Medicine & Child Neurology, 37*(11), 976–984. doi:10.1111/j.1469-8749.1995.tb11952.x

Piek, J. P., & Dyck, M. J. (2004). Sensory-motor deficits in children with developmental coordination disorder, attention deficit hyperactivity disorder and autistic disorder. *Human Movement Science, 23*, 475–488. doi:10.1016/j.humov.2004.08.019

Piek, J. P., & Skinner, R. A. (1999). Timing and force control during a sequential tapping task in children with and without motor coordination problems. *Journal of the International Neuropsychological Society, 5*(04), 320–329. doi:10.1017/S1355617799544032

Piek, J. P., Barrett, N. C., Dyck, M. J., & Reiersen, A. M. (2010). Can the child behavior checklist be used to screen for motor impairment? *Developmental Medicine & Child Neurology, 52*(2), 200–204. doi:10.1111/j.1469-8749.2009.03326.x

Pitcher, T. M., Piek, J. P., & Hay, D. A. (2003). Fine and gross motor ability in males with attention deficit hyperactivity disorder. *Developmental Medicine & Child Neurology, 45*, 525–535. doi:10.1017/S0012162203000975

Querne, L., Berquin, P., Vernier-Hauvette, M. P., Fall, S., Deltour, L., Meyer, M. E., & de Marco, G. (2008). Dysfunction of the attentional brain network in children with developmental coordination disorder: A fMRI study. *Brain Research, 1244*, 89–102. doi:10.1016/j.brainres.2008.07.066

Rai, Y., Chaturvedi, S., Paliwal, V. K., Goyal, P., Chourasia, A., Rathore, R. K. S., . . . Gupta, R. K. (2013). DTI correlates of cognition in term children with spastic diplegic cerebral palsy. *European Journal of Paediatric Neurology, 17*(3), 294–301. doi:10.1016/j.ejpn.2012.11.005

Rasmussen, P., & Gillberg, C. (2000). Natural outcome of ADHD with developmental coordination disorder at age 22 years: A controlled, longitudinal, community-based study. *Journal of the American Academy of Child & Adolescent Psychiatry, 39*(11), 1424–1431. doi:10.1097/00004583-200011000-00017

Reynolds, J. E, Licari, M. K., Reid, S. L, Elliott, C., Winsor, A. M., Bynevelt, M., & Billington, J. (2017). Reduced relative volume in motor and attention regions in developmental coordination disorder: A voxel-based morphometry study. *International Journal of Developmental Neuroscience, 58*, 59–64. doi:10.1016/j.ijdevneu.2017.01.008

Reynolds, J. E., Licari, M. K., Billington, J., Chen, Y., Aziz-Zadeh, L., Werner, J., . . . Bynevelt, M. (2015). Mirror neuron activation in children with developmental coordination disorder: A functional MRI study. *International Journal of Developmental Neuroscience, 47*, 309–319. doi:10.1016/j.ijdevneu.2015.10.00

Rigoli, D., Piek, J. P., Kane, R., & Oosterlaan, J. (2012). Motor coordination, working memory and academic achievement in a normal population of adolescents: Testing a mediation model. *Archives of Clinical Neuropsychology, 27*, 766–780. doi:10.1093/arclin/acs061

Skinner, R. A., & Piek, J. P. (2001). Psychosocial implications of poor motor coordination in children and adolescents. *Human Movement Science, 20*, 73–94. doi:10.1016/S0167-9457(01)00029-X

Taylor, E. A. (1986). Childhood hyperactivity. *British Journal of Psychiatry, 149*, 562–573. doi:10.1192/bjp.149.5.562

Tsai, C. L., Chang, Y. K., Hung, T. M., Tseng, Y. T., & Chen, T. C. (2012). The neurophysiological performance of visuospatial working memory in children with developmental coordination disorder. *Developmental Medicine & Child Neurology, 54*(12), 1114–1120. doi:10.1111/j.1469-8749.2012.04427.x

Tsai, C. L., Pan, C. Y., Cherng, R. J., Hsu, Y. W., & Chiu, H. H. (2009). Mechanisms of deficit of visuospatial attention shift in children with developmental coordination disorder: A neurophysiological measure of the endogenous Posner paradigm. *Brain and Cognition, 71*(3), 246–258. doi:10.1016/j.bandc.2009.08.006

Tseng, M. H., Howe, T. H., Chuang, I. C., & Hsieh, C. L. (2007). Cooccurrence of problems in activity level, attention, psychosocial adjustment, reading and writing in children with developmental coordination disorder. *International Journal of Rehabilitation Research, 30*(4), 327–332. doi:10.1097/MRR.0b013e3282f144c7

Van Waelvelde, H., & Miyahara, M. (2016). Environmental risk factors and children's motor performance. *Developmental Medicine & Child Neurology, 58*(8), 795–796. doi:10.1111/dmcn.13075

Vinay, L., Ben-Mabrouk, F., Brocard, F., Clarac, F., Jean-Xavier, C., Jean-Xavier, C., Pearlstein, E. & Pflieger, J-F.. (2005). Perinatal development of the motor systems involved in postural control. *Neural Plasticity, 12*, 131–139. doi:10.1155/NP.2005.131

Wang, C. H., Lo, Y. H., Pan, C. Y., Chen, F. C., Liang, W. K., & Tsai, C. L. (2015). Frontal midline theta as a neurophysiological correlate for deficits of attentional orienting in children with developmental coordination disorder. *Psychophysiology, 52*(6), 801–812. doi:10.1111/psyp.12402

Waszczuk, M. A., Leonard, H. C., Hill, E. L., Rowe, R., & Gregory, A. M. (2016). Coordination difficulty and internalizing symptoms in adults: A twin/sibling study. *Psychiatry Research, 239*, 1–8. doi:10.1016/j.psychres.2016.02.044

Whyatt, C. P., & Craig, C. M. (2012). Motor skills in children aged 7–10 years, diagnosed with autism spectrum disorder. *Journal of Autism and Developmental Disorders, 42*(9), 1799–1809. doi:10.1007/s10803-011-1421-8

Williams, J., Hyde, C., & Spittle, A. (2014). Developmental coordination disorder and cerebral palsy: Is there a continuum? *Current Developmental Disorders Reports, 1*(2), 118–124. doi:10.1016/j.humov.2010.04.006

Wilson, B. N., Kaplan, B. J., Crawford, S. G., Campbell, A., & Dewey, D. (2000). Reliability and validity of a parent questionnaire on childhood motor skills. *American Journal of Occupational Therapy, 54*(5), 484–493. doi:10.5014/ajot.54.5.484

Yoshida, S., Hayakawa, K., Yamamoto, A., Okano, S., Kanda, T., Yamori, Y., . . . Hirota, H. (2010). Quantitative diffusion tensor tractography of the motor and sensory tract in children with cerebral palsy. *Developmental Medicine & Child Neurology, 52*(10), 935–940. doi:10.1111/j.1469-8749.2010.03669.x

Zarrei, M., MacDonald, J. R., Merico, D., & Scherer, S. W. (2015). A copy number variation map of the human genome. *Nature Reviews Genetics, 16*(3), 172–183. doi:10.1038/nrg3871

Zwicker, J. G., Missiuna, C., Harris, S. R., & Boyd, L. A. (2010). Brain activation of children with developmental coordination disorder is different than peers. *Pediatrics, 126*(3), e678–e686. doi:10.1542/peds.2010-0059

Zwicker, J. G., Missiuna, C., Harris, S. R., & Boyd, L. A. (2011). Brain activation associated with motor skill practice in children with developmental coordination disorder: An fMRI study. *International Journal of Developmental Neuroscience, 29*(2), 145–152. doi:10.1016/j.ijdevneu.2010.12.002

Zwicker, J. G., Missiuna, C., Harris, S. R., & Boyd, L. A. (2012). Developmental coordination disorder: A pilot diffusion tensor imaging study. *Pediatric Neurology, 46*(3), 162–167. doi:10.1016/j.pediatrneurol.2011.12.007

SECTION III
Education and therapy

7

ADAPTED PHYSICAL ACTIVITY IN PHYSICAL EDUCATION

Martin E. Block

Introduction

The goals of the PE class are to instruct more efficient forms of movement, to build a positive attitude to being physically active, to create enjoyment of physical play in its various forms, and to find one's niche for lifelong involvement in physical activity – whether solo or team-based, whether on the playing field or pool-based, whether fitness or motor skill oriented, whether sports or recreational, adventure activities (Elliott, Stanec, & Block, 2016).

Inclusion is the philosophy of educating individuals with disabilities in classes with typically developing peers while providing the necessary support and services for all students to achieve their full potential (Block & Obrusnikova, 2016; Haegele & Sutherland, 2015). Inclusive education takes the responsibility away from the individual student for adapting his/her own learning style and calls for teachers to provide content in ways that encourage diverse learning, successful outcomes and promotes the abilities of all students. Inclusion principles can be successful, if the teacher of PE adopts a positive attitude and applies basic, well established pedagogy to cater for the spectrum of motor abilities in their class (Haegele & Sutherland, 2015).

Adapted physical activity in physical education

Students with disabilities often can be safely and successfully included in general physical education. However, the physical educator must be prepared to make modifications to how the class is organized, how information is presented, the equipment and organization used and how support personnel are utilized. Relatively simple instructional and curricular modifications can make a tremendous difference between success and failure for students with disabilities. For example, students with visual impairments would not understand what to do in physical education if you used only demonstrations. The simple addition of verbal cues would allow these students to be successful. Similarly, a simple accommodation in volleyball for a student with an intellectual disability who has limited strength is allowing the student to stand closer to the net and use a lighter, larger ball when it is his turn to serve.

The purpose of this chapter is to introduce a variety of instructional and curricular modifications to accommodate students with disabilities in general physical education. These modifications illustrate how subtle changes in how you organize your class and present information can better accommodate students with disabilities. The goal of these modifications is to allow all students, including students with disabilities, to participate in a general physical education setting that is safe and challenging and affords opportunities for success. Which techniques you choose to implement will depend on the particular needs of the student with disabilities, the age group you are working with, the skills you are focusing on, the make up of your class, availability of equipment and facilities, availability of support personnel, and your own preference. Although specific examples are provided, it is important that you focus on the general process of how to modify. You can apply this process to a variety of physical education activities and situations if you understand the general process of creating and implementing appropriate instructional and curricular modifications.

Universal models related to modifications

There are two general models for accommodating the needs of diverse learners – differentiated instruction and universal design for learning (UDL). These approaches are designed to account for the wide variability in skills, experiences and learning styles of students within the student body at-large and not just the student with a disability (Janney & Snell, 2013). However, making an effort to make sure all the students in a class are successful and challenged ultimately makes it easier to include students with disabilities. For example, a physical educator may feel intimidated by the prospects of accommodating a 10-year-old student with cerebral palsy who uses canes for walking into a soccer unit. However, using differentiated instruction this physical educator thinks of all the students as individuals with unique strengths and weaknesses and who all need some level of accommodation. There are different size balls for kicking, there are different distances to kick, and there are different size targets. Finally, students are encouraged to set individual goals such as trying to hit a small target 1/5 tries or a large target from 10 feet away 4/5 times. With all these accommodations designed to make sure all the students in the class are successful and challenged at their own levels, the physical educator realizes it is possible to accommodate the student with cerebral palsy.

Differentiated instruction

Differentiating instruction is a model where students are given different options in how they demonstrate understanding and knowledge and how concepts and content are presented (Huebner, 2010; Tomlinson, 2014). Differentiated instruction takes into account individual student readiness, abilities and interests when planning instruction (Gregory & Chapman, 2013; Janney & Snell, 2013). Tomlinson (2014) explained the difference between differentiated instruction and individualized instruction. Individualized instruction involves doing something different for each individual student, which can be extremely difficult in a classroom or physical education setting of 20 or more students. Differentiated instruction offers several options for students, but the model does not assume each individual student would need a separate, unique modification. For example, rather than creating a unique accommodation for a student with autism spectrum disorder (ASD) in a throwing/catching unit, the teacher proactively created a number of ways to experience, practice and measure success in throwing and catching for all students. Thus this student with ASD has the opportunity to be successfully included in the unit not by having unique, individual accommodations but by taking advantage of the planned differentiated options offered to all students in the class.

Differentiated instruction provides multiple choices to three specific areas related to instruction and learning: content, process and product (Janney & Snell, 2013; Tomlinson, 2014).

Content is what the student is expected to learn. Different levels of content can be offered to the students ranging from learning basic skills and a basic understanding of rules of games to advanced skills and team strategies. For example, team handball is presented in a secondary physical education class. Choices of content for passing includes (1) basic fundamental of passing and catching using larger, lighter balls (perhaps even foam balls) while standing stationary relatively close to your partner, (2) moving slowly and farther apart from your partner and (3) moving quickly and still farther away from your partner. Additional challenges, concepts and strategies would be offered to the students in the advanced group such as how to throw to avoid a defender. A student with ASD could be comfortably accommodated and included with a foam ball and standing close to his partner during the practice sessions. Additionally, more skilled peers can be rotated into the area with the lesser skilled students to provide extra instruction and feedback.

Process is how students make sense of the concepts and content presented. This includes providing differentiation in instructional strategies, materials used, conditions in which the student is expected to learn and activities presented. In physical education, instructional strategies might include verbal directions, demonstrations and visual cues such as pictures or video clips showing students how to perform the skill correctly. Some students understand what is expected with a simple verbal cue and demonstration, but others need pictures and videos to understand what is expected. The student with ASD from the example discussed (as well as other students who have limited experiences with team handball) would benefit from seeing a series of pictures showing the step-by-step process for throwing a handball, and slow motion video clips of skilled throwers would provide even more help to these lesser skilled students who are just being introduced to throwing a handball. Again, note how accommodations are planned ahead of time and not designed for any particular student, yet by differentiating all students those with disabilities are accommodated.

Product refers to how students demonstrate what they have learned. For example, with throwing a handball three types of product measurement are used: (1) demonstrating improvement in mastery of the components of a skillful throw, (2) demonstrating improved distance in throwing and (3) demonstrating improved accuracy when throwing. Since the teacher focuses on improvement, all students, regardless of their starting point, will have a chance to show improvement, from the student who shows improvement by mastering one component of the overhand throw, to another student who was close to mastery and shows improvement by mastering that last component, and finally to other students who already mastered all the components who are showing improvement through increased distance and accuracy. See Ellis, Lieberman, and LeRoux (2009) for additional examples of differentiated instruction applied to an inclusive physical education setting.

Universal design for learning (UDL)

Universal design is based on the philosophy that the physical environment and the activities engaged in within the environment, should be used by all individuals without adaptations or specially designed equipment (Null, 2014). Examples of universal design include door handles that are levers and not doorknobs (the latter would not require a person to reach, grab and turn the handle but instead simply pushing the handle down to open the door) and curb cuts which allow you to easily move into the street whether walking or using a wheelchair, pushing a baby stroller or riding a bicycle. UDL can be used in education settings (McGuire, Scott, & Shaw, 2006) and specifically in physical education settings (see Lieberman & Houston-Wilson, 2009 for more detail). Similar to differentiated instruction, UDL focuses on making the environment and program accessible to all students not just those from a single disability group (e.g., student who uses a wheelchair). For example, using UDL when teaching a unit on football, one has to consider what would be a single piece of equipment that could be used to (1) maintain the integrity of the game, (2) include all students and (3) address movement concerns? To answer this question, the teacher must be able to identify all the components of the game from: contextual (e.g., moving the ball across the pitch to score a goal or preventing the other team from scoring a goal), skills (e.g., dribbling, passing, shooting, defending), and student learning (e.g., rule and strategy modifications to make the game accommodating yet challenging for everyone). Again, UDL is not the same planning process when deciding how to "adapt" the game of football for a person who is visually impaired; UDL considers all students. The result of the analysis might be using a larger, softer, more brightly colored ball that still has the feel of a soccer ball for the more skilled students but is easier to see, easier to kick and safer for the less skilled students. In addition, universal rules include only allowing a player to score once in a game (this prevents one student from dominating the game and gives others a chance to score) and the creation of zones to teach positioning, eliminate the one dominant player and allowing a greater chance for everyone to touch the ball during the game.

Principles of universal design for learning

McGuire et al. (2006) suggested nine principles supporting UDL for instruction that can be applied to physical education and used to address the educational needs of students with disabilities. Block, Klavina, and Davis (2016) provided examples of how each of these UDL principles can be applied to a physical education setting (see Table 7.1).

Selecting appropriate modifications

Not all modifications are necessarily "good modifications." For example, making all players sit in chairs when playing volleyball to accommodate a student who uses a wheelchair would result in the other students not enjoying the volleyball unit, not learning and practicing the skills of volleyball, and most likely lead to peers resenting having this student in their class. Before implementing an instructional modification, it is important to determine whether a particular modification will truly help the student with disabilities without negatively affecting the experience of peers without disabilities. If the modification has a negative effect on any or all of these individuals, then it is not the most appropriate modification. Block et al. (2016) created the following three criteria whenever considering a particular modification:

1 *Does the change allow the student with disabilities to participate successfully yet still be challenged?* Finding the balance between success and challenge can be very difficult, but it is critical for students with disabilities. Not providing necessary accommodations can cause the student with disabilities to be confused or to fail, but providing too much support makes the activity too easy for the student. For example, a student with an intellectual disability might simply need a peer helper to find a kicking station, find a ball and then a safe place to stand and practice kicking into the wall, and finally occasional reminders on how to perform the kick and to stay on task and continue practicing. Other simple changes might include allowing the student with a disability to stand closer to the net when serving in volleyball, hitting a ball off a tee rather than a pitched ball in softball, and doing fitness activities differently than peers to accommodate limited strength and endurance. Note that these and similar accommodations are best presented via differentiated instruction where all students in the class have the option of using these modifications.

2 *Does the modification make the setting unsafe for the student with a disability or for peers?* Safety should always be a top priority when determining accommodations. Often relatively simple modifications can make the setting safer for all students. For example, an impulsive student often gets distracted by extraneous equipment

TABLE 7.1 Principles of universal design with application to physical education

Principle	Definition	Application to Physical Education
1 Equitable Use	Instruction is designed to be useful to and accessible by people with diverse abilities; provide same means of use for all students whenever possible	Use of color coded signs to direct movement around the play space (red=stop; green=go) coupled with auditory cues
2 Flexibility in Use	Instruction is designed to accommodate a wide range of individual abilities; provide choice in methods of use	Post pictures or short YouTube videos on exercise equipment demonstrating appropriate use of the machine; support with physical cues as needed. Allow students to select level of difficulty to engage equipment; maintain safety
3 Simple and intuitive	Instruction is designed to be straightforward. . . eliminate unnecessary complexity	Use of iPad videos of desired movement i.e. throwing; support with auditory (one word) and physical cues as needed
4 Perceptible information	Instruction is communicated effectively regardless of students' sensory abilities	Use of stations for activity (fundamental skills or exercise) combine with Principle #2 and provide pictures, videos, or tactile input with peers partners
5 Tolerance for error	Instruction anticipates variation in individual student learning pace and prerequisite	Provide students choices for distance, object, and movement to complete the task i.e. throwing at target, striking a ball, that become developmentally more challenging as they progress
6 Low Physical Effort	Instruction is designed to minimize nonessential physical effort in order to allow maximum attention to learning	*authors indicate this Principle may not apply to physical effort required of a course; in this case physical education
7 Size and Space for approach and use	Instruction is designed with consideration for appropriate size and space for approach, reach, manipulations, and use regardless of the student body size, posture, mobility, and communication needs.	Make sure to consider placement of equipment, entry and exit pathways, areas needed for students using wheelchairs, guide canes, scooters, and be sure to address high volume use of boom boxes, iPads, or videos.
8 A community of learners	The instructional environment promotes interaction and communication among students and between students and teacher	Color code sections of your work space to promote certain activities (blue – group discussions; green – sharing stories; yellow – creative ideas) then allow all students to engage these areas on their own
9 Instructional climate	Instruction is designed to be welcoming and inclusive	Consider using more assistive technology i.e., iPads, tablets, use of program Apps for instruction. Encourage students to teach peers, make their own instructional videos, or role play a sports scenario

such as mats stored to the side of the gym. He has been known to leave the group, climb on the mats, and then jump down before the teacher even knows he is gone. To accommodate this student (and others who have been distracted by the stack of mats), the teacher has stored the mats behind a curtain on a corner of the stage that is connected to the gym. Now the mats no longer distract this student and others in the class. Similarly, using foam balls prevents students from getting hurt by errant balls, and creating safe zones prevent peers from running into less skilled students. On the other hand, some modifications while well intended could actually pose safety issues. For example, a student who uses a wheelchair could be allowed to play in a basketball game. But giving free passes when passing the ball to a teammate and free shots when trying to score a point does not prevent peers from accidently running into the student's wheelchair. Modifications might include having the student play in the game but not go into the three-point arc area where there is a greater chance for contact with peers.

3   *Does the change affect peers without disabilities?* Accommodations that affect the entire class should be used cautiously. As noted earlier, having all students sit in chairs when playing volleyball "ruins" the game for everyone. While it would be fun to play the Paralympic sport of sitting volleyball (sitting on the floor and not in chairs) for a few minutes to introduce the class to the activity, playing sitting volleyball for the entire six-week volleyball unit would not be popular with most students in the class. Similarly, playing volleyball with a beach ball would help a student with slow reaction time and coordination problems, but this would drastically change the game for those who really want to play regulation volleyball. One way to accommodate different abilities is to have multiple games. There can be three volleyball courts set up with one for the more skilled students who play a regulation game, one for moderately skilled students who may use a larger, lighter volleyball and have minor rule changes (stand closer to net when serving, get two tries to serve over the net instead of one, no penalty for lifting or double hitting), and finally one for less skilled students where a beach ball is used some of the time and a larger, lighter volleyball is used some of the time. In this case, the net may also be lower and there are no real rules (students just try and hit the ball back and forth and learn the basic skills).

Instructional modifications

Instructional modifications are accommodations in how you present information and organize the setting. Instructional modifications are particularly important for students who may have difficulty understanding verbal instructions (e.g., those with ASD, intellectual disabilities or hearing impairments) and those who may be challenged by certain class formats (e.g., students with ASD in large group settings as compared to partner activities). This next section provides several suggestions for instructional modifications to accommodate students with disabilities. As noted earlier, it is always preferred to present modification through differentiated instruction for the entire class as opposed to a specific accommodation for the one student with a disability.

Teaching style

Teaching style refers to the learning environment, the general routine, and how the lesson is presented to the class. Mosston and Ashworth (2002) described several different teaching styles commonly used by physical educators that reflected decisions made by the teacher and by the student. On one side of the spectrum, teachers make all or most of the decisions for students regarding what to do, when to do it, how to do it, how long to do it, with whom (if anyone) to do it, and with what equipment to do it. These styles are referred to as *reproductive styles* because students are supposed to reproduce or replicate a particular movement pattern. For example, students learning how to shoot a basketball are given a basketball and asked to follow the step-by-step directions given by the teachers. The goal is for students to copy the teacher's pattern as accurately as possible. Students know exactly what they are supposed to do and teachers are more apt to have control over the class making these styles particularly appropriate for students with intellectual disabilities and ASD. The major disadvantage of these styles is that students are more passive rather than active learners, and students are less likely to be creative and discover unique and different ways to solve movement problems.

At the other end of the spectrum, students make most or all the decisions. Teaching styles on this side of the spectrum are referred to as *productive styles*, because students are supposed to produce or discover the most appropriate movement pattern to solve a particular movement problem. In some cases, there is no absolute right or wrong movement pattern, and students learn through discovery which pattern fits best with which particular situation. For example, a teacher might want her students to discover the best way to kick a football so that it lofted in the air. Students are encouraged to explore different foot placements and parts of the ball to kick and discover the best way to kick a ball to get it up in the air. In productive style teaching approaches students tend to be more invested in their learning and retain what they have learned longer. These approaches might be best for students who use wheelchairs or canes/crutches (e.g., students with cerebral palsy) who have motor challenges that do not allow them to perform skills like their peers. With the productive styles these students can experiment and explore until they find the best movement pattern that matches their unique movement skills and challenges.

Class formats

Class formats refers to how members of the class are organized. Seaman, DePauw, Morton, and Omoto (2003) outlined seven class formats commonly used in physical education settings:

1   One-to-one instruction: one teacher or assistant for every student
2   Small groups: 3–10 students working together with a teacher or teacher assistant
3   Large group: entire class participating together as one group
4   Mixed group: using various class formats within one class period

5   Peer teaching or tutoring: using classmates or students without disabilities from other classes for teaching and assisting students with disabilities
6   Teaching stations: several areas in which smaller subsets of the class rotate through to practice skills
7   Self-paced independent work: each student works on individual goals at his or her own pace following directions on task cards or with guidance from teacher and teacher assistants.

No class format is necessarily wrong or right. It is just important that the goals of your lesson match the learning needs of your class. You want to find the best class format to help your students (including the student with a disability) achieve your goals for the lesson. For example, a student with ASD may struggle in large class formats but will do better in small groups or with a partner. The physical educator can try to divide the group into smaller groups or use partners as often as possible to help this student cope in physical education.

Peer tutoring

Peer tutoring involves students helping students. Because it can be difficult for a general physical education teacher to work individually with students with disabilities, peers without disabilities can be trained and then assigned to provide extra instruction and support. In addition, peer tutoring creates a setting in which the student with a disability receives one-to-one instruction and increased practice and reinforcement (Lieberman & Houston-Wilson, 2009). Peer tutoring programs have been successfully applied to students with mild and moderate disabilities in physical education settings (e.g., Houston-Wilson, Dunn, van der Mars, & McCubbin, 1997; Lieberman, Newcomer, McCubbin, & Dalrymple, 1997; Lieberman, Dunn, van der Mars, & McCubbin, 2000), and also to students with severe and multiple disabilities (Klavina & Block, 2008). Peer tutoring often can replace the support of a paid teacher assistant, which can be cost effective for a school. In addition, peers provide more natural supports, increase social interactions and communication skills and maintain or enhance students' academic engagement (Klavina & Block, 2008). There are different types of peer tutoring the teacher can use including traditional *one-on-one peer tutoring* (one student supports the student with a disability), *classwide peer tutoring* (all students in the class are paired off and take turns serving as tutor or tutee), *small group tutoring* (4–6 students per group) with the student with a disability placed in a group that knows the student and is comfortable giving support, and *cross-age peer tutoring*, in which an older student from the same school or even a different school (e.g., student from a secondary school comes to the primary school 1–2 times per week to serve as a tutor).

Cooperative learning

Another class format option is *cooperative learning* in which students work together to accomplish shared goals. Group goals can only be accomplished if individual students in the group work together (Luvmor & Luvmour, 2013; Orlick, 2006). In cooperative learning, students are instructed to learn the assigned information and to make sure that all members of the group master the information (at their level). For example, each student in the group must perform a set number of push-ups for the team to reach its shared goal of 180 push-ups. One girl who is very strong and who is trying to break the school record is trying to do 100 push-ups. Another student in the group usually can do 35 push-ups, two other students in the group are trying to do 20 push-ups, and a student with an intellectual disability is trying to do 5 push-ups. In order for the team to be successful, each person must meet his or her individual goal. Members of the team encourage each other to reach these goals that, in turn, help the team reach their shared goals.

Often individuals in the group are given specific jobs or tasks that contribute to goal attainment. Cooperative learning encourages students to work together, help each other, and constantly evaluate each member's progress toward individual and group goals (Grineski, 1996). For example, in a gymnastics unit a team of four members must balance so that a total of two feet, two hands, two elbows, and two knees touch the ground. The team, which includes a student who is blind and has poor balance, together decides the best way to solve the challenge. After much discussion and experimentation, the team comes up with the following solution: The student who is blind stands on two feet and holds the ankles of another student who is standing on her hands (she needs the support or she will fall). Another student gets on his elbows and knees (feet up) while a fourth student sits on his back. The student sitting on his back helps balance the person standing on his hands. The only way this team could be successful was for everyone to work together.

Accommodations in how information is presented

Verbal instructions

Verbal instructions refer to the length and complexity of commands or verbal challenges used to convey information to the class. Students with a specific language impairment or intellectual disabilities who cannot understand complex commands or students with hearing impairments who cannot hear verbal commands may need to have instruction delivery modified. Seaman et al. (2003) suggested the following ways in which instructions can be modified for students who have difficulty understanding verbal language: simplify words used, use single-meaning words (e.g., run to the base versus go to the base), give only one command at a time, ask the student to repeat the command before performing it, say the command and then demonstrate the task and or physically assist the student. Although these modifications might be helpful for a student with a specific language impairment or an intellectual disability, such modifications might not be needed for the majority of students in the class. The physical educator can continue to give complex verbal directions including information about abstract strategies and team concepts to the class. When the teacher is finished instructing the class, a peer could repeat key directions to the student with an intellectual disability. The peer can demonstrate some strategies and concepts, while abstract concepts can be translated into more concrete examples or skipped altogether.

Demonstrations

Demonstrations can vary in who gives demonstrations, how many are given, how often they are given, and the best location for a demonstration. Modifications to demonstrations could be as simple as having students with poor vision stand close to the teacher. For students with intellectual disabilities, the teacher might need to highlight key aspects of the demonstration or have a peer repeat the demonstration several times. For example, the teacher could demonstrate the starting preparatory position, backswing, trunk rotation, and follow-through for the overhand throw to the class. For a student with an intellectual disability just learning to throw, the teacher (or peer) might repeat the demonstration, focusing on just one aspect (stepping with the opposite foot) so that this student knows what component he should focus on.

Visual supports

Many students with ASD are thought to be visual learners (Quill, 1997; Mesibov & Shea, 2008). Temple Grandin, a person with ASD who is now a successful college professor and author of several books, explained how she was a visual learner:

> I think in pictures. Words are like a second language to me . . . when some-body speaks to me, his words are instantly translated into pictures . . . One of the most profound mysteries of ASD has been the remarkable ability of most autistic people to excel at visual spatial skills while performing so poorly at verbal skills.
>
> *(Grandin, 1995, p. 19)*

To accommodate these visual strengths, many have suggested the use of visual support for students with ASD (e.g., Bernard-Opitz & Häußler, 2011; Bondy & Frost, 2011; Cohen & Sloan, 2008). *Visual supports* refer to any kind of visual prompt that helps a student understand and interact with his or her world (Bondy & Frost, 2011), and the use of visual supports to accommodate students with ASD in physical education has been recommended in several papers (Block & Taliaferro, 2014; Blubaugh & Kohlmann, 2006; Fittipaldi-Wert & Mowling, 2009; Green & Sandt, 2013). One study showed that visual supports significantly improved scores on the Test of Gross Motor Development (TGMD-2) in students with ASD compared to just a verbal cue or demonstration (Breslin & Rudisill, 2011). Visual supports help students understand and follow rules, know what is happening in their day, understand how to complete an assignment and when an assignment is complete, transition from one activity to another, and make choices about what they want.

Visual support also allows the student to become more independent (Bondy & Frost, 2011). There are many different kinds of visual supports that can be used in physical education.

- *Visual schedules:* Visual schedules set out a plan for the entire day, for part of the day, or for a particular class (e.g., for physical education). The amount of time as well as the number of activities placed on a schedule varies from student to student. Visual schedules are easily created for physical education. For example, a student with ASD is given a new physical education schedule each day. Before class, the physical educator places select pictures on a special clipboard. The pictures show the student doing various activities in the order in which these activities will be presented during physical education that day. Every time an activity is completed, the student is prompted to point to the next picture on the schedule. This type of schedule helps this student understand the physical education activities of the day.
- *Checklists/organizers:* Checklists and organizers break skills into manageable steps so that the student can complete them. Many students can complete the beginning or end of a task or perhaps one or two steps in the middle of a task. Checklists and organizers promote independence by prompting the student to remember and then execute the various steps needed to complete a task. For example, a checklist in physical education might have pictures of the 10 stretching and strengthening activities that all students are expected to do upon arrival into the gym. Checklists also can be used to help middle and high school students become more independent in the locker room by visually reminding them exactly what to do.
- *Visual behavioral supports:* Visual behavioral supports remind the student of behavior expectations. Visual behavioral support systems usually include the expected behaviors, such as how to act in physical education, along with reinforcement. For example, Samantha has trouble sitting and keeping her voice down when the teacher takes roll/the register at the beginning of her middle school physical education class. After Samantha changes into her physical education clothes and sits in her squad, she looks at her visual behavioral support (a file card she brings with her to physical education). The card has a small picture of Samantha sitting nicely in her squad. It also has a picture of a person with their mouth closed. A smiley face reminds Samantha that if she sits quietly in her squad during role/register, she will earn a star. Samantha has learned that if she receives five stars during physical education, she can help the general physical educator put the equipment away (a favorite activity of Samantha's). This visual behavior prompt allows Samantha to be more independent in general physical education and more responsible for her own behavior.
- *Countdown strips and visual timers:* Visual supports can also be very useful for keeping students on-task and help them know when a task is finished. Many students, particularly those with ASD and Attention deficit hyperactive disorder (ADHD), will be more inclined to stay on task if the activity has a clear,

observable end point. A countdown strip is a visual support that allows the students to countdown how many times they must complete an activity. This could be a simple visual such as a strip of paper, with the numbers 0 to 10. Each time an activity is completed (for example each time the student practices the overhand throw), the student moves a clothes peg to the next number until they have reached 0. An alternative strategy may be to stand up ten cones; each time the student completes the activity, he knocks down a cone. All the cones knocked down signify the task is complete.

Curricular modifications

Curricular modifications refer to any adaptation made to the general education curriculum in order to prevent a mismatch between a student's skill level and the lesson content and promote student success in learning targeted individual education program (IEP) objectives and appropriate skills (Block & Vogler, 1994; Giangreco & Putnam, 1991). Curricular modifications might include changes to equipment and changes to the rules of games. As with instructional modifications, changes that affect the entire class should be implemented cautiously to avoid negatively affecting the program for students without disabilities. However, as with instructional modifications, some changes that affect the entire class can be positive. Utilizing the differentiated instruction and universal design principles presented earlier in this chapter provides all students with more choices and opportunities to be successful yet challenged at their own levels. For example, rather than having a lower basket and smaller ball just for a student with a disability to accommodate limitations in strength, have multiple height baskets and multiple sized balls available for all students in the class to choose to match their unique levels of strength and coordination. No doubt there will be other students in the class besides the student with a disability who would be more successful and thus more motivated to try harder and to use proper basketball shooting technique if a lower basket and smaller ball were made available. The following presents modifications designed to accommodate students who present specific challenges related to success in physical education including limited strength, power, endurance and coordination.

Specific adaptations for students with impairments in strength, power and endurance

Lowering the target

Students who cannot reach a 10-foot basket in basketball can shoot at a 6- or 8-foot basket. Similarly, a student who cannot hit a ball over a regulation volleyball or badminton net can have the net lowered. By lowering the target, students will have a greater opportunity for success that in turn will encourage them to continue to practice the skill.

Reduce the distance

Many physical education activities require students to throw, pass, serve, or shoot a ball or run a certain distance. Distances can be reduced so students with disabilities can be successful. For example, safe spaces can be added to tagging games so that a student who walks with crutches can walk a shorter distance without concern for being tagged. For games that require running up and down an entire floor or field (e.g., basketball or soccer), games can be played using the width of the field rather than the length, or half court games can be played. Another modification that would not affect the entire class is allowing a particular student to play in just half the field (just play defense or offense), or place the student in a position that requires less movement (playing defensive back in soccer rather than midfielder; playing lineman in football rather than wide receiver).

Shorten/lighten racquets and balls

Students with limited arm or grip strength or who have smaller than normal hand size may have difficulty holding large/heavy striking implements or balls. Permitting this student to use a racquetball or badminton racket or a tennis racket with the handle cut off would allow this student more success. Some students might need to simply be encouraged to hold the racket a few inches from the bottom of the racquet to make it shorter. Similarly, balloons, beach balls, or foam balls can be a good substitute for balls that are too heavy or too intimidating for a student.

Use deflated balls or suspended balls

By their nature, balls tend to roll when put in motion. Balls that are deflated or paper balls (crumpled up piece of paper wrapped with a few pieces of masking tape) do not roll away. Also, balls suspended from a basket or ceiling or balls tied to a student's wheelchair are easy to retrieve.

Decrease activity time/increase rest time

Games and practice sessions can be shortened for students who fatigue easily. Students can be allowed to play for 5 minutes, then rest for 5 minutes, or all students play for 3 minutes, then rotate to an activity that requires less endurance. For example, a game of sideline basketball could be played in which three players from each team play for 3 minutes while the other players on each team stand on opposite sidelines prepared to assist their teammates. Another possibility is to allow free substitutions in a game. For example, a student with asthma can come out of a soccer game every 2 or 3 minutes.

Reduce speed of game/increase distance for peers without disabilities

Modifications can be made so that races and games are more equitable for students with limits in speed and endurance. For example, slower students in a relay race need only go up and back one time, while more skilled students go up and back two times. Similarly, a special zone in soccer can be marked off for a student who has limited speed. When the ball goes into the zone, this student is the only one who can kick the ball.

Specific adaptations for students with problems of coordination and accuracy

Use large, light, soft balls

Large balls are easier to catch and strike than smaller balls. If a student is unsuccessful or frightened of small, hard balls (e.g., softball) then the use of a large foam ball, balloon, or punch ball is appropriate.

Decrease distance ball is thrown and reduce speed

Reduce the distance that balls are thrown for students who have difficulty tracking balls. For example, some students might be allowed to hit a tennis ball tossed from 10 feet away while other students are expected to hit a ball tossed from 20 feet. Similarly, a ball can be tossed slowly for some students, faster for others, and still faster for more skilled students.

Strike or kick stationary balls

Allow students to first kick a stationary ball or strike a ball on a tee. Suspended balls that move at slower speeds and at a known trajectory are also easier than moving balls. Again, allow the student to be successful and demonstrate a skillful pattern with adaptations, then gradually fade away the adaptations as the student gains confidence and skill.

Increase the surface of the striking implement

Allow students to use lighter bats with a larger striking surface or a racket with a larger striking surface. Again, have a variety of striking implements for students to choose.

Use backstops

Students who miss the ball often may spend most of their time retrieving the ball rather than practicing the skill. This does not promote good use of practice time, and it can become very frustrating for the student. When working on striking, kicking, or catching activities, have a backdrop, backstop, net, or rebounder available. You can also attach a string to a ball and then to a student's wheelchair for ease of recovery.

Increase size of target

Allow students to throw or kick to larger targets, or allow students to shoot at larger baskets. In addition, give points for coming close to target such as hitting the rim or backboard in basketball. Less skilled students can be allowed to stand closer to the target in order to promote initial success, and then gradually allow them to move back as they become more accurate.

Use light, unstable pins when bowling

In games or activities in which the goal is to knock something down, use light objects (e.g., milk cartons, aluminum cans) so that any contact with the object will result in success. In addition, use more pins and spread them out farther than normal so that tosses or kicks that would normally miss the target still result in success.

Summary

Students with disabilities can have positive experiences in general physical education when physical educators are willing to make relatively simple instructional and curricular modifications. In many cases, modifications can and should be universally designed to accommodate the range of abilities seen in a typical physical education class from very skilled students to those who struggle to perform even simple motor skills. The goal of these modifications is to allow all students, including students with disabilities, to participate in a general physical education setting that is safe and challenging and affords opportunities for success and enjoyment. Which techniques you choose to implement will depend on the particular needs of the student with disabilities, the age group you are working with, the skills you are focusing on, the makeup of your class, availability of equipment and facilities and availability of support personnel.

References

Bernard-Opitz, V., & Häußler, A. (2011). *Visual support for children with autism spectrum disorders: Materials for visual learners.* Shawnee Mission, KS: AAPC Publishing.

Block, M. E., & Obrusnikova, I. (2016). What is inclusion? In M. E. Block (Ed.), *A teacher's guide to adapted physical education* (4th ed., pp. 19–34). Baltimore, MD: Paul H. Brookes Publishing.

Block, M. E., & Taliaferro, A. (2014). Assessment and the IEP process. In M. Grenier (Ed.), *Physical education for students with autism spectrum disorders* (pp. 47–62). Champaign, IL: Human Kinetics.

Block, M. E., & Vogler, E. W. (1994). Including children with disabilities in regular physical education: The research base. *Journal of Physical Education, Recreation, and Dance, 65*(1), 40–44.

Block, M. E., Klavina, A., & Davis, R. (2016). Instructional modifications. In M. E. Block (Ed.), *A teacher's guide to adapted physical education* (4th ed., pp. 93–124). Baltimore, MD: Paul H. Brookes Publishing.

Blubaugh, N., & Kohlmann, J. (2006). TEACCH model and children with Autism. *Teaching Elementary Physical Education, 17*(6), 16–19.

Bondy, A., & Frost, L. (2011). *A picture's worth: PECS and other visual communication strategies in autism* (2nd ed.). Bethesda, MD: Woodbine House.

Breslin, C. M., & Rudisill, M. E. (2011). The effect of visual supports on performance of the TGMD-2 for children with autism spectrum disorder. *Adapted Physical Activity Quarterly, 28*(4), 342–353.

Cohen, M. J., & Sloan, D. L. (2008). *Visual supports for people with Autism: A guide for parents and professionals*. Bethesda, MD: Woodbine House.

Elliott, S., Stanec, A., & Block, M. E. (2016). What is physical education? In M. E. Block (Ed.), *A teacher's guide to adapted physical education* (4th ed., pp. 3–18). Baltimore, MD: Paul H. Brookes Publishing.

Ellis, K., Lieberman, L., & Leroux, D. (2009). Using differentiated instruction in physical education. *Palaestra, 24*(4), 19–23.

Fittipaldi-Wert, J., & Mowling, C. M. (2009). Using visual supports for students with autism in physical education. *JOPERD: The Journal of Physical Education, Recreation & Dance, 80*(2), 39–43.

Giangreco, M. F., & Putnam, J. W. (1991). Supporting the education of students with severe disabilities in regular education environments. In M. H. Meyer, C. A. Peck, & L. Brown (Eds.), *Critical issues in the lives of people with severe disabilities* (pp. 245–270). Baltimore: Paul H. Brookes Publishing.

Grandin, T. (1995). *Thinking in pictures and other reports from my life with Autism*. New York: Vintage Books.

Green, A., & Sandt, D. (2013). Understanding the picture exchange communication system. *The Journal of Physical Education, Recreation & Dance, 84*(2), 33–39.

Gregory, G. H., & Chapman, C. M. (2013). *Differentiated instructional strategies*. Thousand Oaks, CA: Corwin.

Grineski, S. (1996). *Cooperative learning in physical education*. Champaign, IL: Human Kinetics.

Haegele, J. A., & Sutherland, S. (2015). Perspectives of student with disabilities towards physical education: A qualitative inquiry review. *Quest, 67*(3), 255–273. doi:10.1080/00336297.2015.1050118

Houston-Wilson, C., Dunn, J. M., van der Mars, H., & McCubbin, J. (1997). The effects of peer tutors on the motor performance in integrated physical education classes. *Adapted Physical Activity Quarterly, 14*, 298–313.

Huebner, T. A. (2010). Differentiated instruction. *Educational Leadership, 67*(5), 79–81.

Janney, R., & Snell, M. E. (2013). *Modifying schoolwork* (3rd ed.). Baltimore: Paul H. Brookes Publishing.

Klavina, A., & Block, M. E. (2008). The effects of peer tutoring on interaction behaviors in inclusive physical education. *Adapted Physical Activity Quarterly, 25*, 132–158.

Lieberman, L. J., Dunn, J. M., van der Mars, H., & McCubbin, J. (2000). Peer tutors' effects on activity levels of deaf students in inclusive elementary physical education. *Adapted Physical Activity Quarterly, 17*, 20–39.

Lieberman, L. J., Newcomer, J., McCubbin, J., & Dalrymple, N. (1997). The effects of cross-aged peer tutors on the academic learning time of students with disabilities in inclusive elementary physical education classes. *Brazilian International Journal of Adapted Physical Education Research, 4*(1), 15–32.

Lieberman, L., & Houston-Wilson, C. (2009). *Strategies for inclusion: A handbook for physical educators* (2nd ed.). Champaign, IL: Human Kinetics.

Luvmour, J., & Luvmour, B. (2013). *Everyone wins: Cooperative games and activities* (2nd ed.). Gabriola Island: New Society Publishers.

McGuire, J. M., Scott, S. S., & Shaw, S. F. (2006). Universal design and its applications in educational environments. *Remedial and Special Education, 27*(3), 166–175.

Mesibov, G., & Shea, V. (2008). Structured teaching and environmental supports. In K. D. Buron K. D., & P. Wolfberg P. (Eds.), *Learners on the autism spectrum: Preparing highly qualified educators* (pp. 114–137). Shawnee Mission, KS: Autism Asperger.

Mosston, M., & Ashworth, S. (2002). *Teaching physical education* (5th ed.). Upper Saddle River, NJ: Pearson Benjamin Cummings Publishers.

Null, R. (2014). *Universal design: Principles and models.* Boca Raton, FL: Taylor & Francis Group.

Orlick, T. (2006). *Cooperative games and sports: Joyful activities for everyone* (2nd ed.). Champaign, IL: Human Kinetics.

Quill, K. A. (1997). Instructional considerations for young children with autism: The rationale for visually cued instruction. *Journal of Autism and Developmental Disorders, 27,* 697–714.

Seaman, J. A., DePauw, K. P., Morton, K. B., & Omoto, K. (2003). *Making connections: From theory to practice in adapted physical education.* Scottsdale, AZ: Holcomb Hathaway.

Tomlinson, C. A. (2014). *The differentiated classroom: Responding to the needs of all learners* (2nd ed.). Alexandria, VA: ASCD.

8

PHYSICAL EDUCATION AND ACTIVITY IN CHILDREN AND ADOLESCENTS WITH DCD

Beth Hands and Helen E. Parker

Introduction

The primary aim for a physical educator or sports coach of children and adolescents is to find developmentally appropriate positive ways to ensure they engage with, rather than avoid, physical activity opportunities. The physical inadequacies of children with DCD, such as being a slow runner or unable to catch a ball, are very visible in the playground and physical education classes. In contrast, a student who has difficulties with mathematics or spelling is less visible to his or her peers. Public events that expose a student's physical inadequacies such as the school athletic or swimming carnival cause high levels of stress, anxiety and even psychosomatic illnesses (Wagner, Jekauc, Worth, & Woll, 2016). Yet engagement in the many sports related physical and social activities after school and on weekends is important to minimise social isolation.

The previous chapter presented the general principles of adapting physical activity in physical education. In this chapter we will focus on ways to include children and adolescents with DCD into physical activity opportunities in the school and community setting. Students with DCD will learn best in a supported environment in which the teacher or coach applies the principles of basic, effective teaching methods. It is likely that most students with DCD are included in regular PE classes rather than in specially segregated physical activity settings. Given that there is low recognition of this learning disability and access and funding for individual therapy programs are scarce, we present how inclusive PE classes can be designed and teaching methods adapted to improve motor competence and enjoyment of physical activity for children with DCD. The key, best practice principles for DCD interventions should be evidence-based, foster participation and prevent secondary consequences. In this regard, Camden, Wilson, Kirby, Sugden, and Missiuna (2014) highlighted evidence calling for programs "focusing on daily activities, teaching specific skills and fostering generalization of learning" (p. 153) and creating opportunities for children with DCD to experience a range of sports and leisure activities to 'find their niche'. A successful intervention approach is one that builds capacity among both parents and teachers via information and support for children rather than relying on scant resources for one-on-one or group therapy interventions. School-based PE provides the ideal avenue for this.

Recognising the student with DCD in schools

Teachers should be alert to students who are often alone in the playground, are socially isolated and tend to be on-lookers rather than participants. Many students with DCD develop strategies to avoid participation in physical activities to minimise exposure of their physical inadequacies such as discounting or devaluing physical activity, saying "This is boring" or feigning illness or injury, going to the toilet, acting out, or saying "I'm tired". These students actually mean that they cannot do these activities, they may look foolish or be laughed at, or they are not confident nor sure how to do it. Other coping strategies include choosing like-minded friends who do not enjoy sports, particularly in adolescence, when self-awareness of their physical limitations is heightened. Indeed, research highlights some distinctions in the ratings of adolescents who have differing degrees of motor competence, adolescents with poor motor competence rated the outcomes of physical activity participation, such as improving health and fitness, socialising and having fun, significantly less likely than their typically coordinated peers. Nevertheless, these outcomes were also ranked as highly important to them (Hands, Parker, Rose, & Larkin, 2016). Further, Barnett and colleagues (2012) found that while adolescent boys with poor motor competence desired to be more physically active than their current level they favoured recreational games and activities rather than competitive team sports. This is important information for high school PE teachers – finding the most suitable activity niche is critical to student engagement.

Conceptual framework for physical education teaching

Block (chapter 7) has outlined the general goals of Physical Education and the philosophy of inclusion in teaching sessions, which we also advocate. Furthermore, to engage and support students with DCD, effective PE teachers base their practice and instruction on key conceptual frameworks and principles. In the last chapter, Block introduced instructional and curricular modifications, differentiated instruction and the universal design for learning models. Here, we present alternative guiding frameworks for PE program design, teaching strategies and lesson formats which is a blend of two leading motor control models – the Systems Constraints Theory of Newell (1986, see chapter 3 of this volume) and the Task Ecological Framework of Gentile, Higgins, Miller, and Rosen (1975). Further, we introduce a developmental spectrum which considers age-related activities appropriate for students with DCD. Lastly, we review motor learning principles relevant for teaching students with DCD as advanced by Magill and Anderson (2014).

Unified ecological task rubric

Newell's (1986) Constraints Theory posits that the dynamic interplay of three factors – person, task and environment, mutually constrain (or enable) motor skill coordination. Applied to teaching, this model challenges the teacher to consider, firstly, the *student with DCD* – what capabilities and difficulties they bring to the PE class. Such aspects as current motor and fitness capabilities, their interests, motivation and temperament, their motor ability and their verbal ability provide essential information to support the learner.

Secondly, *characteristics of the task* to-be-learned should be analysed by the PE teacher. What dynamics, timing, speed and power demands are involved? What coordination complexities? What performance cues are required? What aspects should be simplified? Which are potential learning blockers? What elements should be simplified in the instruction and practice for graded success? Can choices in outcomes offer success to all? The third constraining factor is the *learning environment*. There are many aspects of the classroom environment that you can modify to create positive student engagement for all, such as, setting a positive class climate, instructional methods, types of practice, types of feedback, visual cues, teaching style and positive social support by peers. Task and Environment factors are specifically incorporated into the Task Ecological Framework of Gentile and colleagues (Gentile et al., 1975) via practical examples (see Tables 8.1 and 8.2).

The Unified Ecological Task Rubric denotes how the interaction of Task and Environment factors allows the teacher to map the variations of motor tasks within a skill to be mapped from easiest to most difficult and allows a comparison between tasks (see Tables 8.1 and 8.2), adapted from Magill and Anderson (2014). PE teachers can classify any motor skill, from easier or simpler to harder or more complex to perform. Therefore, by locating a motor skill to-be-learned within the rubric and considering which elements (either Task or Environment) make it less difficult the teacher of PE can systematically organise learning tasks from simple to complex, in easy steps suited to the student with DCD.

The *Task factor* considers body movement (whether stable or in motion/moving) and implement used (whether none or ball, bat). In this rubric the *Learning Environment* factor highlights the source of performance cues (closed task or open task) and their stability (fixed or variable). Cues in a stable or closed environment are internally paced and predictable, whereas cues in an open or moving environment such as a game situation are externally paced and less predictable. In open game environments, such as in football or basketball, the player must concentrate on what is happening around them and has less time to concentrate on how to perform the skill. Consider the examples in the following rubrics. Table 8.1 maps the relative simplicity or complexity within an exemplar sample skill. Table 8.2 compares different motor tasks.

TABLE 8.1 Unified ecological task rubric – mapping progressions within a skill e.g., basketball lay up

			Task Factors			
			Body Stable / Stable stance		Body Moving / Locomoting	
			No implement	Implement/Ball used	No implement	Implement/Ball used
Learning Environment	Stable cues (Closed)	No variability	Practice forward and reverse pivot on right foot	Ball dribbling on the spot	Walk through 3-step lay up pattern; Agility and cut runs using marker cones for run through	Walk through 3-step and lay up with ball; Dribble ball around cones
		Variable cues	Coach calls randomly forward and back pivot direction	Ball dribbling on the spot with stationary defender shielding area	Defence players in various static positions on court in run through zone	Walk through lay up from different angles on each run-through; defence players in static positions
	Moving cues (Open)	No variability	Not relevant	Ball dribbling on the spot; stationary defender shielding R and L sides alternately; or 2 R; 2 L, etc.	4:1 drill Defence players in known positions and move in consistent same direction each time; evade run through to keyway	4:1 Defence in fixed positions; Dribble with ball during run though
		Variable	Not relevant	Ball dribbling on spot; stationary defender randomly shielding R & L sides trying to reach in for bouncing ball	4:1 drill Defence players move in variable patterns; try to block evasive run though	4:2 drill Full play; game context – receive ball up field and drive for goal and layup

TABLE 8.2 Unified ecological task rubric – comparing different skills

		Task Factors			
		Body Stable/ Stable stance		Body Moving/ Locomoting	
		No implement	Implement/Ball used	No implement	Implement/Ball used
Learning Environment	Stable cues (Closed) — No variability	Gymnastics – Balance scale;	Hit ball off a tee; weights machine; stationary exercise cycle	Footprint markings for locomotor task; hopscotch; Swimming strokes	Archery to target; kick ball into goal – soccer
	Variable cues	Balance game on coloured spots (twister)	Horse riding; track cycling	Running among cones in an agility course	10 pin bowling; Rock climbing; soccer goal with active goalie to defend ball
	Moving cues (Open) — No variability	Dance gestural movements; martial arts moves	Hula hoops; Rhythmic gymnastics ribbon	Partner dance routine; Cheerleading routine	Tennis rally from ball machine
	Variable cues	Wii skiing game	Surfing; Mountain biking	Tag game 1:1; or more players	Coach hitting balls for forehand practice Tennis game

Developmental spectrum

Students with DCD report less enjoyment of PE than do other children (Cairney et al., 2007). However, if teachers and coaches engage students with DCD in appropriately chosen physical activities, where accommodation of motor skill level is made, they may build positive perceived (and sometimes actual) motor competence and enhance their enjoyment of physical activity. The developmental spectrum in Table 8.3 presents age-related activity foci, performance constraints and identifies appropriate activities for students with DCD.

Motor learning principles

To teach motor skills effectively, the PE teacher will assimilate key motor learning principles that relate to instructions, practice and feedback (see Magill & Anderson, 2014). In the previous chapter, Block described the difference between differentiated and universal design for learning (individualised) instruction applied to the content, process and product of learning. This section expands on how UDL for learning is applied within inclusive PE settings.

Instructions

Teacher instructions create focus and motivation for learning. The PE teacher states the goal of the session (e.g., Who saw the cricket match on TV? Lots of hits go along the ground. A fielder must run around behind to trap the ball. Did you see that? Today, we're going to learn to trap a rolling ball and throw it back underarm to the wickets). They use meaningful simple language and give brief verbal instructions to convey key teaching points (e.g., watch the ball to your hands, fingers down to grass; get behind the ball). Use picture words/phrases (e.g., your hands are a scoop, a small basket). Show via demonstration (e.g., look at how I bend my knees, fingers to ground, little fingers crossed over; Be my shadow and copy). Use physical modelling (e.g., help your partner – place their finger tips on the grass; overlap their little fingers; position behind rolling ball; change over).

Of course, children learn in different and individual ways. Contemporary approaches to PE curriculum emphasise instructing from a capability-based (also called strength-based) perspective with students. This approach treats the student as an individual whose motor learning is contingent on their current learning, their needs, strengths and level of performance, and not on age-based expectations of typical motor skill competency. Some students with DCD may first be able to verbally describe, draw or write how to perform a task before being able to perform it efficiently. Their linguistic strengths enable them to make greater gains when language is the mediating role in teaching skills (Green, Chambers, & Sugden, 2008). For them, Q&A strategies may be used to check for understanding of how to perform a skill (e.g., Tell me what you need to do to make a soft landing when you

TABLE 8.3 Developmental spectrum for students with DCD

	Early Childhood Kindergarten to Year/Grade 2	Middle Childhood Year/Grade 3–5	Late Childhood Year /Grade 6–7	Adolescence Year/Grade 8+
Key sport focus	SKILL DEVELOPMENT and MASTERY OF FUNDAMENTAL MOTOR SKILLS (FMS)	MODIFIED GAMES, SPORTS and CONSOLIDATION	MODIFIED GAMES, SPORTS and SKILL	SPORTS, GAMES AND RECREATIONAL SKILLS
Performance constraints	Simple skills in closed, stable environment Body management/ balance skills	Minor games in more open, moving environment. Implements/objects used	Modified sports	Modified youth sports. Indoor and outdoor recreational pursuits
Sports/Activities most suited to students with DCD	Learn to swim, Sledding simple challenges/non-competitive games FMS – run, skip, leap, gallop, jump, throw, catch, bounce, kick, roll, dodge	Swimming, Sledding, dance, gymnastics, martial arts, multi-sports	Swimming, martial arts, soccer, sailing, outdoor education Avoid sports that involve odd shaped balls (rugby, grid iron), small balls (baseball), bats or racquets	Swimming, soccer, dance, martial arts, long distance running, outdoor education– canoeing, hiking, cross-country skiing, cycling, fitness gyms Solo, non-competitive pursuits are easier than team sports

jump?).You seek responses such as – "swing my arms, land on toes, bend my ankles and knees, and look ahead", performance cues that you used in your instructions. Others may find music that is the same rhythm as the skill (e.g., skipping, marching, galloping) is helpful.

Visual imagery as a mediator of performance

Raymond was participating in a movement enhancement program to help improve his coordination. He had ASD and very little control of his body. One day the group was playing "Musical Statues" except this time the spotter was a Tyrannosaurus Rex that can only catch and eat his prey if he can see them move. Raymond had just been to see the movie Godzilla. When the music stopped and T-Rex turned to face the group – Raymond was able to freeze every single muscle group – his arms, legs, eyes, eyelashes! He had the mental image and could translate it perfectly to the task.

Practice

Motor learning theory also guides the most effective ways to practice and master a skill and for students with DCD, progression in practice is typically slower than their peers. Simpler versions of a task are the scaffold to more complex whole task learning (see rubric in Table 8.1) and provide revision steps at the next session. A number of practice principles that could be applied when teaching children with DCD are **part practice before whole** skill practice (e.g., elements of ball handling and dribbling before running layup to shoot a basket); **simple to complex** practice (e.g., set shot from set positions to receiving ball on the run, pivoting, cutting through defender screen to basket); **slower before faster** pace practice (e.g., walking before cut-running at pace); **stationary before dynamic** cues (e.g., pivoting, dribbling on the spot before mobile dribbling and pivoting to avoid a defender); and **task generalisation** through context variations (e.g., over-arm throw pattern is common to volleyball and tennis serve).

A PE teacher should be mindful that repetition is the key to skill improvement and consider class format, student groupings, and equipment availability to maximise frequent practice attempts. Repeated, **quality practice** of achievable steps with relevant, **coherent feedback** are important factors to enhancing skill acquisition for students with DCD.

Feedback

An effective teacher gives feedback in a way that is meaningful and maximises the learning for each student. It is important to consider its **timeliness** (if too delayed the student forgets what they did) and whether given to an **individual or group** (feedback to the individual is more meaningful, although a common performance error can be conveyed to the whole group). Feedback should be **coherent** with the previous teaching points, such as a student concentrating on a soft hand contact, as instructed, may be confused by feedback drawing attention to body posture. Finally, various **modalities** of feedback such as visual, verbal, or tactile should be used. Some examples of the various way in which information can be provided for students with disabilities are given by Block in the previous chapter. Students with DCD may have difficulty translating visual demonstrations and/or verbal feedback into an appropriate kinaesthetic response. Even visual feedback such as demonstrating a task may be a challenge particularly if the teacher or coach is facing them and they need to mirror the movement. Often appropriate tactile, physical guidance is the most effective. For example, gently move their arm or leg through the proficient pattern of movement, touch the arm they use to throw the ball or the leg they use to kick.

Teaching approaches

Learning fundamental motor skills has been described as the founding alphabet of physical literacy (Gallahue, Ozmun, & Goodway, 2012) providing students with a repertoire of movement patterns that can be applied and generalised across sporting or recreational activities. Much research on DCD shows that without targeted intervention, those with DCD are unlikely to improve their motor skill efficiency (Cantell, Smyth, & Ahonen, 1994). This section covers the task specific approach to PE teaching, the importance of identifying motor difficulties and how to systematically modify the task challenge.

Task specific instruction

Intervention programs for students with DCD traditionally are classified as either process, 'deficit-oriented' or the task 'specific functional' approaches (Sugden, 2007). Teaching students with DCD in PE is most successful via the task-oriented approach which concentrates on the development of functional skills, sometimes with a particular skill in mind, such as riding a bike or playing volleyball (Revie & Larkin, 1993; Sugden & Chambers, 2003) or sometimes with a focus on task groupings, such as ball, kicking or balance skills (Mannisto, Cantell, Huovinen, Kooistra, & Larkin, 2006).

When the focus is on a specific skill, basic motor competency and confidence in managing one's own body is built by direct instruction. The priority is usually on functional skills of the playground considering those with which a student experiences problems and those they wish to learn, e.g., swim freestyle, run fluently, jump high, catch or strike a ball or boot-scoot (Schoemaker, Neimeijer, Reynders, & Smits-Engelsman, 2003; Sugden, 2007).

For younger students, teaching of fundamental motor skill groupings, such as, locomotor, body management and object control skills, provides an opportunity to develop those beneficial, foundation motor patterns from which basic game skills can be developed. For example, the teacher instructs the key teaching points of the catch but then introduces variations of the skill (ball size, distance, ball path) to challenge and extend the student's learning in a sequential way. The following boxes elaborate sequential practice for learning to trap and catch a ball, and dribbling a ball, from easy to difficult; from simple (closed, body stationary) to more complex (open, body moves to intercept).

Sequential practice – trapping and catching – closed, body stationary

Trap a rolling ball. *Teaching points (TP): watch ball, bend low, hands behind ball, finger towards ground, grip ball*

1   Practice of ball rolled directly to child.
2   Increase challenge by rolling ball a bit faster, or by varying the angle so player runs off a central spot. It requires concentration and visual motor tracking.

Catching. *Teaching points: watch ball into hands, grasp with hands, thumbs behind like a web, and give with elbows.*

1   Large ball, then medium ball thrown directly, but softly to student (simple).
2   Change to smaller ball thrown directly to student.
3   Once reliably catching, throw ball higher or lower to practice hand positioning (*Additional TPs – fingers high, fingers low*).
4   Vary throw to either side of central position (*Additional TP – Move feet to get in line with ball path*).
5   Combine 3 and 4, child learns to move quickly and to reach out to grip and control the object.

Throughout, the PE teacher reinforces the common TPs – "watch the ball, move body behind it, extend arms to ball, grip and give". The teacher can focus on one-to-one coaching for the child with DCD and their less skilled peers while scanning the whole class performing the activity.

Sequential practice – dribbling the ball – open, body in motion

The student wants to be able to dribble a ball and play basketball in the playground games (an object control task, dynamic movement, open variable cues). He can barely bounce and catch a ball with two hands while standing still – he has difficulty with adequate force control, hands are stiff, rather than fingers being the last to push the ball, he uses extended arms through the action of bouncing, elbows are stiff; he hugs the rebounded ball to catch.

1   Place the student close to a wall and show them how to bounce the ball against the wall and catch it. They can stand as close as they like to be successful. They are in control!
2   Focus on learning the correct force for rebound height – practice releasing ball to rebound at knee height, then waist height, then shoulder height to learn different force required emphasising fingers and wrist action at release with elbows tucked by side.
3   Focus on hand contact – like a cap covering top of ball. Control of ball with two hands.
4   Push ball with one hand – at knee, waist, chest height but still catch with 2 hands.
5   Progress to repeated bouncing at waist height, from 2 to 3 to 5 bounces in a row etc., with control.
6   Increase challenge by varying number of repetitions and bounce height combinations – e.g., 3 bounces at waist height, then 3 at knee height; 2–3–2 and so on.

Therefore, when initially teaching a motor skill, the effective PE teacher will adapt the demands of the task to match the students' current capabilities and previous learning. How do you achieve this? Consider the following aspects – diagnostic performance analysis and modifying the challenge.

Diagnostic performance analysis

PE teachers should systematically observe the motor performance of the student with DCD to identify their general difficulties and which particular elements of the task are deficient. A diagnostic analysis of the performance by the teacher is critical not only for the student with DCD but also for novice performers in the class (Larkin & Parker, 2002). It is inadvisable to set up a formal skill testing session, as this further stresses the student with DCD and takes time away from learning and

TABLE 8.4 Diagnostic matrix for sprint run performance (a continuous action)

Overall learning goal	Components	Phase of action	Dynamic	Motor fitness
To run fast and efficiently	Leg action Head and eyes Trunk posture Arm action Breathing rhythm	Foot strike/ support Recovery Flight Landing	Speed Stride length Gait width Stable head and trunk Amplitude and direction of forward knee lift and swing Amplitude and direction of arm swing	Leg strength and power Hip flexibility Anaerobic power Endurance

practice. Observation can be done informally while the child is playing with others, in the playground or during skill practices in PE class.

Table 8.4 is an example of a diagnostic performance checklist for the PE teacher, guiding the focus of observation on four performance elements – components, phases, dynamics and motor fitness. Locomotor or swimming tasks (continuous skills) can be observed across repeated cycles of the action (Table 8.4). The run may be slow and awkward because the child's eyes are not focusing forward and their head is unstable; their arms may be flailing out to the side; poor leg strength means the stride is short and uneven. Diagnostic analysis allows the teacher to concentrate teaching on the primary causes of performance inefficiency.

Modifying the learning challenge

PE has traditionally been taught from a normative perspective (Wilson, 2005), such that pupils learn to reproduce movement patterns to look 'normal'. However, with our greater understanding of interacting performance constraints (see the earlier discussion), especially as expressed in the DCD population, effective physical educators increasingly adapt and modify the learning task and the learning environment in consideration of the student's capabilities.

It is important to provide activities in a way all students can achieve success (also see previous chapter by Block). This can be achieved by differentiating or varying the levels of challenge to ensure it is appropriate to each student's level of achievement, or by grouping the students in ways best suited to the activity. Often, it is most successful to group the students according to their ability and then individualise the activity, examples are in Tables 8.5 and 8.6. For students with DCD, providing cues for learning is important. These cues could be auditory or visual and draw attention to the necessary sensory input. Image phrases can often trigger a more proficient movement pattern (e.g., when balancing "use your arms like airplane wings"). Physical reminders are also helpful. These include tying a ribbon around a preferred foot, or placing a small dot on the preferred throwing hand.

TABLE 8.5 Varying the demands or rules of the task

	Skill Example	Simpler, Easier	More Complex, Harder
Demands	Balance	Hands outstretched Eyes open Flat surface	Hands on hips Eyes closed Small block
Rules	Volleyball	Bounce the ball once Catch the ball	No bounce
Count	Catch	5 successful catches	15 successful catches
Teaching cues	Throw or kick	Visual cues such as foot shapes for starting position Picture cards	No foot marking
Path of ball	Throw or roll	Along the ground	In the air
Distance	Throw for accuracy Run	Close to target Run 30 metres	Further from target Run 50 metres
Playing Area	Tag	Large playing area	Small playing area
Time	Bounce a ball	5 bounces in 15 seconds	5 bounces in 5 seconds
Number of players	Tag	Many players (greater chance of tagging, despite lower agility)	Fewer players (less chance of tagging, greater physical demands)

TABLE 8.6 Varying the equipment

	Example	Simpler Easier	More Complex Harder
Size/Width of target	Soccer goal	Big Wide	Little Narrow
Height of target	Goal post	Low	High
Number of targets	Skittles	Many	Few
Size	Ball Racquet	Large (balloon, basketball) Large hitting surface	Small (tennis ball) Small hitting surface
Length of handle of bat/racquet	Tennis racquet	Short	Long
Height of equipment	Incline board beam	Low	High
Weight	Tee-ball bat	Light	Heavy

Some studies have shown that simple playground markings increase the physical activity level of children (Ridgers, Stratton, Fairclough, & Twisk, 2007). Such strategies could also engage students with DCD in more physical activity. Table 8.5 and 8.6 summarise modifications to task and equipment appropriate to students with DCD, also discussed in the broader context of adapted physical education in the previous chapter by Block.

Teaching styles

Of necessity, the teacher should use different teaching styles for different student outcomes. Block discussed the Mosston and Ashworth (2002) teaching styles spectrum in the previous chapter. We explain how particular styles from that spectrum are relevant for students with DCD. Table 8.7 identifies those styles which are most appropriate in teaching students with DCD, noting that in each cluster each successive style becomes more student-centric and less teacher-centric.

Command and practice

In the command and practice styles the teacher decides the content, instructs the student via demonstrating the skill accompanied with verbal instructions and sets the form of practice. The student practices the skill and the teacher/coach provides specific feedback coherent with the key teaching points. For new, unskilled students (those with DCD) when the goal is to teach a particular, efficient motor pattern (swim stroke) and for skills where an element of danger or injury risk is a factor if the task is wrongly performed (shot put, FMS, gymnastics, swimming, sports skills with implements), these styles are very appropriate. Teachers focusing on *task-specific instruction* (see the next paragraph) often rely on these traditional styles. These formal, direct instruction styles often become copy-and-drill with the student being required to reproduce the model action. For students with DCD this can be an impossible goal and highly demotivating. They struggle to coordinate limbs in the fluid, normal motor pattern. A student with DCD needs more inventive, individualised approaches to PE instruction that encourage cognitive-motor engagement and recognise that some variations to the 'normative' movement pattern are perfectly acceptable motor solutions.

Reciprocal

The reciprocal teaching style groups peers to instruct each other (also see the previous chapter section on Peer Tutoring). It is effective in enhancing inclusion and

TABLE 8.7 Outline of Spectrum of Teaching Styles (Mosston & Ashworth, 2002)

Reproduction Teaching Styles (replicate a specific model – concrete facts, rules, specific skills)	Production Teaching Styles (discover new movements – problem solving, creating, inventing, critical thinking)
Command*	Guided discovery*
Practice*	Convergent discovery*
Reciprocal*	Divergent discovery*
Self-check	Individual program-learner design
Inclusion*	Learner-initiated
	Self-teaching

* Most commonly used styles in PE – shaded are most appropriate for students with DCD

learning (Houston-Wilson, Dunn, van der Mars, & McCubbin, 1997; Ward & Ayvaso, 2006). For older students with DCD, in particular, it is likely that their class peers could tutor motor skill techniques under guidance of the PE teacher. Peer-coaches can provide instructional assistance to students with DCD, which naturally leads to more frequent instruction of key teaching points, feedback and motivation. In using this approach, the teacher needs to prepare the class for the purposes of this approach, and the explicit role for the 'pupil teacher' and the 'pupil learner'. Roles are reversed by the duos or trios within teaching and practice episodes, so that the student with DCD also acts as 'teacher' and can cognitively reinforce their knowledge of the skill by helping another.

In the disability literature, trained peer tutors, have been shown to enhance PE experiences of students with disabilities (Houston-Wilson et al., 1997; Ward & Ayvaso, 2006). Recent, research also confirms that positive skill learning comes from having the intention to teach. It is intriguing to consider that peer teaching/reciprocal strategies advantage both students, including those with DCD, as they take turns being the learner and the teacher in practice dyads.

Guided discovery

Guided discovery is a pedagogical approach that promotes skill practice with greater cognitive engagement and problem solving in students. They learn to discover new ways of moving or new strategies for achieving goals (such as rock climbing, outdoor pursuits, games strategies, or dance routines). One advantage of this approach to teaching is an individualised movement solution/response to a common movement challenge, students work at their own level, students are not singled out by failing to meet a too-difficult motor challenge, pupil motivation and confidence to have a try is encouraged, and the class climate is supportive and non-threatening. Consequently, for students with DCD, success is framed at the individual level rather than at a seemingly impossible performance standard. The PE teacher readily and naturally caters for the range of motor competency within the class.

For example, challenge instructions from the teacher may be "Show me a balance on your feet and two hands; can you remove one foot and stay balanced? Now what about one hand? How about balancing on your knees? Can you now show me three ways you could support your weight?" Each student responds at their own level and with their movement solution including the student with DCD. There is neither a single answer nor one correct answer. They are learning 'in', 'through', and 'about' movement (Arnold, 1979).

Regardless of teaching style adopted teachers should also consider the following:

- Minimise any pressure to publicly demonstrate a skill. Alternatively, if you know they can verbalise the information ask them to tell the class.

  o Q: what do you need to remember when throwing a ball a long way?
  o A: Stand side-on, bring my arm down and back and step forward with this leg!

- Be patient. Sometimes it is one step forward then two steps back.
- Give students choice in the task and allow them to spend time practicing a task they enjoy or need to improve.
- Provide a meaningful explanation about why a skill is best performed in a certain way, why it is useful to do a particular activity.
- Acknowledge and accept a student's negative feelings and welcome their thoughts, feelings, goals and behaviours (Katartzi & Vlachopoulos, 2011).
- When possible, stand close to those students with difficulties.

Curriculum approaches

Research specifically testing the effectiveness of PE curriculum approaches for students with DCD is relatively rare (Caçola & Romero, 2015; Larkin & Parker, 2002; Smits-Engelsman, Blank et al., 2013). From practical experience, the following approaches have some promise in engaging older students with DCD along with skill improvement, positive participation and attitudinal outcomes.

Activity stations

Activity or play stations enable a range of learning and practice activities in the one lesson with each station providing more practice opportunities than one where all the class completes the same learning activity. The station approach allows for effective use and distribution of PE equipment when the amount of equipment is scarce. Small student groups (5–6) rotate around the activity stations after a fixed period of time during the lesson.

This allows the teacher flexibility in how to assist those with difficulties.

- Rotate with the least able students to provide extra assistance.
- Base yourself at the activity that is most challenging for students with DCD.
- Balance your time among each of the stations.
- Base yourself at a single station and offer individual feedback to each student as they practice that task.

Key features of activity stations:

- Arrange the activity space into a grid – for example 2 x 3 grid of 3m squares.
- Organise small group learning activities. The students very quickly learn how to set up stations.
- Divide the class into six (or fewer) small, like-ability or peer paired groups.
- Demonstrate the learning activity for each group. Each grid square offers a different learning activity. Ensure each activity can be individualised to vary the challenge. This ensures success for all. Task cards illustrating the activity station and activities can be provided.
- Each group performs the learning activity for a defined length of time e.g., 10 minutes then rotates to the next station.

Sport education

Sport education curriculum models have gained popularity as a student-centred means of engaging students of all abilities in meaningful physical activity. It developed in response to the unintended effect of focusing on sports skill performance and competition games, which inevitably excluded the less skilled, less confident and de-motivated class members.

It is called SEPEP (Sport Education in Physical Education Program) and introduces students to all roles within sport. For an example, see www.achper.org.au/blog/blog-sepep-revisited. There are many practical resources and examples freely available on the internet (Presse, Block, Harvey, & Horton, 2011).

Key features of this model are:

- Team sports such as soccer, basketball, volleyball, softball.
- Students actively investigate the sport – skills, rules, game tactics/strategies, social importance and history of the sport.
- Students take on a variety of leadership roles in addition to being players – sports board, team captain, coach, first aid advisor, the publicity officer, records keeper, coordinator organising competition fixtures, referee, and rules and disputes officer in addition to player.
- Even teams are selected – ability, gender, physique; team members remain with that team for the whole competition 'season' (typically one term or semester).
- Rules are modified as required e.g., for small sided team games.

Sport education in practice

Paul, a secondary specialist PE teacher is new to the school, has been allocated a class of 32, 14-year-old boys and girls among whom are three youths with motor learning difficulties (DCD). He has been warned that this class is difficult, de-motivated and has a higher than usual withdrawal from PE class. Their previous PE teacher was a traditionalist who ran drills and skills classes, with a boot-camp atmosphere. This teacher was unconcerned by the same cluster of bench warmers, including the three with coordination difficulties, who brought sick-notes from parents to excuse them from participating. How could Paul turn these pupils onto PE class and to introduce them to the joy and fun of playing again?

- Discussion with class about their sporting interests – he runs with their real interest in the soccer World Cup.
- Paul plans a 10-week, semester-long soccer program using the sport education approach.
- Forms mini clubs with weekly, 5-a-side, round-robin soccer matches culminating in the final.

- Class members will take on varying roles as well as player to support their 8-member clubs.
- Balance ability, gender and physical size and students choose roles of skill coach, fitness trainer, referee as well as player.
- Across the weeks of the program, basic skill coaching and fitness activities are developed by both Paul and class members.
- Coaching activities are instructed by the 'club' officials and teachers rules as they get along. Paul is a facilitator of learning activities.
- Class teaching becomes less teacher-centric and more student-centric across the semester.
- 'Club' officials devise their own new skill and fitness activities and work on playing strategies for the mini-games.
- The referee practices rule adjudication and schedules playing fixtures in concert with the other clubs' referees.
- The unit of work culminates in celebration of all roles and contributions are acknowledged and celebrated.
- An authentic context in which students learn to value the contributions of a variety roles that enable sport to run.

Fitness education and health

One PE approach that is pertinent to adolescents is that of fitness education. This curriculum approach taps into what teenagers across a spectrum of motor abilities perceive as important to them and likely to be an outcome from being physically active. Our research has shown that adolescents with DCD rated the same health and fun outcomes as highly likely and highly important compared to their motor competent peers (Hands et al., 2016). When teenagers with DCD participate in gym work, they are doing something that is meaningful, individualised and non-judgmental, and the fact they are in a group setting is beneficial for feelings of inclusion (Caçola & Romero, 2015). A fitness education approach provides knowledge, skills and motivation in an authentic setting that is also readily available in many communities for post-school participation. Much of the equipment in a gymnasium, such as the pin-loaded machines constrains the movement pattern so that specific muscle groups can be exercised.

Key features:

- Individualised health-related fitness goals in strength, endurance, flexibility.
- Initial evaluation and measurable progress.
- Self-evaluation of progress on one's own goals rather than class rankings or averages.
- Peers can partner to support and encourage each other.

- Direct instruction, command, practice styles of teaching to instruct the correct technique.
- Increase repetitions and keep weights low to ensure safety and avoid injury.

New game-based technologies such as Wii Fit or WiiGames may also assist in building motor fitness, or enhancing skills in children with DCD (Ferguson, Jelsma, Jelsma, & Smits-Engelsman, 2013). Nevertheless, we must consider the principle of training specificity ("you get what you train for") in expecting broader skill improvement from students with DCD participating in these otherwise engaging activities. Improved ball skills or better sports agility skills need to be practiced and the degree of transfer to new physical game contexts need to be specifically introduced, especially for students with DCD. Their relative inability to transfer old learnings into new skills is characteristic of their motor learning difficulty.

Teaching games for understanding (TGFU)

This curriculum approach values the learning of problem solving and decision making and is sometimes also referred to as 'Game Sense'. This approach places the learning of motor skills within the context of that games' strategic purpose (Pill, 2015) and embraces the production teaching styles of Mosston. TGFU considers skill learning in game clusters – net, court, wall games; running games; invasion games, and facilitates students transferring their learning within game classification types. Students learn to read the play, to make relevant decision about appropriate motor responses and thereby develop thinking players. Skill is only meaningful in a game context and students learn not only what, but why and how to adapt the skills for the game circumstance.

For high school students of all abilities, this appears to re-engage students into authentic sport-play from lesson one. The teacher uses a variety of teaching styles (see above) as necessary within the lesson and students finish a unit of PE learning in-depth about the game, its strategic intent and what cues and decisions are important for successful play.

A sequence of the steps to follow are:

1. Begin with a representative task of the sport, e.g., for invasion games of soccer or basketball, students play 'keeping off'.
2. Enquiry learning via Q&A – What do the rules allow us to do? What are the boundaries/opportunities/creative options in play? What are the risks/rewards of the choice? That is, explore outcomes of action rather than process to get there at this stage.
3. Shape the play by modifying constraints on play, e.g. use width, timing, constrict space. At this stage one may revert to direct instruction of specific motor skill to improve performance.
4. Shape play by increasing complexity – increase number of players, increase speed, increase distance of passes. Set up small group practices that introduce these variations.

5   Focus play – by asking questions and monitoring change in play – ask Q's coherent with the intention of the tactics of play, e.g., how might you create space in offence? Where could you run to use the space better? How might you crowd space as a defending team? Each of these scenarios are played and skill practice is interleaved with game play.

For students who have mastered some basic skills, this curriculum approach may allow learning:

- 'In' sport – technical and tactical capability for recreation;
- 'About' sport – how sport is structured in certain ways to bring about societal, social, health and fitness, economic benefits;
- "Through" sport – social, emotional, moral, cognitive learning, and team work and resilience; and
- "Because" sport – brain and cognitive development (Pill, 2015).

There are many free resources available on the internet to support your teaching of this approach (www.playsport.net/about-playsport; www.ciraontario.com/home.).

Conclusion

The effective PE teacher will evaluate the competencies of students with DCD to identify strengths and weaknesses. Importantly, inclusion-focused teaching practices which consider task/environment factors to understand potential learning constraints will be most successful. When instructions and feedback are delivered in meaningful ways with a variety of curriculum, teaching styles and lesson formats, then participation, success and social connection between class members will be maximised. A class climate of respect, achievement, fun and confidence will evolve.

References

Arnold, P. (1979). *Meaning in movement, sport and physical education*. London: Heinemann.

Barnett, A. L., Dawes, H., & Wilmut, K. (2012). Constraints and facilitators to participation in physical activity in teenagers with Developmental Co-ordination Disorder: An exploratory interview study. *Child: Care. Health & Development, 39*, 393–403. doi:10.1111/j.1365-2214.2012.01376.x

Caçola, P., & Romero, P. (2015). Strategies to accommodate children with developmental coordination disorder in physical education lessons. *Journal of Physical Education, Recreation and Dance, 86*(9), 21–25. doi:10.1080/07303084.2015.1085341

Cairney, J., Hay, J., Mandigo, J., Wade, T., Faught, B. E., Flouris, A. (2007). Developmental coordination disorder and reported enjoyment of physical education in children. *European Physical Education Review, 13*(1), 81–98.

Camden, C., Wilson, B., Kirby, A., Sugden, D., & Missiuna, C. (2014). Best practice principles for management of children with Developmental Coordination Disorder (DCD): Results of a scoping review. *Child: Care, Health and Development, 41*(1), 147–159. doi:10.1111/cch.12128

Cantell, M. H., Smyth, M. M., & Ahonen, T. P. (1994). Clumsiness in adolescence: Educational, motor, and social outcomes of motor delay detected at five years. *Adapted Physical Activity Quarterly, 11*, 115–129.

Ferguson, G. D., Jelsma, D., Jelsma, J., & Smits-Engelsman, B. C. M. (2013). The efficacy of two task-oriented interventions for children with developmental coordination disorder: Neuromotor task training and Nintendo Wii Fit training. *Research in Developmental Disabilities, 34*, 2449–2461. http://dx.doi.org/10.1016/j.ridd.2013.05.007

Gallahue, D., Ozmun, J., & Goodway, J. (2012). *Understanding motor development: Infants, children, adolescents, adults.* New York: McGraw-Hill.

Gentile, A. M., Higgins, J. R., Miller, E. A., & Rosen, B. M. (1975). The structure of motor tasks. *Movement, 7*, 11–28.

Green, D., Chambers, M. E., & Sugden, D. (2008). Does subtype of developmental coordination disorder count? Is there a differential effect on outcome following intervention? *Human Movement Science, 27*(2), 363–382.

Hands, B., Parker, H. E., Rose, E., & Larkin, D. (2016). Gender and motor competence affects perceived likelihood and importance of physical activity outcomes among 14 year olds. *Child: Care, Health and Development, 42*(2), 246–252. doi:10.1111/cch.12298

Houston-Wilson, C., Dunn, J. M., Van Der Mars, H., & McCubbin, J. (1997). The effect of peer tutors on motor performance in integrated physical education classes. *Adapted Physical Activity Quarterly, 14*(4), 298–313.

Katartzi, E. S., & Vlachopoulos, S. P. (2011). Motivating children with developmental coordination disorder in school physical education: The self-determination theory approach. *Research in Developmental Disabilities, 32*(6), 2674–2682. doi:10.1016/j.ridd.2011.06.005.

Larkin, D., & Parker, H. E. (2002). Task-specific intervention for children with developmental coordination disorder: A systems view. In S. Cermak & D. Larkin (Eds.), *Developmental coordination disorder* (pp. 234–247). Albany, NY: Delmar.

Magill, R. A., & Anderson, D. (2014). *Motor learning and control: Concepts and applications* (10th ed.). New York: McGraw-Hill.

Mannisto, J. P., Cantell, M., Huovinen, T., Kooistra, L., & Larkin, D. (2006). A school-based movement programme for children with movement difficulty. *European Physical Education Review, 12*(3), 273–287. doi:10.1177/1356336X06069274

Mosston, M., & Ashworth, S. (2002). *Teaching physical education* (5th ed.). San Francisco: Pearson Benjamin Cummings.

Newell, K. M. (1986). Constraints on the development of coordination. In M. Wade & H. T. A. Whiting (Eds.), *Motor development in children: Aspects of coordination and control* (pp. 341–360). Dordrecht: Martinus Nijhoff Publishers.

Pill, S. (2015). Valuing learning in, through and about sport-physical education and the development of sport literacy. In H. Askell-Williams (Ed.), *Transforming the future of learning with educational research.* Hershey, PA: IGI Global.

Presse, C., Block, M. E., Harvey, W., & Horton, M. (2011). Adapting the sports education model for children with disabilities. *Journal of Physical Education, Recreation, and Dance, 82*(3), 32–39.

Revie, G., & Larkin, D. (1993). Task-specific intervention with children reduces movement problems. *Adapted Physical Activity Quarterly, 10*, 29–41.

Ridgers, N., Stratton, G., Fairclough, S., & Twisk, J. (2007). Long-term effects of a playground markings and physical structures on children's recess physical activity levels. *Preventive Medicine, 44*(5), 393–397.

Schoemaker, M. M., Neimeijer, A. S., Reynders, K., & Smits-Engelsman B. C. M. (2003). Effectiveness of neuromotor task training for children with developmental coordination disorder: A pilot study. *Neural Plasticity, 10*, 155–163.

Smits-Engelsman, B. C. M., Blank, R., Van der Kaay, A., Mosterd-Van der Meijs, R., Vlugt-Van Den Brand, E., Polatajko, H., & Wilson, P. (2013). Efficacy of interventions to improve motor performance in children with developmental coordination disorder: A combined systematic review and meta-analysis. *Developmental Medicine and Child Neurology, 55,* 229–237. doi:10.1111/dmcn.12008

Sugden, D. A. (2007). Current approaches to intervention in children with developmental coordination disorder. *Developmental Medicine and Child Neurology, 49,* 467–471.

Sugden, D. A., & Chambers, M. E. (2003). Intervention in children with developmental coordination disorder: The role of parents and teachers. *British journal of Educational Psychology, 73*(4), 545–561.

Wagner, M., Jekauc, D., Worth, A., & Woll, A. (2016, December 15). Elaboration of the environmental stress hypothesis – results from a population-based 6-year follow-up. *Frontiers in Psychology, 7,* 1904. doi:10.3389/fpsyg.2016.01904. eCollection 2016.

Ward, P., & Ayvaso, S. (2006). Class wide peer tutoring in physical education: Assessing its effects with kindergarteners with Autism. *Adapted Physical Activity* Quarterly, *23,* 233–244.

Wilson, P. H. (2005). Practitioner review: Approaches to the assessment and treatment of children with DCD: An evaluative review. *Journal of Child Psychology, 46*(8), 806–823. doi:10.1111/j.1469-7610.2005.01409.x

9

OCCUPATIONAL THERAPY

Current approaches

Sylvia Rodger and Ann Kennedy-Behr

Defining occupational therapy

In this chapter we use the term 'client/s' to refer to individuals who seek the input of occupational therapists or whose parents/carers/guardians seek this input on their behalf. Other terms you may find in the literature are consumers, end users, patients, residents, depending on the area of practice.

According to the World Federation of Occupational Therapists (WFOT) (2012), occupational therapy is a:

> client-centred health profession concerned with promoting health and well-being through occupation. The primary goal of occupational therapy is to enable people to participate in the activities of everyday life. Occupational therapists achieve this outcome by working with people and communities to enhance their ability to engage in the occupations they want to, need to, or are expected to do, or by modifying the occupation or the environment to better support their occupational engagement.

Occupation

A key term that needs to be understood to make sense of the role of occupational therapists is 'occupation'. Occupation in the context of the health profession and this chapter refers to the everyday activities or things that people need to do, have to do, and most importantly want to do. Some examples of things that people need to do or have to do are getting themselves washed, dressed, toileted, fed as well as the associated tasks of ensuring there is food to eat (shopping, putting groceries away), living space is clean, tidy, hygienic, garbage is removed, housework completed, pets and or dependents cared for, and the person's health care needs (such as taking medications) are taken care of. Hence these are the everyday occupations that must be done to live a healthy life.

The 'have to do occupations' may include going to work to a job each day to earn a living for self and or family/dependents, for children this is most often going to school as this is a requirement in most countries for children into their late teens, and doing chores like homework tasks, tidying away toys, clothes, emptying the dishwasher etc. The 'want to do' occupations might include engaging in leisure interests (such as sports, hobbies, creative pursuits, spiritual activities, relaxation, visiting friends and family etc.). Hence occupational therapists are interested in assisting people to achieve all of the everyday activities that make up their daily lives so that they can participate meaningfully in their societal roles.

Roles

Roles are both social and occupational. For example, a child may be a sibling, grandson or daughter, a friend, a school student, a basketball team member, a dancer or gymnast, among others. An adult woman may be a wife/partner, mother, daughter, granddaughter, sibling, friend, worker, volunteer, choir member, gardening club member, neighbour etc. These roles have certain societal expectations associated with them, some of which are implicit and others explicit. Being a parent implicitly requires that children are adequately cared and provided for and are safe as well as protected from harm, abuse or neglect. Certain occupational roles are associated with explicit responsibilities such as a police officer is expected to respect the law, provide assistance, keep the community safe, and enforce the law where required. We all have self-care roles that relate to looking after ourselves (eating, dressing, grooming, toileting, taking medication if required) known as basic activities of daily living (BADL) and the space around us where we live (cleaning, tidying, gardening) known as instrumental activities of daily living (IADL). IADL also refers to activities such as shopping, personal transportation, going to the doctor when not well etc. These activities change across the lifespan in terms of what they are, who does them, and how much assistance is required.

Whether an occupation is viewed as something that an individual either 'has to do' or 'wants to do', depends on his or her roles at anyone point in time, amongst other things. For example, a chef has to do various cooking activities as part of his/ her paid job, and a parent has to ensure that children are fed. However, an adolescent may enjoy baking for friends and family and would consider cooking biscuits on the weekend as something they do because they want to. How much choice one has about these daily activities varies from person to person and over time as well. Hence it is important for occupational therapists to understand how the individuals they are working with view or perceive the daily activities they do.

Types of occupations

Commonly, occupational therapists categorise broadly the activities that individuals do as work or productivity occupations (jobs, school work, chores), leisure or play

FIGURE 9.1   Different types of occupations

Source: Sylvia Rodger, created November 2016.

occupations (basketball, playing an instrument, going for a walk, playing with a train set), or self-care (looking after ourselves) frequently also referred to as activities of daily living (dressing, bathing etc.). See Figure 9.1.

It is important to have a good grasp of these terms as in chapter 10 we will discuss how a condition such as Developmental Coordination Disorder (DCD) can affect a person's ability to carry out these tasks due to the perceptual, cognitive and motor difficulties with which they often present. The other concept to keep in mind is that occupational therapists work with individuals across the lifespan, from pre-term infants, through to toddlers and preschool-aged children who have a range of physical, emotional, sensory, social and cognitive challenges, students at school, university, adults at work who may have work related injuries, and older people who tend to experience age-related conditions that impact on their ability to independently care for themselves. What occupational therapists do at different ages and stages of a person's life will look very different, but essentially the therapist will be considering the person's roles and the occupations or activities that are crucial for those roles.

Interdisciplinary teamwork

Occupational therapists typically work with other health, social care, education and allied health disciplines (e.g., medicine, nursing, social work, speech pathology, physiotherapy, dentistry, podiatry, optometry, psychology, as well as teachers). This type of work requires collaboration across disciplines and is commonly referred to as interprofessional teamwork. The challenge for occupational therapists is that sometimes they work in primarily health and social care/disability teams with professionals from health backgrounds, while at other times they work with educational teams in school settings. Hence, therapists need to have a good grounding in the contribution and backgrounds of all these professionals and the impact of the context in which they work. For example, in a health setting the focus may well be on diagnosis of the child's condition (e.g., DCD) and its initial assessment and related interventions. While in a school setting, therapists must focus on the child's ability to engage in the tasks they are required to do at school. In these settings, the teachers' priorities in the classroom and in physical education lessons necessarily become the priority. Thus, the focus may be on interventions that address handwriting, computer skills, arts and crafts and ball skills relevant to ball games in physical education classes. Discussion with the teachers, parents and child him/herself will be important in order to prioritise goals. In a community clinic or private practice setting, bike riding, rollerblading or skating or community leisure skills may well be addressed rather than education focused skills; however, this will depend on the child's roles and goals.

Teamwork, communication and planning are important for therapists and all team members if they are to ensure person- or client-centred care whatever setting they work in. In some settings, roles may overlap. For example if there is a physiotherapist and an occupational therapist, the child's goals may determine which professional is involved; handwriting (occupational therapist) vs bike riding or improving physical education skills (physiotherapist). However, if there is only one or other the OT may become involved with both activities. In smaller community or regional centres, there tend to be fewer team members and hence roles are more likely to be shared and professional boundaries more blurred. The heart of the issue is ensuring that the client's goals are met and concerns are addressed by a competent professional.

Occupational therapy in different workplaces

Occupational therapists work across a range of sectors – health, education, disability, employment, aged care, social welfare. They may be employed privately (as private practitioners) or for private companies (such as providers of injury prevention, workplace rehabilitation, and workplace health and safety services), by government or public organisations (such as public schools, hospitals, disability service providers, nursing homes) or private organisations that run private schools, hospitals, respite and home care or nursing facilities), or not for profit organisations. Increasingly occupational therapists are employed in other areas such as by City Councils who are looking to improve their provision of accommodations for people with disabilities, auditing public spaces and buildings for accessibility, provision of playgrounds for children with a range of needs, consulting on the provision of assistive technologies in aged care, smart technologies, adapting vehicles for drivers with various conditions, consulting with architects on aged care design etc. Occupational therapists also work with individuals with a range of challenges resulting from disease processes impacting on physical, perceptual and cognitive functioning (e.g., stroke, Parkinson's disease), mental ill health (e.g., depression, anxiety, psychotic conditions), sensory issues (e.g., hearing, visual impairment, sensory sensitivities), chronic conditions (e.g., cancer, cardiovascular), and environmental deprivation (e.g., refugees and asylum seekers).

Disability practice models

Occupational therapists obtain a theoretical grounding in the human physical sciences, social sciences, and medical sciences. In addition, they spend a significant amount of time learning about occupational therapy theories and practice models, which provide a basis to their learning to 'think and reason like occupational therapists'. They also have a solid grounding in the International Classification for Functioning Disability and Health (ICF) (World Health Organisation) (WHO, 2001). This classification describes the impact of a health condition on an individual's body structure and function, activities (what they do), and participation (ability to engage in society and their roles). These three aspects are also influenced by personal factors (that are relatively stable and unique to the individual) such as ethnicity, gender, socio-economic factors, personality, as well as environmental factors (family structure, culture, geographic location, institutional context, dwelling, school layout) (WHO, 2001, 2007). These concepts are closely related to occupational therapy practice models. Not surprisingly a number of occupational therapists were very involved in the development of the ICF framework. When body structure/function issues impact on a person's abilities these are known as impairments such as a broken arm (impairment) limits a child's ability to bat a ball or field. Inability to do these things is known as an activity limitation which also impacts on the child's ability for participation in playing cricket in the local team (social role as team member). A fracture is a short-term limitation to participation, however, many of the children and adults with whom occupational therapists work have impairments that are chronic (e.g., cerebral palsy), pervasive (e.g., autism) or degenerative (e.g., muscular dystrophy), hence the potential limitations to their activities and participation are long term, and frequently life-long.

Occupational therapy models

While there are a number of occupational therapy specific models of practice that therapists draw upon, there are a number of key concepts which are germane to all of these theories. Rather than provide a lot of detail about these different models, we will focus in this chapter on the key concepts. These are often referred to as person, occupation, environment and performance or occupational performance (Rodger & Kennedy-Behr, 2017).

The person

So, let us first look at the concept of the person. This represents a therapist's understanding of the client as an individual. Critical to this understanding are a number of values, enshrined in the Occupational Therapy Code of Ethics (e.g., Occupational Therapy Australia, 2001; WFOT, 2016) such as those of human rights, dignity, worth and respect. At the person level, the occupational therapist considers a range of aspects of that individual as outlined in Box 9.1.

BOX 9.1   SOME EXAMPLES OF CONSIDERATIONS ABOUT THE PERSON

Age (chronological, developmental)
Gender
Family situation
Referring/presenting challenges/issues
Personality, learning style, preferences
Strengths, talents
Physical, medical, neurological conditions
Cognitive, perceptual, attentional, sensory abilities/ needs
Social emotional status

Source: Sylvia Rodger, created November 2016.

Information about these may be obtained through referral sources, interview with the person and relevant others, discussions, observations or other forms of assessment.

The occupations

In addition, the occupational therapist will want to understand the occupations (see Figure 9.1) that are challenging for the individual and which may have prompted self or other referral. Most particularly, he/she will need to know about the occupations the person needs to, has to and wants to be able to do, what the current barriers or limitations to engaging in these occupations that are preventing the person's optimal participation in his/her life roles and society. This understanding can occur through discussion with the individual and relevant others, observations and particular occupation–centred assessments.

The environment

The third critical concept is that of the environment. This is a complex concept and is understood by the therapist under a number of broad headings as outlined in Box 9.2.

People conduct their daily lives within a range of environments each with their own supports and challenges and these vary across the lifespan. For example, a school-aged child will likely spend their day between their home environment complete with family members, pets; their school classroom, playground, library and other special facilities (physical education gymnasium) and perhaps the local park where they ride to play after school. Weekends typically involve other environments in the community (shopping centres, movie theatres, fun parks) and natural

BOX 9.2 THE ENVIRONMENT

Physical – Built or Natural (surfaces, size, space, objects, temperature, other features etc.)

Human or Social – the other people (including pets) in the environments where the person functions – home, school, work, neighbourhood/ community, elder care facility.

Sensory – visual, auditory, olfactory, etc.

Institutional – culture, rules, guidelines, expectations (e.g., classroom in school, workplace, community).

Temporal – time constraints.

Source: Sylvia Rodger, created November 2016.

environments such as the beach, forests, lakes or camping grounds. Hence it is important for therapists to understand as much as possible about the environments in which occupational challenges occur and what might be the barriers and potential supports that naturally occur in these contexts or those that might be included to accommodate performance issues. These may not always be physical things like a foot rest under the child's desk, a laptop, or a sloping table, but may also involve changes to the social environment (who the child sits with) and instructional environment (how the teacher provides instructions to the child, provision of additional visual supports or repetition, etc.).

Occupational performance

Occupational performance refers to the individual's ability to carry out their daily occupations. The better the match between the supports and affordances of the environment, the capacity of the person, and the requirements of the occupation, the better an individual's occupational performance will be. Hence each of the three aspects of person, environment and occupation, commonly known as the P, the E, and the O (Law et al., 1996), need to be understood, with the therapist and client problem solving how each might need adjustment, modification or support to optimise performance. At the heart of this reasoning is that people's engagement in purposeful and meaningful occupation (to perform these occupations) affects their health and well-being (Wilcock, 1998).

There are many occupational therapy models to choose from such as Person – Environment – Occupation (Law & Dunbar, 2007), Occupational Performance Model (Australia) (OPMA) (Chapparo & Ranka, 1997), the Model of Human Occupation (MOHO) (Kielhofner, 2007; Kramer & Bowyer, 2007), the Ecological Human Performance Model (Dunn, 2007), Person – Environment – Occupation – Performance

Model (Christiansen, Baum, & Bass, 2015), and the Canadian Model of Occupational Performance – Enablement (CMOP-E) (Townsend & Polatajko, 2007). These models tell us what occupational therapy is about and delineate our expertise and scope or domain of practice.

Client-centred practice

Clients can refer to: 'individuals, families, groups, communities, organizations, or populations who participate in occupational therapy services' (Townsend & Polatajko, 2007, p. 96). In this chapter our focus is on clients as individuals and their families. Client-centredness originated with the work of Carl Rogers in psychology who promoted person-centred therapies that embraced a humanistic approach to counselling exchanges (Rogers, 1946, 1951). Essentially being client-centred reflects how the occupational therapist engages with the client from the perspective of the values held by him/her as a professional about human dignity, respect and worth, and having a clear desire to try to understand the world from the client's perspective, ascertaining his/her goals and priorities and working with the client's strengths and abilities.

There are a number of elements that go together to makeup/inform client-centred practice. These include that:

- Clients, their families and their choices are respected.
- Information, emotional support and person-centred communication are provided.
- Clients are facilitated to participate fully in occupational therapy services.
- Clients and families have the ultimate responsibility for decisions about their daily occupations and services.
- Occupational therapy service delivery is flexible and individualised.
- Clients are enabled to solve their own occupational performance issues.

(Rodger & Keen, 2017, p. 46)

An important part of being client-centred is listening to the client's desires, wishes, wants and expectations. Through guided conversations, the therapist is able to determine with the client (and family especially where the child is the person at the centre of the service) where the focus of their time together needs to be spent.

The occupational therapy process

Irrespective of which occupational therapy theoretical model the therapist uses for practice, there is a process that is consistent across almost all therapeutic encounters. We call this the occupational therapy process and it consists of seven stages which may be iterative rather than linear. These stages are: (1) referral for input, (2) information gathering, (3) goal setting and prioritising, (4) occupation-centred assessment, (5) intervention, (6) evaluation and either (7) discharge, re-engagement, or refer on if needed or re-engage with further goal setting etc. (Rodger, 2010). See Figure 9.2.

While there may be exceptions, typically an occupational therapy encounter will begin with a suggestion from a friend, teacher, or formal referral from a doctor or other allied health practitioner that a child might benefit from seeing an occupational therapist. Initially the therapist will discuss the referring concern with the parent or guardian who is typically the person who will make contact with the service system. This allows the therapist to ensure that the referral is appropriate (that they are the right person to manage the concern) and the parent or the client in the case of adults understands what will ensue and what to expect. If the referral is not appropriate, suggestions will be made as to where else the person might go. If it is, an initial appointment will be made.

The first phase is one of information gathering or finding out more about the concern/s and how it/they manifest and in which contexts (e.g., home, school, neighbourhood for children) and under what conditions (e.g., timing/speed, stress, anxiety etc.) and whether there are other situations/ conditions where there may be no concerns. This phase of information gathering typically involves discussion via interview, taking a history of the situation, development history and status (in child's case), interests, preferences, learning styles, strengths, other approaches/strategies/ therapies previously used/engaged in and what has worked or not worked, and why that may/may not be the case.

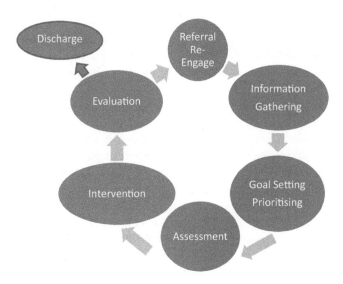

FIGURE 9.2   The occupational therapy process

Source: Sylvia Rodger, created November 2016.

The second phase involves goal setting followed by prioritising. Therapists can use a range of goal setting tools to help children identify their own goals such as using the activity card sorts like the Pediatric Activity Card Sort (PACS) (Mandich, Polatajko, Miller, & Baum, 2004), Perceived Efficacy and Goal Setting (PEGS) (Pollock & Missiuna, 2015) which was originally designed for children who have DCD, or through a 24-hour log and Canadian Occupational Performance Measure (COPM)(Law et al., 2014) with parents (and child if he/she is old enough). Obtaining information from teachers, parents and child can be very useful and help to triangulate and further understand concerns. These tools will be considered in more detail in the next chapter.

Importantly the individual is much more likely to be motivated to change and engaged with intervention if they have had involvement in choosing the goals they wish to work on. Choice is well known to promote both motivation and engagement, which is particularly important when working with children (Poulsen, Ziviani, & Cuskelly, 2013). Goals should be specific, measurable, achievable, realistic and time based (SMART). A number of other words have been associated with SMART and some of these are listed below:

- S – specific, significant, stretching
- M – measurable, meaningful, motivational
- A – agreed upon, attainable, achievable, acceptable, action-oriented
- R – realistic, relevant, reasonable, rewarding, results-oriented
- T – time-based, time-bound, timely, tangible, trackable

(www.projectsmart.co.uk/smart-goals.php.
Retrieved 14 October 2016)

An example might be that the client wants to be able to dress herself without help from her husband in a reasonable time (15 minutes) or that a student wishes to write more neatly when using cursive script so that he does not have to stay in at recess by the end of the school term.

The next important step is to ensure that goals are prioritised by rating them from 1 to 5 or so in terms of which is the most important to the client, then the next and so forth. When children are involved in this activity, parents need to be agreeable to working with the child's most important goal, even if this is not the parents' highest priority (such as improving with basketball goal shooting rather than improving speed of handwriting).

From, this point the occupational therapist will engage in assessing how the person performs the particular task or activity embedded in the agreed upon goal. This may involve observation (such as how the child now shoots goals) at clinic or watching a video taken at home of goal shooting, and or undertaking specific assessments that may shed some light on the child's ball skills, eye hand coordination etc. from a standardised assessment. When these assessments are used, it is critical that observation of the individual's actual task performance occurs and where appropriate videotaped. This can provide evidence of progress and improvement that can enhance children's motivation especially when the going gets tough as it does at times.

Intervention involves the therapist choosing an occupation-centred approach to facilitate the achievement of the particular goal. The approach used will be varied and depend on the individual's age, stage of development, strengths and interests, resources available, therapist's expertise, the available evidence, and the therapist's clinical experience with working with this type of client in the past (the condition, the goal, etc.). This is what is known as the therapist's professional reasoning and this will be grounded in his/her knowledge of the condition, the client and his/her preferences, the evidence, and his/her past experience (Copley, Bennett, & Turpin, 2017).

For example, the goal of accurately shooting more goals may be approached using a teaching and learning approach using forward chaining, a task specific approach using blocked practice, a graded approach using balls of various sizes, hoops of particular heights, and child standing at various distances from the goal post; or a cognitive strategy based approach such as Cognitive Orientation for daily Occupational Performance (CO-OPApproach™) (Polatajko & Mandich, 2004; Dawson, McEwen, & Polatajko, 2017). Whereas for a person who has sustained a low-level spinal injury, who wants to be more successful at independent dressing – transferring from a lying position (bed) where lower limb dressing is undertaken using loops on underpants, loose shorts/slacks laid out in correct position, to the wheelchair to undertake upper limb dressing seated would use both a teaching approach coupled with assistive technology and appropriate supervised practice.

Evidence based practice and professional reasoning

Copley et al. (2017) provide a comprehensive overview of how occupational therapists make decisions about intervention approaches in real world occupation-centred practice with children, particularly when choices are not clear and the empirical research evidence in many areas of practice continues to emerge. Professional reasoning is the meta-cognitive process that therapists use to make complex decisions about interventions taking into account client preferences, the research evidence, and the therapist's practice experience (wisdom). A number of terms have been used to describe reasoning processes including narrative, interactive, scientific, ethical, procedural, pragmatic and conditional reasoning (Schell, 2014).

In the face of uncertainty, clear foundations for decision making are both more critical and more obvious. This is why therapy is as much an art (Hinojosa & Kramer, 2009) as a science. Rycroft-Malone et al. (2004) described therapists using information from: (1) clients, their families, and their contexts (environments), (2) the practice context where the service is being provided and available resources, (3) empirical research (evidence), and (4) their clinical lived experience. Having information from multiple sources enables the therapist to decide whether to focus intervention on a child's skill development (person level focus) and/or changing the environment, the task (occupation level) or the expectations such as from the child's teacher (environment level).

Therapists report that a lack of available research regarding specific techniques or intervention approaches and particular client groups (e.g., children with learning difficulties) as challenging for translating research to practice (Copley & Allen, 2009). Where there is limited research or competing and equivocal findings, therapists still have a responsibility to consider broader information to make decisions and apply the best evidence available (Copley, Bennett, & Turpin, 2010). When integrating information from different sources therapists work at different levels simultaneously such as at the *hands-on level* (using embedded practices such knowing how to engage a child's motivation), and at a *conceptual level* (using their theoretical knowledge) to determine how therapy might progress (Copley et al., 2010).

The influence of occupational science

Occupational science is a relatively new academic discipline that generates knowledge about human occupation and humans as occupational beings. As already described in this chapter, occupation refers to all the things that people do in their everyday life. Occupational scientists research what people do in their daily lives and what influences their occupational potential (Asaba & Wicks, 2010).

The basic research undertaken in this field informs occupational therapy theory and practice. In particular the meaning of occupations to people, how these are experienced, the impact of culture, and its importance, and the health-giving benefits of engaging in occupation alone and with others, as well as how space and time impact on occupational engagement for people in the community, in elder care facilities, at school etc. For example, without safe and accessible spaces to play such as parks and neighbourhood playgrounds, children are unable to engage in specific play occupations such as outdoor play on equipment that challenges their physical abilities, riding bicycles and skateboards. Without sufficient time as well as the right space, children do not have the opportunity to develop elaborate pretend play schemas that let them explore social relationships, give and take, and various endings to games they create etc. Hence temporal (time) and spatial features of the environment are important to which occupations are performed as well as how they are performed.

Conclusion

In this chapter, occupational therapy has been described as a profession that facilitates an individual's engagement in the occupations of daily life. The occupations encompass a range of activities that make up productivity (e.g., school, chores, volunteering, work), play/leisure, and self-care (looking after yourself). Occupational therapists focus on helping people to achieve their personal goals in relation to various aspects of their daily lives. Using a structured process of information gathering, goal setting with the person, assessment and intervention, the occupational therapist works collaboratively with the person to help them to achieve their desired goals so that they can reach their occupational potential. Regular evaluation enables checking for success and enables revision of intervention as required.

Occupational therapists work in a range of hospital, health care, educational, community, private practice and non-government settings with people whose everyday occupations are impacted by a range of social disadvantage, health care, developmental and educational difficulties. They work not only with individuals and groups but also at a societal level, seeking to influence policy and practice across a range of contexts (e.g., occupational health and safety, community access, provision of environments that facilitate occupations) etc.

The following chapter will specifically address the role of occupational therapists when working with children with Developmental Coordination Disorder.

References

Asaba, E., & Wicks, A. (2010). Occupational terminology. *Journal of Occupational Science, 17*(2), 120–124. doi:10.1080/14427591.2010.9686683

Chapparo, C., & Ranka, J. (1997). Towards a model of occupational performance: Model development. In C. Chapparo & J. Ranka (Eds.), *Occupational performance model (Australia): Monograph 1* (pp. 24–45). Sydney: Total Print Control.

Christiansen, C., Baum, C., & Bass, J. (2015). *Occupational therapy: Performance, participation and well-being* (4th ed.). Thorofare, NJ: SLACK.

Copley, J., & Allen, S. (2009). Using all the available evidence: Perceptions of paediatric occupational therapists about how to increase evidence-based practice. *International Journal of Evidence-Based Healthcare, 7*(3), 193–200. doi:10.1111/j.1744-1609.2009.00137.x

Copley, J., Bennett, S., & Turpin, M. (2010). Decision making for occupation-centred practice with children. In S. Rodger (Ed.), *Occupation-centred practice with children: A practical guide for occupational therapists* (pp. 320–341). Chichester, West Sussex: Wiley-Blackwell.

Copley, J., Bennett, S., & Turpin, M. (2017). Decision-making for occupation-centred practice with children. In S. A. Rodger & A. Kennedy-Behr (Eds.), *Occupation-centred practice with children: A practical guide for occupational therapists* (2nd ed., pp. 349–371). Chichester: Wiley-Blackwell.

Dawson, D., McEwen, S., & Polatajko, H. (2017). *Enabling participation across the lifespan: Advancements, adaptations, and extensions of the Co-Op Approach.* Bethesda, MD: AOTA Press.

Dunn, W. (2007). Ecology of human performance model. In S. B. Dunbar (Ed.), *Occupational therapy models for intervention with children and families* (pp. 127–156). Thorofare, NJ: SLACK.

Hinojosa, J., & Kramer, P. (2009). Frames of reference in the real world. In P. Kramer & J. Hinojosa (Eds.), *Pediatric occupational therapy* (3rd ed., pp. 571–581). Philadelphia, PA: Lippincott, Williams & Wilkins.

Kielhofner, G. (2007). *The model of human occupation: Theory and application* (4th ed.). Philadelphia, MD: Lippincott, Williams & Wilkins.

Kramer, J. M., & Bowyer, P. (2007). Application of the model of human occupation to children and family interventions. In S. B. Dunbar (Ed.), *Occupational therapy models for intervention with children and families* (pp. 51–90). Thorofare, NJ: SLACK.

Law, M., & Dunbar, S. B. (2007). Person-environment-occupation model. In S. B. Dunbar (Ed.), *Occupational therapy models for intervention with children and families* (pp. 27–50). Thorofare, NJ: SLACK.

Law, M., Baptiste, S., Carswell, A., McColl, M., Polatajko, H., & Pollock, N. (2014). *The Canadian occupational performance measure* (5th ed.). Ottawa, ON: CAOT Publications ACE.

Law, M., Cooper, B., Strong, S., Stewart, D., Rigby, P., & Letts, L. (1996). The person-environment-occupation model: A transactive approach to occupational performance. *Canadian Journal of Occupational Therapy, 63*(1), 9–23.

Mandich, A., Polatajko, H. J., Miller, L. T., & Baum, C. (2004). *Paediatric activity card sort.* Ottawa, ON: CAOT Publications ACE.

Occupational Therapy Australia (2001). *Code of ethics.* Retrieved from https://otaus.com.au/sitebuilder/onlinestore/files/14/codeofethics.pdf

Polatajko, H., & Mandich, A. (2004). *Enabling occupation in children: The Cognitive Orientation to daily Occupational Performance (CO-OP) approach.* Ottawa, ON: CAOT Publications ACE.

Pollock, N., & Missiuna, C. (2015). *The perceived efficacy and goal setting system* (2nd ed.). Hamilton, ON: CanChild.

Poulsen, A. A., Ziviani, J., & Cuskelly, M. (2013). Understanding motivation in the context of engaging children in therapy. In J. Ziviani, A. A. Poulsen, & M. Cuskelly (Eds.), *The art and science of motivation.* London: Jessica Kingsley.

Rodger, S. (2010). Becoming more occupation-centred when working with children. In S. Rodger (Ed.), *Occupation-centred practice with children: A practical guide for occupational therapists* (1st ed., pp. 21–44). Chichester: Wiley-Blackwell.

Rodger, S., & Keen, D. (2017). Child and family-centred service provision. In A. Rodger & A. Kennedy-Behr (Eds.), *Occupation-centred practice with children: A practical guide for occupational therapists* (2nd ed., pp. 45–71). Chichester: Wiley-Blackwell.

Rodger, S., & Kennedy-Behr, A. (2017). Becoming an occupation-centred practitioner. In S. Rodger & A. Kennedy-Behr (Eds.), *Occupation-centred practice with children: A practical guide for occupational therapists* (2nd ed., pp. 21–43). Chichester: Wiley-Blackwell.

Rogers, C. R. (1946). Significant aspects of client-centered therapy. *The American Psychologist, 1*(10), 415–422.

Rogers, C. R. (1951). *Client-centred therapy: Its current practice, implications and theory.* Boston, MA: Houghton Mifflin.

Rycroft-Malone, J., Seers, K., Titchen, A., Harvey, G., Kitson, A., & McCormack, B. (2004). What counts as evidence in evidence-based practice? *Journal of Advanced Nursing, 47*(1), 81–90. doi:10.1111/j.1365-2648.2004.03068.x

Schell, B. A. B. (2014). Professional reasoning in practice. In B. A. B. Schell, G. Gillen, & M. E. Scaffa (Eds.), *Willard and Spackman's occupational therapy* (12th ed., pp. 384–397). Philadelphia, PA: Lippincott, Williams & Wilkins.

Townsend, E., & Polatajko, H. (2007). *Enabling occupation II: Advancing an occupational therapy vision for health, well-being and justice through occupation.* Ontario, ON: CAOT Publications ACE.

Wilcock, A. (1998). *An occupational perspective of health.* Thorofare, NJ: SLACK.

World Federation of Occupational Therapists (WFOT) (2012). *Definition of occupational therapy.* Retrieved October 14, 2016, from www.wfot.org/aboutus/aboutoccupationaltherapy/definitionofoccupationaltherapy.aspx

World Federation of Occupational Therapists (WFOT). (2016). *Code of ethics.* Retrieved from www.wfot.org/SearchResults.aspx?Search=Code+of+Ethics

World Health Organisation (2001). *International classification of functioning, disability, and health (ICF).* Geneva: Author.

World Health Organisation. (2007). *International classification of functioning, disability and health (ICF): Children and youth version.* Geneva: Author.

10

OCCUPATIONAL THERAPY FOR CHILDREN WITH DCD

Ann Kennedy-Behr and Sylvia Rodger

Introduction

According to the best practice principles for children with DCD identified by Camden and colleagues (Camden, Wilson, Kirby, Sugden, & Missiuna, 2015), health professionals should use the following five principles when working with these children and young people:

1.1 Increase awareness of DCD and coordination among professionals and community groups
1.2 Implement clearly defined pathways to ensure access to diagnosis, evaluation and intervention
1.3 Use a graduated/staged approach of assessment and interventions to foster capacity building and to efficiently address all the needs of children with DCD and their families
2.1 Integrate child and family views in assessment, goal-setting and intervention
2.2 Use interventions which are evidence-based, foster function and participation and prevent secondary consequences

(adapted from Camden et al., 2015, p. 150)

In this chapter, we will use these principles as a framework to discuss the role of the occupational therapist in working with children with DCD. We will outline how occupational therapists can contribute towards the diagnosis of DCD, how to empower children and families through goal setting, and describe relevant assessments and the interventions that can be used to effectively work with these children and young people. Finally, a case scenario will illustrate one of these interventions. While there is some overlap between the five best-practice principles, and occupational therapists may be involved in enacting some principles more than others, for the sake of comprehensiveness, clarity and transparency, all five will be addressed.

1.1 Increase awareness of DCD and coordination among professionals and community groups

Awareness of a condition and diagnosis are closely linked, so this principle has considerable overlap with the next one which is specifically concerned with diagnosis. It is difficult to seek a diagnosis or indeed diagnose a condition, if one does not know that a condition exists. Despite affecting an estimated one child in every classroom (Missiuna et al., 2008), DCD is under-recognised by general practitioners, paediatricians, teachers and the general public (Wilson, Neil, Kamps, & Babcock, 2013). One of the first ways an occupational therapist can support a family is through raising awareness of the condition and assisting with diagnosis (Missiuna et al., 2008). As discussed in chapter 9, in the occupational therapy process, a family will frequently come to an occupational therapist with a referral which is often quite general and nonspecific. During the information gathering process, the occupational therapist will ask about the child's ability to do the things he/she needs to do and wants to do, and the parent and child responses might indicate motor difficulties (Missiuna et al., 2008). If motor skills are thought to be limiting a child's ability to participate, then an occupational therapist can conduct a motor test to support Criterion A of the Diagnostic and Statistical Manual – Fifth edition (DSM-5) (American Psychiatric Association, 2013) DCD diagnostic criteria. Appropriate motor tests include the Movement Assessment Battery for Children – Second Edition (MABC-2) (Henderson, Sugden, & Barnett, 2007) and the Bruininks-Oseretsky Test of Motor Proficiency – Second Edition (BOT-2) (Bruininks & Bruininks, 2005). Additionally, an occupational therapist can provide information to satisfy Criterion B by determining whether the motor difficulties significantly impact on the child's ability to complete activities of daily living (ADLs), participation in school and leisure roles and related academic and recreational activities. Asking caregivers to complete either the Developmental Coordination Disorder Questionnaire 2007 (DCDQ'07) (Wilson & Crawford, 2007) or the Little Developmental Coordination Disorder Questionnaire (Little DCDQ) (Rihtman, Wilson, & Parush, 2011) can provide some of this information, as can observation of the child completing ADLs and engaging in play. For school-aged children, a careful analysis of written school work may provide evidence to support Criterion B.

Communicating the findings of these assessments with the child's caregivers and referring doctor can assist not only with diagnosis but also with raising awareness of the condition (Missiuna et al., 2008). Occupational therapists have contributed to the many resources available at the CanChild website for adolescents, parents, teachers and physicians which aim to further understanding of DCD and also provide information on how to encourage children's participation (see www.canchild.ca/en/diagnoses/developmental-coordination-disorder/dcd-educational-materials-for-home-school-physicians-and-other-health-professionals). Some of these resources are now available in up to 10 languages, which assists with access in different cultural communities in Canada as well as in countries around the world.

Not all people who have DCD are diagnosed during childhood. Adolescents and young adults who struggle with learning new motor tasks such as driving a car or participating in community sports are often not aware of the existence of DCD but sense they are different to their peers (Gagnon-Roy, Jasmin, & Camden, 2016; Kirby, Edwards, & Sugden, 2011; Lingam, Novak, Emond, & Coad, 2013; Timler, McIntyre, Cantell, Crawford, & Hands, 2016). Promoting awareness of DCD amongst adolescents and adults and providing access to self-report questionnaires such as the Adolescent Motor Competence Questionnaire (Timler et al., 2016), or the Adult Developmental Coordination Disorders/Dyspraxia Checklist (ADC) (Kirby, Edwards, Sugden, & Rosenblum, 2010) may assist with diagnosis, open up avenues for support and potentially reduce the sense of isolation (Timler et al., 2016).

Occupational therapists can raise awareness of DCD within their work environment. Occupational therapists working in schools, for example, are ideally positioned to provide information for teachers and parents in an accessible and appropriate way on what DCD looks like, and how children with the condition can be supported (Camden et al., 2015; Missiuna, Pollock, Levac et al., 2012).

Diagnosis is important for reasons that go beyond the obvious. Families have spoken of their relief when understanding that their child had a diagnosable condition (Alsonso Soriano, Hill, & Crane, 2015; Missiuna, Moll, King, Law, & King, 2006); in some countries, diagnosis can lead to funding for intervention (Blank, Smits-Engelsman, Polatajko, & Wilson, 2012). In countries where DCD is not prioritised, families who receive a diagnosis have an even greater need to be supported with education and understanding.

1.2 Implement clearly defined pathways to ensure access to diagnosis, evaluation and intervention

"Pathways" in health care refers to a clearly defined entry into the health service and defined roles for health care professionals to play (Camden et al., 2015). The role of the occupational therapist in the pathway is determined by the health care or educational service and country in which they work. Some European countries have developed clear pathways specifically for children with DCD and the role of the occupational therapist is defined within this, typically involving providing information that can lead to diagnosis and intervention where necessary (Blank et al., 2012; Forsyth, Maciver, Howden, Owen, & Shepherd, 2008). Other countries do not have clearly defined pathways, making it even more important for occupational therapists to recognise the condition and understand how they can best support a diagnosis and access to intervention.

1.3 Use a graduated/staged approach of assessment and interventions to foster capacity building and to efficiently address all the needs of children with DCD and their families

Camden et al. (2015) suggest that support for children with DCD should at first take a population-based approach and only children who do not respond well to this approach or for whom this approach is not sufficient should be referred for individual intervention. Capacity-building approaches which benefit all children are thought to be more efficient than one on one therapy (Camden et al., 2015; Campbell, Missiuna, Rivard, & Pollock, 2012; Missiuna, Pollock, Levac et al., 2012; Stephenson & Chesson, 2008). In Canada, Partnering for Change (P4C) was developed as a school population level approach to facilitate participation for all children including those with DCD (Campbell, Missiuna, Rivard et al., 2012; Dancza, Missiuna, & Pollock, 2017; Missiuna, Pollock, Campbell et al., 2012; Missiuna, Pollock, Levac et al., 2012). The advantage of this approach is that occupational therapists collaborate with educators and families to create a more enabling environment for all children, not just those with specific conditions. In P4C, the "4 C's" also refer to "Building Capacity through Collaboration and Coaching in Context"(Dancza et al., 2017). Working together with educators means that professionals are able to share knowledge and build capacity. An example of this might be a school occupational therapist who notices a child who is often slumped at a desk at school and appears to struggle with the physical demands of many school-related activities such as organising his/her schoolbag, packing up in a timely manner and having the required school materials organised. In a whole class approach it is not necessary for the child to have a confirmed diagnosis. The occupational therapist could collaborate with the class teacher to find solutions that would work for all children, for example, checking desk/chair height and whether all children are able to place their feet flat on the floor; considering arrangements of furniture in the classroom and organisation of coats and bags outside the classroom (Dancza et al., 2017). These small adaptations are likely to benefit all children. By working collaboratively, the teacher has a greater understanding of the challenges a child with DCD may experience and is potentially in a position to address these in future classes without the input of a therapist.

Being a guest speaker at a parent-teacher evening and describing how one can support a child with DCD to succeed at the things they want to do and need to do is another example of a way an occupational therapist can help build capacity. Not all parents want or have access to individual intervention for their child, however, being directed to quality resources on the internet (e.g. the CanChild website: www.canchild.ca, the Move.Grow.Engage website www.movegrowengage.com.au or the Movement Matters website www.movementmattersuk.org) may assist them to provide their child with the needed support.

In the United Kingdom, Dancza has developed a model to support occupational therapy students implement a whole class or whole school approach (Dancza et al., 2017). While the focus of this approach is on supporting occupational therapy students in their clinical reasoning, the intended outcome of this approach is that the students have the knowledge and ability to provide whole class and whole school intervention. This is in itself a capacity building approach – by teaching a new generation of occupational therapists how to implement a school population level intervention, health educators are expanding the capacity of the healthcare workforce.

The implication of using a graduated or staged approach to assessment and intervention is that if a population approach has been tried and the child is still experiencing difficulties, then the next step is to try a small group intervention followed by individual intervention.

2.1 Integrate child and family views in assessment, goal-setting and intervention

Previous research has indicated that the needs of the child and family have on occasion been overlooked or not sufficiently recognised by health care professionals during assessment goal-setting and intervention (e.g. Mandich, Polatajko, & Rodger, 2003; Missiuna, Moll, Law, King, & King, 2006; Stephenson & Chesson, 2008). While occupational therapy is ideally a client-centred intervention, practicalities and competing interests such as directives from physicians and health care providers can mean that this is not always prioritised.

Involving clients in the goal-setting process is acknowledged as best practice in health care (Brewer, Pollock, & Wright, 2014; Law et al., 2003; Pollock et al., 2014). Although collaborative goal-setting can be time-intensive, it is associated with increased motivation to engage in therapy and improved outcomes (Locke & Latham, 2002; Löwing, Bexelius, & Brogren Carlberg, 2009). It is even suggested that goal-setting has an intervention effect (Graham & Rodger, 2010; Locke & Latham, 2002) i.e. that through the process of goal-setting, individuals may become aware of and use knowledge and strategies related to the goal they have just set.

While parent and care-giver involvement in goal-setting is part of everyday practice, it is important not to exclude children from this process. In a recent Austrian study examining collaborative goal-setting, Costa, Brauchle, and Kennedy-Behr (2017) found that children (including those with DCD) had quite different goals to their parents and teachers. Surprisingly, the children chose goals related to ADLs (e.g. tying shoes, fastening clothing) more frequently than their parents whose goals tended to focus on school-related tasks. These findings support those of Dunford, Missiuna, Street, & Sibert (2005) who found that children with DCD identified quite different areas of concern to either their parents or teachers. The implication of both these studies is that children should always be involved in the goal-setting process so that their perspectives are captured.

The Perceived Efficacy and Goal Setting System (PEGS) (Missiuna & Pollock, 2000, 2004; Pollock & Missiuna, 2015) is a tool occupational therapists can use to assist children and their parents to set therapy goals. PEGS was initially developed for children with motor difficulties (Missiuna, 1998) and features 24 paired cards of typical activities for children aged between 5 and 9 years. Each pair of cards includes one picture of a child struggling with an activity and one picture of a child doing the same activity in a competent manner. In the goal-setting process, the child is asked to choose which card he/she is most like (i.e. the child who is competent at that particular activity or the child who is less competent). Although the cards are not diagnosis specific, the illustrations are of activities that children with DCD typically find challenging and so are very appropriate when working with this population. The PEGS includes questionnaires for parents and teachers which ask about the same activities as the 24 paired cards, and blank cards are also provided so that the child can name other activities that might be important to them.

When working with adolescents and adults with DCD, a generic tool, such as the Canadian Occupational Performance Measure (Law et al., 2014), can be used to support goal-setting conversations as well as be used to gauge the individual's perceptions on how effective therapy has been.

2.2 Use interventions which are evidence-based, foster function and participation and prevent secondary consequences

Once goals have been collaboratively set, the occupational therapist moves on to assessing how well the child or adolescent is currently able to perform the task, activity or occupation which is embedded in the identified goal. As described in chapter 9, observation of the child's task performance and analysing what else is going on in the environment is a key part of the occupational therapist's reasoning and decision making process. From this process, the occupational therapist will identify appropriate interventions to use. Two interventions appropriate for using with children and adolescents with DCD are described next. Through the use of effective interventions, therapists are able to empower children to solve their own motor performance issues, which enhances their self-esteem. By focusing on child chosen goals therapists tap into the child's motivation and interests. This sense of autonomy (choice and control), relatedness (relationship with therapist), and competence (satisfaction with success) as defined by self-determination theory (Deci & Ryan, 2000) epitomises the approaches described next.

CO-OP Approach™

The CO-OP Approach™, originally referred to as the Cognitive Orientation for daily Occupational Performance (CO-OP), is an intervention that was specifically developed for children with DCD (Polatajko, Mandich, Miller, & Macnab, 2001). Drawing on learning theory rather than developmental theory, the CO-OP Approach™ focuses on teaching a child/adolescent how to use cognitive strategies to achieve chosen goals (Rodger & Polatajko, 2017). In this intervention, instead of addressing the child's motor difficulties, the therapist facilitates the child's discovery of strategies that assist him/her to goal achievement; "*Goal-plan-do-check*" is taught as a global problem-solving strategy which the child is then encouraged to apply to other goals (for further details on implementing CO-OP, see Rodger & Polatajko,

2017). Therapists identify areas of performance breakdown based on their obser-vation of successive performances, based on this process of dynamic performance analysis, they help the child to identify plans or strategies that might assist. These are trialled and then checked to see if the strategy worked. Iteratively further plans are identified and trialled. Practice is hence directed by strategy development rather than learning that is based in repeated errors.

The evidence base on the effectiveness of CO-OP with children with DCD is solid and expanding (e.g. Anderson, Wilson, & Williams, 2016; Armstrong, 2012; Bernie & Rodger, 2004; Capistran & Martini, 2016; Rodger & Liu, 2008; Sangster, Beninger, Polatajko, & Mandich, 2005; Scammell, Bates, Houldin, & Polatajko, 2016; Taylor, Fayed, & Mandich, 2007; Thornton et al., 2016; Ward & Rodger, 2004). In a meta-analysis of interventions, CO-OP was identified by Smits-Engelsman and colleagues (2013) as one of the two task-oriented approaches recommended as an evidence-based intervention for children with DCD. The other, neuromotor task training (NTT), is more commonly used in physiotherapy (Niemeijer, Smits-Engelsman, & Schoemaker, 2007) and mostly in Europe. It focuses on training a child to complete a functional task by improving motor planning and motor control processes and there is less emphasis on teaching the child to use cognitive strategies.

Occupational performance coaching

Occupational performance coaching (OPC) is an intervention that focuses on caregivers rather than children/adolescents (Graham & Rodger, 2010; Graham, Rodger, & Kennedy-Behr, 2017; Graham, Rodger, & Ziviani, 2009). In this solution-focused intervention, caregivers are encouraged to set goals for themselves as well as their child, and the occupational therapist coaches the caregiver or parent in analysing the environment, the task and the individual's strengths and challenges related to a specific goal. For example, a caregiver might identify mealtimes as an issue. Through using the Canadian Occupational Performance Measure (Law et al., 2014), the therapist would work with the caregiver to set a positively worded spe-cific goal, such as *"Jack will sit at the table with the family for 15 minutes and use cutlery while eating his meal"*. The occupational therapist would then coach the caregiver through identifiying what is happening now at mealtimes: *where does Jack sit, do his feet touch the floor? Does he know how to use cutlery, which cutlery do you expect him to use? What else is going at mealtimes (e.g. is the television on; are other siblings present). Tell me about Jack's best ever use of cutlery . . . what was different on that day?* By asking questions related to the environment or child's task performance rather than just suggesting solutions, in OPC, the therapist is recognising the caregiver's expert role as well as building on the caregiver's capacity to find solutions for other areas of difficulty.

OPC was designed to be used with caregivers of children with a range of issues, including DCD. Research on OPC is still emerging (e.g. Graham, Rodger, & Ziviani, 2013; Graham, Rodger, Ziviani, & Jones, 2015; Hui, Snider, & Couture, 2016; Kennedy-Behr, Rodger, Graham, & Mickan, 2013). Studies conducted with mothers who were coached through the OPC process indicate that the mothers' satisfaction with their child's ability to achieve identified goals increased significantly and that these achievements had a "spillover" effect – OPC led to improvement in areas which were not the specific focus of the intervention (Graham et al., 2013). In another study, Graham et al. (2015) also found that the mothers came to view their child's needs differently through the OPC process. This is particularly pertinent in the case of DCD which has often been misunderstood. In a small study piloting the use of OPC with preschool teachers, Kennedy-Behr et al., found that kindergarten teachers of children with DCD changed the way they interpreted a child's behaviour once they understood more about the condition. Instead of viewing the child as "naughty" e.g. deliberately knocking over another child's creation, one teacher then interepreted the child's behaviour in a more favourable light and came up with strategies to change the environment so that the child was less likely to bump into other children or their constructions. OPC with teachers could potentially be a population level approach (see principle 1.3).

Other interventions

In a systematic review evaluating the effectiveness of interventions for children with DCD, Smits-Engelsman and colleagues (2013) found that task-oriented interventions, such as CO-OP, NTT, and traditional occupational therapy and physiotherapy, were supported by more evidence than process-oriented interventions, such as sensory integration and perceptual training. The review evaluated studies published between 1995 and 2011. Given Smit-Engelsman et al.'s findings, occupational therapists should continue to use task-oriented interventions when working with children and young people with DCD.

The final point of principle 2.2, to "prevent secondary consequences", is perhaps the most fundamental one. Children do not grow out of DCD (Cantell, Smyth, & Ahonen, 2003; Forsyth et al., 2008; Green, Baird, & Sugden, 2006; Smits-Engelsman et al., 2013). Several studies have shown that in addition to motor difficulties, many children and adolescents with DCD also experience anxiety and depression (Piek et al., 2007; Pratt & Hill, 2011) and that this can continue into adulthood (Hill & Brown, 2013). There is also some evidence that children with DCD are stigmatised and excluded by their peers (Campbell, Missiuna, & Vaillancourt, 2012; Kennedy-Behr, Rodger, & Mickan, 2013). Due to the potential secondary consequences of DCD, it is imperative that any occupational therapy intervention focus on participation, coping skills and well-being. Qualitative studies investigating the experience of DCD have found that from the parents' perspective, supporting their child to find something they are good at and enjoy and to develop coping strategies were key to the well-being of their child and their family (Mandich et al., 2003; Missiuna, Moll, King, King, & Law, 2007; Rodger & Mandich, 2005; Stephenson & Chesson, 2008).

The following case study will illustrate how some of these best practice principles can be implemented.

Case study

Marco is an eight year old boy referred to occupational therapy due to "difficulty with fine motor and gross motor skills". Through the information gathering process with both Marco and his mother, the occupational therapist established that Marco found the academic tasks at school very easy, however, his handwriting was holding him back. Marco's mother was concerned about his "disorganisation" at home.

As the health fund provider required motor difficulties to be confirmed, the occupational therapist asked Marco's mother to complete the DCDQ'07 and assessed Marco's gross and fine motor skills using the MABC-2. Results from the DCDQ indicated Marco was "probably DCD". His overall MABC-2 score of 61 (9th percentile) indicated significant motor difficulties compatible with a diagnosis of DCD.

Following completion of the initial assessments, the occupational therapist used the PEGS cards to engage Marco in the therapy process and to discover his perspective on his own abilities. Marco identified that his handwriting was like the "less competent" picture card as was doing up his shoelaces. On the outdoor play card he said he wasn't really like any of the children there but what he would really like to do was to climb to the top of the climbing frame "just like the other kids". Together with his mother, the following goals were set: 1) climb to the top of the climbing frame at school, 2) tie his shoelaces independently, 3) write a sentence and stay between the lines, and 4) pack his schoolbag neatly (without tearing papers/books) and independently. While Marco did not share his mother's concerns regarding his schoolbag or his handwriting he was willing to work on that goal as she said it was very important to her and he accepted (albeit grudgingly) that staying between the lines was important for school.

Over the next eight sessions, the occupational therapist then used the CO-OP Approach™ with Marco to work on his goals. Climbing to the top of the climbing frame was chosen as the first goal as it was the most important to Marco and from conversations she had had with both Marco and his mother, it was clear that achieving this goal was important for his self-esteem and participation at school. The occupational therapist introduced Marco to Goal-Plan-Do-Check which he quickly understood. Marco's mother brought a photo of the climbing frame at Marco's school so that the therapist would know exactly what kind of equipment Marco was wanting to climb and they found a similar frame in a nearby park (while it might have been possible to visit the school and practise on the actual equipment with Marco, due to concerns that Marco might be stigmatised by this, the occupational therapist chose to work on climbing at a different location). With the occupational therapist guiding him, Marco discovered that saying the order of movements quietly to himself helped him remember how to start climbing, for example, repeating "hand, hand, foot, foot". Marco also found that even though he was left handed, he preferred to start climbing with his right hand as he felt it was stronger. At one point he froze while climbing and the occupational therapist used that as an opportunity to problem solve ways Marco could cope with "freezing" at school and either climb down or continue climbing up. Marco found that continuing with his "hand, hand, foot, foot" mantra helped. Once progress had been made on the first goal, he started work on the second, that of tying his shoelaces. As using verbal self-guidance had worked well with climbing, the same strategy was trialled with tying shoelaces. A ditty was developed with Marco which talked him through the tying process. As with the first goal, any strategies that were found useful for the second goal were also then applied to the third and fourth goals. Marco was asked to re-evaluate his ability on all four goals using a scale customised with his terms (1= hmmm, 2= alright I suppose, 3= ok, 4= good, 5 = awesome). At the end of the intervention, in his eyes, Marco's climbing was "awesome".

Conclusion

This chapter has used Camden et al.'s (2015) best practice principles to describe the role of occupational therapists when working with children and young people with DCD. Occupational therapists can contribute to raising awareness of DCD and access to appropriate services and resources. Using population-level interventions can support all children, including those without a diagnosis, as well as build capacity amongst teachers and other groups. Goal-setting methods which incorporate the child/young person's view as well as that of the family is recommended. When offering individual interventions, task-oriented approaches such as CO-OP Approach™ should be favoured over process-oriented interventions. Finally, supporting children and young people's well-being and preventing the secondary consequences of DCD should be a priority for all health care practitioners.

References

Alonso Soriano, C., Hill, E. L., & Crane, L. (2015). Surveying parental experiences of receiving a diagnosis of Developmental Coordination Disorder (DCD). *Research in Developmental Disabilities, 43–44,* 11–20. doi:10.1016/j.ridd.2015.06.001

American Psychiatric Association (2013). *Diagnostic and statistical manual of mental disorders, Fifth Edition (DSM-V).* Arlington, VA: American Psychiatric Association.

Anderson, L., Wilson, J., & Williams, G. (2016). Cognitive Orientation to daily Occupational Performance (CO-OP) as group therapy for children living with motor coordination difficulties: An integrated literature review. *Australian Occupational Therapy Journal.* doi:10.1111/1440-1630.12333

Armstrong, D. (2012). Examining the evidence for interventions with children with developmental coordination disorder. *British Journal of Occupational Therapy, 75*(12), 532–540. doi:10.4276/030802212x13548955545413

Bernie, C., & Rodger, S. (2004). Cognitive strategy use in school-aged children with developmental coordination disorder. *Physical and Occupational Therapy in Pediatrics, 24*(4), 23–45.

Blank, R., Smits-Engelsman, B., Polatajko, H., & Wilson, P. (2012). European Academy for Childhood Disability (EACD): Recommendations on the definition, diagnosis and intervention of developmental coordination disorder (long version). *Developmental Medicine & Child Neurology, 54*(1), 54–93. doi:10.1111/j.1469-8749.2011.04171.x

Brewer, K., Pollock, N., & Wright, F.V. (2014). Addressing the challenges of collaborative goal setting with children and their families. *Physical & Occupational Therapy in Pediatrics, 34*(2), 138–152. doi:10.3109/01942638.2013.794187

Bruininks, R. H., & Bruininks, B. D. (2005). *Bruininks-Oseretsky test of motor proficiency* (2nd ed.) *(BOT-2)*. Minneapolis, MN: Pearson.

Camden, C., Wilson, B., Kirby, A., Sugden, D., & Missiuna, C. (2015). Best practice principles for management of children with Developmental Coordination Disorder (DCD): Results of a scoping review. *Child: Care, Health and Development, 41*(1), 147–159. doi:10.1111/cch.12128

Campbell, W. N., Missiuna, C., & Vaillancourt, T. (2012). Peer victimization and depression in children with and without motor coordination difficulties. *Psychology in the Schools, 49*(4), 328–341. doi:10.1002/pits.21600

Campbell, W. N., Missiuna, C., Rivard, L., & Pollock, N. (2012). "Support for everyone": Experiences of occupational therapists delivering a new model of school-based service. *Canadian Journal of Occupational Therapy, 79*(1), 51–59. doi:10.2182/cjot.2012.79.1.7

Cantell, M. H., Smyth, M. M., & Ahonen, T. P. (2003). Two distinct pathways for developmental coordination disorder: Persistence and resolution. *Human Movement Science, 22,* 413–431.

Capistran, J., & Martini, R. (2016). Exploring inter-task transfer following a CO-OP approach with four children with DCD: A single subject multiple baseline design. *Human Movement Science, 49,* 277–290. doi:10.1016/j.humov.2016.07.004

Costa, U. M., Brauchle, G., & Kennedy-Behr, A. (2017). Collaborative goal setting with and for children as part of therapeutic intervention. *Disability and Rehabilitation, 39*(16), 1589–1600. doi:10.1080/09638288.2016.1202334

Dancza, K., Missiuna, C., & Pollock, N. (2017). Occupation-centred practice: When the classroom is your client. In S. Rodger & A. Kennedy-Behr (Eds.), *Occupation-centred practice with children: A practical guide for occupational therapists* (2nd ed., pp. 257–287). Chichester: Wiley-Blackwell.

Deci, E. L., & Ryan, R. M. (2000). The "what" and "why" of goal pursuits: Human needs and the self-determination of behavior. *Psychological Inquiry, 11*(4), 227–268.

Dunford, C., Missiuna, C., Street, E., & Sibert, J. (2005). Children's perceptions of the impact of developmental coordination disorder on activities of daily living. *British Journal of Occupational Therapy, 68*(5), 207–214.

Forsyth, K., Maciver, D., Howden, S., Owen, C., & Shepherd, C. (2008). Developmental coordination disorder: A synthesis of evidence to underpin an allied health professions' framework. *International Journal of Disability, Development and Education, 55*(2), 153–172.

Gagnon-Roy, M., Jasmin, E., & Camden, C. (2016). Social participation of teenagers and young adults with developmental co-ordination disorder and strategies that could help them: Results from a scoping review. *Child: Care, Health and Development, 42*(6), 840–851. doi:10.1111/cch.12389

Graham, F., & Rodger, S. (2010). Occupational performance coaching: Enabling parents' and children's occupational performance. In S. Rodger (Ed.), *Occupation-centred practice with children: A practical guide for occupational therapists* (pp. 203–226). Chichester: Wiley-Blackwell.

Graham, F., Rodger, S., & Kennedy-Behr, A. (2017). Occupational performance coaching: Enabling caregivers' and children's occupational performance. In S. Rodger & A. Kennedy-Behr (Eds.), *Occupation-centred practice with children: A practical guide for occupational therapists* (2nd ed., pp. 209–231). Chichester: Wiley-Blackwell.

Graham, F., Rodger, S., & Ziviani, J. (2009). Coaching parents to enable children's participation: An approach for working with parents and their children. *Australian Occupational Therapy Journal, 56*, 16–23.

Graham, F., Rodger, S., & Ziviani, J. (2013). Effectiveness of occupational performance coaching in improving children's and mothers' performance and mothers' self-competence. *American Journal of Occupational Therapy, 67*(1), 10–18.

Graham, F., Rodger, S., Ziviani, J., & Jones, V. (2015). Strategies identified as effective by mothers during occupational performance coaching. *Physical and Occupational Therapy in Pediatrics*, 1–13. doi:10.3109/01942638.2015.1101043

Green, D., Baird, G., & Sugden, D. A. (2006). A pilot study of psychopathology in developmental coordination disorder. *Child: Care, Health and Development, 32*, 741–750.

Henderson, S. E., Sugden, D. A., & Barnett, A. L. (2007). *The movement assessment battery for children, Second Edition (Movement ABC-2)*. London: Harcourt Assessment.

Hill, E. L., & Brown, D. (2013). Mood impairments in adults previously diagnosed with developmental coordination disorder. *Journal of Mental Health, 22*(4), 334–340. doi:10.31 09/09638237.2012.745187

Hui, C., Snider, L., & Couture, M. (2016). Self-regulation workshop and occupational performance coaching with teachers: A pilot study: Étude pilote sur un atelier d'autogestion et des séances d'encadrement du rendement occupationnel à l'intention des enseignants. *Canadian Journal of Occupational Therapy, 83*(2), 115–125. doi:10.1177/0008417415627665

Kennedy-Behr, A., Rodger, S., Graham, F., & Mickan, S. (2013). Creating enabling environments at preschool for children with developmental coordination disorder. *Journal of Occupational Therapy, Schools, & Early Intervention, 6*, 301–313. doi:10.1080/19411243.20 13.860760

Kennedy-Behr, A., Rodger, S., & Mickan, S. (2013). Aggressive interactions during free-play at preschool of children with and without developmental coordination disorder. *Research in Developmental Disabilities, 34*(9), 2831–2837. doi:10.1016/j.ridd.2013.05.033

Kirby, A., Edwards, L., & Sugden, D. A. (2011). Emerging adulthood in developmental co-ordination disorder: Parent and young adult perspectives. *Research in Developmental Disabilities, 32*(4), 1351–1360. doi:10.1016/j.ridd.2011.01.041

Kirby, A., Edwards, L., Sugden, D., & Rosenblum, S. (2010). The development and standardization of the Adult Developmental Co-ordination Disorders/Dyspraxia Checklist (ADC). *Research in Developmental Disabilities, 31*(1), 131–139. doi:10.1016/j.ridd.2009.08.010

Law, M., Baptiste, S., Carswell, A., McColl, M., Polatajko, H., & Pollock, N. (2014). *The Canadian occupational performance measure* (5th ed.). Ottawa, ON: CAOT Publications ACE.

Law, M., Hanna, S., King, G., Hurley, P., King, S., Kertoy, M., & Rosenbaum, P. (2003). Factors affecting family-centred service delivery for children with disabilities. *Child: Care, Health and Development, 29*(5), 357–366. doi:10.1046/j.1365-2214.2003.00351.x

Lingam, R. P., Novak, C., Emond, A., & Coad, J. E. (2013). The importance of identity and empowerment to teenagers with developmental co-ordination disorder. *Child: Care, Health and Development*, n/a–n/a. doi:10.1111/cch.12082

Locke, E. A., & Latham, G. P. (2002). Building a practically useful theory of goal setting and task motivation: A 35-year odyssey. *American Psychologist, 57*(9), 705–717. doi:10.1037/0003-066x.57.9.705

Löwing, K., Bexelius, A., & Brogren Carlberg, E. (2009). Activity focused and goal directed therapy for children with cerebral palsy – Do goals make a difference? *Disability and Rehabilitation, 31*(22), 1808–1816. doi:10.1080/09638280902822278

Mandich, A. D., Polatajko, H., & Rodger, S. (2003). Rites of passage: Understanding participation of children with developmental coordination disorder. *Human Movement Science, 22*, 583–595.

Missiuna, C. (1998). Development of "All about Me," a scale that measures children's perceived motor competence. *OTJR: Occupation, Participation and Health, 18*(2), 85–108. doi:10.1177/153944929801800202

Missiuna, C., & Pollock, N. (2000). Perceived efficacy and goal setting in young children. *Canadian Journal of Occupational Therapy, 67*(2), 101–109.

Missiuna, C., & Pollock, N. (2004). *The perceived efficacy and goal setting system*. San Antonia, TX: Psychcorp.

Missiuna, C., Moll, S., King, S., King, G., & Law, M. (2007). A trajectory of troubles: Parents' impressions of the impact of developmental coordination disorder. *Physical and Occupational Therapy in Pediatrics, 27*(1), 81–101.

Missiuna, C., Moll, S., King, S., Law, M., & King, G. (2006). "Missed and misunderstood": Children with coordination difficulties in the school system. *International Journal of Special Education, 21*(1), 53–67.

Missiuna, C., Moll, S., Law, M., King, S., & King, G. (2006). Mysteries and mazes: Parents' experiences of children with developmental coordination disorder. *Canadian Journal of Occupational Therapy, 73*(1), 7–17.

Missiuna, C., Pollock, N., Campbell, W. N., Bennett, S., Hecimovich, C., Gaines, R., . . . Molinaro, E. (2012). Use of the medical research council framework to develop a complex intervention in pediatric occupational therapy: Assessing feasibility. *Research in Developmental Disabilities, 33*(5), 1443–1452. doi:10.1016/j.ridd.2012.03.018

Missiuna, C., Pollock, N., Egan, M., DeLaat, D., Gaines, R., & Soucie, H. (2008). Enabling occupation through facilitating the diagnosis of developmental coordination disorder. *Canadian Journal of Occupational Therapy, 75*(1), 26–34.

Missiuna, C., Pollock, N., Levac, D., Campbell, W. N., Whalen, S. D. S., Bennett, S. M., . . . Russell, D. J. (2012). Partnering for change: An innovative school-based occupational therapy service delivery model for children with developmental coordination disorder. *Canadian Journal of Occupational Therapy, 79*(1), 41–50. doi:10.2182/cjot.2012.79.1.6

Niemeijer, A. S., Smits-Engelsman, B. C. M., & Schoemaker, M. M. (2007). Neuromotor task training for children with developmental coordination disorder: A controlled trial. *Developmental Medicine and Child Neurology, 49*(6), 406–411.

Piek, J. P., Rigoli, D., Pearsall-Jones, J. G., Martin, N. C., Hay, D. A., Bennett, K. S., & Levy, F. (2007). Depressive symptomatolgy in child and adolescent twins with attention-deficit hyperactivity disorder and/or developmental coordination disorder. *Twin Research and Human Genetics, 10*(4), 587–596.

Polatajko, H., Mandich, A. D., Miller, L. T., & Macnab, J. J. (2001). Cognitive Orientation to daily Occupational Performance (CO-OP): Part II – The evidence. *Physical and Occupational Therapy in Pediatrics, 20*(2/3), 83–106.

Pollock, N., & Missiuna, C. (2015). *The perceived efficacy and goal setting system* (2nd ed.). Hamilton, ON: CanChild.

Pollock, N., Sharma, N., Christenson, C., Law, M., Gorter, J. W., & Darrah, J. (2014). Change in parent-identified goals in young children with cerebral palsy receiving a context-focused intervention: Associations with child, goal and intervention factors. *Physical & Occupational Therapy in Pediatrics*, *34*(1), 62–74. doi:10.3109/01942638.2013.799627

Pratt, M. L., & Hill, E. L. (2011). Anxiety profiles in children with and without developmental coordination disorder. *Research in Developmental Disabilities*, *32*(4), 1253–1259. doi:10.1016/j.ridd.2011.02.006

Rihtman, T., Wilson, B. N., & Parush, S. (2011). Development of the little developmental coordination disorder questionnaire for preschoolers and preliminary evidence of its psychometric properties in Israel. *Research in Developmental Disabilities*, *32*(4), 1378–1387. doi:10.1016/j.ridd.2010.12.040

Rodger, S., & Liu, S. (2008). Cognitive orientation to (daily) occupational performance: Changes in strategy and session time use over the course of intervention. *OTJR Occupation, Participation and Health*, *28*(4), 168–179. doi:10.3928/15394492-20080901-03

Rodger, S., & Mandich, A. (2005). Getting the run around: Accessing services for children with developmental co-ordination disorder. *Child: Care, Health and Development*, *31*, 449–457.

Rodger, S., & Polatajko, H. (2017). Cognitive orientation for daily occupational performance (CO-OP): A uniquely occupation-centred intervention for children. In S. Rodger & A. Kennedy-Behr (Eds.), *Occupation-centred practice with children: A practical guide for occupational therapists* (2nd ed., pp. 165–187). Chichester: Wiley-Blackwell.

Sangster, C. A., Beninger, C., Polatajko, H. J., & Mandich, A. (2005). Cognitive strategy generation in children with developmental coordination disorder. *Canadian Journal of Occupational Therapy*, *72*(2), 67–77.

Scammell, E. M., Bates, S. V., Houldin, A., & Polatajko, H. J. (2016). The Cognitive Orientation to daily Occupational Performance (CO-OP): A scoping review. *Canadian Journal of Occupational Therapy*, *83*(4), 216–225. doi:10.1177/0008417416651277

Smits-Engelsman, B., Blank, R., Van Der Kaay, A. C., Mosterd-Van Der Meijs, R., Vlugt-Van Den Brand, E., Polatajko, H. J., & Wilson, P. H. (2013). Efficacy of interventions to improve motor performance in children with developmental coordination disorder: A combined systematic review and meta-analysis. *Developmental Medicine & Child Neurology*, *55*(3), 229–237. doi:10.1111/dmcn.12008

Stephenson, E. A., & Chesson, R. A. (2008). "Always the guiding hand": Parents' accounts of the long-term implications of developmental co-ordination disorder for their children and families. *Child: Care, Health and Development*, *34*, 335–343.

Taylor, S., Fayed, N., & Mandich, A. (2007). CO-OP intervention for young children with developmental coordination disorder. *OTJR: Occupation, Participation and Health*, *27*(4), 124–130.

Thornton, A., Licari, M., Reid, S., Armstrong, J., Fallows, R., & Elliott, C. (2016). Cognitive orientation to (Daily) occupational performance intervention leads to improvements in impairments, activity and participation in children with developmental coordination disorder. *Disability and Rehabilitation*, *38*(10), 979–986. doi:10.3109/09638288.2015.1070298

Timler, A., McIntyre, F., Cantell, M., Crawford, S., & Hands, B. (2016). Development and evaluation of the psychometric properties of the Adolescent Motor Competence Questionnaire (AMCQ) for Adolescents. *Research in Developmental Disabilities*, *59*, 127–137. http://dx.doi.org/10.1016/j.ridd.2016.08.005

Ward, A., & Rodger, S. (2004). The application of Cognitive Orientation to daily Occupational Performance (CO-OP) with children 5–7 years with developmental coordination disorder. *British Journal of Occupational Therapy, 67*, 256–264.

Wilson, B. N., & Crawford, S. G. (2007). *The Developmental Coordination Disorder Questionnaire 2007 (DCDQ'07)*. Retrieved from www.dcdq.ca

Wilson, B. N., Neil, K., Kamps, P. H., & Babcock, S. (2013). Awareness and knowledge of developmental co-ordination disorder among physicians, teachers and parents. *Child: Care, Health and Development, 39*, 296–300. doi:10.1111/j.1365-2214.2012.01403.x

INDEX

Note: page numbers in *italic* indicate a figure, page numbers in **bold** indicate a table on the corresponding page and numbers preceded by n indicate a note number.